NIGHTMARES IN THE DREAM SANCTUARY

NIGHTMARES IN THE DREAM SANCTUARY

WAR AND THE ANIMATED FILM

DONNA KORNHABER

THE UNIVERSITY OF CHICAGO PRESS || CHICAGO AND LONDON

The University of Chicago Press, Chicago 60637
The University of Chicago Press, Ltd., London
© 2020 by Donna Kornhaber
Published 2020
Printed in the United States of America

29 28 27 26 25 24 23 22 21 20   1 2 3 4 5

ISBN-13: 978-0-226-47268-3 (cloth)
ISBN-13: 978-0-226-47271-3 (e-book)
DOI: https://doi.org/10.7208/chicago/9780226472713.001.0001

Library of Congress Cataloging-in-Publication Data

Names: Kornhaber, Donna, 1979– author.
Title: Nightmares in the dream sanctuary : war and the animated film / Donna Kornhaber.
Description: Chicago ; London : The University of Chicago Press, 2020. | Includes
    bibliographical references and index.
Identifiers: LCCN 2019017187 | ISBN 9780226472683 (cloth : alk. paper) |
    ISBN 9780226472713 (e-book)
Subjects: LCSH: War films—History and criticism. | Animated films—History and criticism.
Classification: LCC PN1995.9.W3 K66 2020 PN1997.5 | DDC 791.43/34—dc23
LC record available at https://lccn.loc.gov/2019017187

♾ This paper meets the requirements of ANSI/NISO Z39.48–1992 (Permanence of Paper).

For Cyrus, Sophia, and Gabriel

What art is possible for the invisible? For the unthinkable?

JULIA KRISTEVA

CONTENTS

ILLUSTRATIONS

I t is one of my earliest memories of any film: the image of an amiable, middle-aged Dick Van Dyke decked out in military fatigues and lounging—not sitting, *lounging*—on a US Army tank, expounding on the patriotism of Donald Duck. For the longest time, this memory stayed in my consciousness surrounded by a riot of surrealist bricolage: flashes of Donald parachuting out of a US military plane, Donald wearing a doughboy uniform and carving potato skins into the word *phooey*, Donald wrapped in an American flag and hugging a miniature Statue of Liberty, and then what seemed like the strangest part of all—Donald in full Nazi dress saluting pictures of Hitler and building bombs on a factory line while some madman on the soundtrack sang about "der Fuehrer's face." And for the longest time I wasn't really sure if any of it was real.

It was. And it was broadcast on national television. To the best I can determine, these memories stem from the wartime segment of *Donald Duck's 50th Birthday* special, which played on CBS in 1984. In fact, the actual special is even stranger than my childhood memory. The war-themed portion of the show starts with Henry Winkler, aka The Fonz, standing in front of a giant American flag wearing a crisp blazer and a wrinkled dress shirt, talking about Donald getting drafted and ruminating on the character's middle name, Fauntleroy, which we then see on a draft card. There is something about Donald never being properly discharged from the military and thus being the longest serving World War II veteran in the country. And the whole thing ends with a parade down the middle of Disneyland. And

right there in the middle of the segment are all of the clips that I remember: *Donald Gets Drafted* (1942), *Commando Duck* (1944), and a
nearly minute-long sequence from *Der Fuehrer's Face* (1942), one of
the most famous Disney propaganda films from the Second World
War and the winner of the 1943 Academy Award for Best Short Subject (Cartoon). And also, in a brief interstitial segment, Dick Van Dyke
lounging on that tank.

Something about those clips fascinated me as a child. My grandfather was a World War II veteran, and he would occasionally share
his memories of being in the service. I loved animation, as any child
does, but also more so: deeply, in a way that would never really change,
even to this day. There was something about the freedom of the form
that always spoke to me. But there was also something about the continuity of the medium, the fact that my mother, grandparents, and
I might enjoy the same cartoon characters, even the very same cartoons as the ones they once watched years ago in the movie theaters
downtown, the ones that had long since closed. Those early Disney
and *Looney Tunes* shorts seemed ageless but also at the same time like
portals to a world long gone. And none would prove more fascinating
to me than those mysterious wartime shorts.

They truly were mysterious, and not just to me. This was long before the days of DVDs (let alone the internet); even VHS was relatively
new. Those shorts teased in *Donald Duck's 50th Birthday* and others of
their ilk were nowhere to be found, locked away in archives and in
most cases inaccessible to the public. In fact, the clips included in the
Birthday special would mark the first time those wartime shorts had
been broadcast to the public since the middle of the century. (The
Washington Post even ran a story timed to Donald's birthday bemoan-
ing Disney's refusal to rerelease those films.)[1] For a time it seemed the
curious collage of imagery involving Donald Duck and Dick Van Dyke
that swirled through my head would be the only record I would ever
have of these films.

But I found them, long before they were ever released to the public. Or rather, I found someone who had them. His name was John

Culhane, though if you're a Disney fan you might know him better as Mr. Snoops, the comical villain from *The Rescuers* (1977). Culhane was a real person, not a cartoon, though he was possibly the closest the former might ever come to the latter: buoyant, inquisitive, with an absolutely boundless energy that I have known only a few real people to ever possess (it is quite common among cartoons). The cousin of Disney icon Shamus Culhane, one of the lead animators on *Snow White and the Seven Dwarfs* (1937) and the figure behind the famous "Heigh-Ho" sequence, John Culhane was one of the first historians of animated film—the author of multiple books and a regular fixture in the Disney Animation Studios, where he often found himself on assignment for newspaper and magazine pieces. It was this combination of omnipresence and inquisitiveness that earned Culhane his surreptitious starring role on screen: searching for a model for the as-yet-unnamed character, the animators working on *The Rescuers* settled on Culhane himself, whom they then appropriately named Mr. Snoops. Culhane was delighted: there is probably nothing he wanted more in the world than to actually become a cartoon, and few people are ever granted that wish.

The name was apropos, because Culhane had the goods. Somehow he had in his possession a library of animated propaganda films from the Second World War—and he would show them to his students. This was back in the 1990s, long after that Donald Duck television special from 1984 and long before any of these films would start to be released to the public on DVD editions in the 2000s. I met Culhane when I was a student in his course on the history of animation at New York University's Tisch School of the Arts. For me, it was a transformative class. Culhane was a witness to history (the man had known Disney himself), and he made the story of animation come alive in a way that few others could. And nothing was more exciting to me than his unit on wartime animation.

The films themselves were absolutely fascinating. And also completely depressing. And actually quite difficult to endure. We watched the entirety of *Der Fuehrer's Face*, which includes over thirty *sieg heils* (the last one being interrupted in the middle when Donald wakes up in America and realizes his service to the Nazi cause has all been a terrible dream). We watched *Education for Death* (1943), about a young child brainwashed into fascist ideology and sent to be slaughtered on the battlefield, which also showed us what a Disney-animated version of a Nazi book burning looked like. We watched Donald defeat the Japanese in *Commando Duck*. Then we watched Daffy Duck defeat the Germans in *Daffy the Commando* (1943). We watched a fake newsreel from *Looney Tunes*, *Tokio Jokio* (1943), which reveled in the implied starvation and death by exposure of Japanese civilians in the wake of American firebombing campaigns. We even watched the infamous *Snafu* training films commissioned from Warner Bros. by the US Army, which married their open racism to equal doses of sexism and misogyny, using busty sexpots to make the operation of military machinery and the adherence to military code seem passably interesting. And we watched endless streams of what can only be described as animated glamor shots of American military vehicles, so many planes flying into so many sunsets.

Before taking Culhane's class, I thought I might one day want to write about animation and its relationship to war, if I could ever find the films. But after seeing them, I didn't ever want to touch the material again. Bellicose, vicious, impervious to sympathy, and often astonishingly racist, the films offer a blistering view of wartime culture in America. By the end of Culhane's course, there was little wonder as to why the executives at Disney kept them locked away for so long, acknowledging their existence only in the dribs and drabs of carefully cropped excerpts like those in the *Birthday* special.

At the time, Culhane was letting us in on a secret by showing us these films, the secret being the major American animation studios' complicity in the apparatus of war, however justified the cause. That secret is now long since out. Disney itself took the lead in acknowledging what it had once kept hidden. In 2004, the company released the DVD *Walt Disney Treasures: On the Front Lines*, containing thirty-two of their wartime shorts, dutifully introduced by film critic and historian extraordinaire Leonard Maltin, who somberly reminds us that "in time of war, it's typical, sometimes even useful, to demonize your enemy." Warner Bros. followed suit with a similar collection in 2008, and now you can buy glossy coffee table books with images from the films published by the studios themselves. With the release of the materials, film scholarship has followed suit, examining, contextualizing, and analyzing the films I watched with Culhane and many, many others besides in numerous books and journal articles.[2] And not just Disney or Warner Bros. either. The rediscovery of an important Japanese animated propaganda film from the war, *Momotarō, Sacred Sailors* (1945), long thought lost in the American firebombing campaigns of the war's later years or destroyed during the American occupation afterward, has prompted renewed attention to animated films made against the Allied powers.[3] Even Nazi animated films, among the most unwatchable species of film on the planet, have started to receive sustained attention from scholars.[4] That attention has spread to animated propaganda films of the First World War as well as Soviet animated propaganda from across the period of the wars.[5] What once seemed like a secret so well kept that I doubted my own memories is now a vibrant area of scholarship in my own field of study.

And yet, I've often wondered: Is there not more to this story? Does the history of animation's relationship to war really begin and end with parodies of dictators and stirring images of tanks set to martial music? Is there not another, still undiscovered secret hiding behind the one now exposed in all of those DVDs and books and articles? For their many individual differences, something about all those propaganda films just seemed *the same*: the same anger, the same exaggeration, the same jingoistic images, the same set of very disturbing jokes. But animation is so many different things. As a child it made me laugh; as an adult it has made me cry. I am moved nearly to tears every time I watch Adam Benjamin Elliot's 1999 Claymation short *Brother*, about the premature death of a beloved sibling. I gaze in wonder at Don Hertzfeldt's 2015 stick-figure masterpiece *World of Tomorrow*, one of the most profound reflections on the human condition I have ever encountered. I am mesmerized by Konstantin Bronzit's *We Can't Live without Cosmos*, from 2014, among the most tragic love stories ever put to film, told within the span of only fifteen minutes. I chill at the otherworldly imagery of a film like *Madame Tutli-Putli* (2007) by Maciek Szczerbowski and Chris Lavis or the surreal melancholy of Julia Potts's *Belly* (2011). Where is the animation that tells the story of war in the way that these animators use the form to tell their stories: stories that are personal, idiosyncratic, humane, and born from experience? Are there really no films that do this work?

There are. There are hundreds of them. They span the whole history of animation, from its first years to last year. They span the globe. And they have never been written about before, not together. Some of them are well known to the public: *Waltz with Bashir* (2008), *Persepolis* (2007). Some of them have won major awards: *Bear Story* (2014), winner of the Academy Award for Best Short Film (Animated) in 2016, or *The Hole* (1962), which won the same award in 1962. Some are famous in the world of animation: Jiří Trnka's *The Hand* (1965) or Yuri Norstein's *Tale of Tales* (1979), frequently listed as two of the greatest animated films ever made. Many are obscure, even to those who study and follow animation. Some have never been written about in English before. And a few, posted online by their creators, have never been written about at all until now. I have come to these films, all of them, because I knew they were out there: because I knew that animation had more to say about the experience of war than the world of rabid propaganda would allow, because I knew there were artists who had suffered through terrible atrocities and who had turned to animation as a means of expressing those experiences. The films included here come from every corner of the world: from Syria and Sarajevo, from the Congo and Korea. They cover conflicts ranging from the end of the nineteenth century to the beginning of the twenty-first. They encompass worldwide conflagrations like the First World War and unnamed conflicts in stateless territories. They touch on genocide and nuclear annihilation. They cover the experiences of child soldiers and kamikazes, invaders and occupiers, insurgents and partisans, and terrified bystanders. And all of them use the medium of animation to tell their stories.

There is no single name for this type of film. Some have been examined before under the rubric of documentary animation, but most of them far exceed the boundaries of that genre and almost none of them have been expressly constructed in that mode.[6] A few bear connections to certain efforts in the realm of comic books and graphic novels to tell the story of war and atrocity, though the vast majority are original, standalone films.[7] Together these works do not necessarily constitute a tradition in the way that most scholars would define the term: some are in conscious conversation with one another; a great many others are not. But they represent, all of them, a common effort: a shared attempt to communicate the lived experience of war, the gravest of human enterprises, using the tools that only animation can provide. All of them, I argue, constitute acts of witness.

These are the films I had been searching for, really for nearly all of my life, somehow knowing they were always there. It is my great honor to tell their stories.

INTRODUCTION: WITNESS

I want to begin with two scenes from the history of animation.

The first: London. The Empire Theatre in Leicester Square on a mild December afternoon in 1899. The Ladies Welfare Committee for Soldiers and Sailors has just announced that very morning a special matinee performance of a charitable program to benefit the soldiers then fighting overseas—only two months prior Britain had entered into war with the independent Boer states north of their South African colonies, hastily dispatching an initial wave of ten thousand troops in what would eventually become the largest military deployment in the nation's history. The facade of the Empire Theatre, four stories of imposing masonry with the columns and arches of a fine concert hall, towers over the busy city street and nearby Shakespeare fountain. The inside is a giant jewelry box, all ornament and fabric: an imposing staircase leads to the grand foyer, the decor throughout a stately cream, gold, and white. One could easily still mistake the slightly tawdry music hall for the stately opera house it had been just twelve years before. But the bill that afternoon includes no arias or ballets. On the stage, above the fourteen-piece orchestra pit, is instead a screen. And on it, the flickering image of two matchsticks come suddenly alive in a quirky, one-minute photoplay called *Matches Appeal*, a new concoction by the slightly eccentric Hertfordshire photographer Arthur Melbourne-Cooper (plate 1). It is the world's first recorded viewing of an animated film.[1]

That afternoon in London, history and animation met for the first time. *Matches Appeal* did not just hold its premier in the early days of the Second Boer War. Nor did it merely play on a charity bill for the soldiers and sailors shipped off to fight in that war. The very appeal of the matches on screen—the actual *appeal* of *Matches Appeal*—was a plea that the patrons in the audience in Leicester Square donate money, at least a guinea, to send some much-needed matchbooks to the undersupplied soldiers on the front. Watching Melbourne-Cooper's peculiar anthropomorphs construct this message made up the very substance of the entertainment itself. Painstakingly built from matchsticks strung together with thin copper wire and meticulously shot so that their every incremental movement could be captured on its own frame of film (the process is now known as stop-motion animation and remains much the same today), the wooden men of Melbourne-Cooper's fantasy stumble around the screen like dizzy stick figures just born into three dimensions. Silently and diligently they assemble a scaffolding made of matchsticks, take up a matchstick as a writing implement, and climb their improvised matchstick rig to begin spelling out their matchstick petition on the blank chalkboard wall behind them: "An appeal. For one guinea, Messrs Bryant & May will forward a case containing sufficient [*sic*] to supply a box of matches to each man in a battalion: with name of the sender inside." Their work done, the first matchstick man drags the matchstick scaffolding off camera, but the second stays behind to add one final note—slowly and with great precision he spells out in extra-large type: "N.B. Our soldiers need them." One last confirmation of the dire reality that lay behind and motivated this short glimpse of fantasy.

Surely, the audience in the Empire Theatre that day was stupefied. The medium of film itself was still practically brand new, having first premiered in Berlin and in Paris just four short years before in 1895. To watch a film, any film, for spectators of that era was an exercise in wonderment: to gape at the moments of a human life captured and replayed, at the faraway and nearby spaces of the world etched onto celluloid strips and projected onto a screen in long streams of light. Early cinema was premised first and foremost on "its ability to *show* something," to use the words of film historian Tom Gunning: it was a *cinema of attractions*, per his famous phrase.[2] But the attraction that Melbourne-Cooper showed that afternoon was something altogether new: this was no scratched recording of the common world replayed for a crowd's brief amusement. *Matches Appeal* was something closer to a projected hallucination, a glimpse of an impossible realm made real for a few fleeting moments; a "dream sanctuary," in the words of film historians Tjitte de Vries and Ati Mul.[3] Like in some dimly remembered story from childhood, the stolid and inanimate objects of daily existence had here come boisterously to life and sent a message to the human beings with whom they quietly shared the world. In animation, writes the philosopher Stanley Cavell, "we are presented with drafts of the world's animism."[4] In the service of his cause, Melbourne-Cooper offered to his patrons that day a shocking brush with that animism, presenting nothing less than a total enchantment of the everyday, the mundane rendered suddenly and unforgettably miraculous. *Matches Appeal* must have seemed like a minute's worth of magic: a guinea for a matchbook would have been a small price to pay for such a vision.

The second: Moscow. A freezing winter's day nearly a century later, in 1983, in an imposing concrete-block building looming over Dolgorukovskaya Street. Though it is utterly lacking in ornamentation, the building looks something like a stripped-down version of the Empire Theatre back in London: four stories tall with a row of columns on the second level of its facade and another longer row of columns high up on the fourth. But whatever glory it once had has long since passed. The place looks washed out and exhausted now, even more so with the gray skies and the snow. Inside, though, it is vibrant: long lines of drafting tables and stacks and stacks of shelving holding piles of paper and slips of celluloid sheets, men and women everywhere drawing and tracing and inking and coloring. In a separate section of the building, the shelves hold papier-mâché and clay, small wooden dolls, and elaborate puppets. The building even houses a kind of theater of its own, though infinitely smaller than the grand circle of the Empire Theatre: large enough to fit just matchsticks on a tiny rigged platform. It is the home of Soyuzmultfilm, the Soviet animation studio first founded in 1936, and inside it a former stage actor turned puppeteer turned animator, Garri Yakovlevich Bardin, is fiddling with a set of matchsticks, trying to get all of their positions just right. Alongside him is a skeleton crew: four other animators and his cinematographer. They are working on a film about war: a bracingly graphic account of a silly conflict between matchsticks that turns into a terrible conflagration. They will have to get it past the censors at the State Committee for Cinematographers, of course, but for the most part, the keepers of the state ideology let the animators at Soyuzmultfilm do what they want. The studio's script editors are well practiced at explaining each film to the committee officials in the best possible light, and as far as the censors are concerned this is just children's entertainment anyway. But Bardin and his fellow animators see it differently. For them, this is utterly serious work.

You wouldn't know it, though, from the opening moments of the film on which Bardin is working, with its miniature set and matchstick stars. Despite its rather somber title—*Conflict*—the seven-minute film begins with just a matchbook on a bright white background, playful children's music scoring the movement of the matches as they happily spring out of the book and start to divide themselves into green-headed matches and blue-headed. There's a little pushing and shoving, but it seems no worse than children on a playground. Soon the matches gather into groups on either side of the frame, and the geography of the world bends a little to accommodate their chosen arrangements: a striped line appears down the middle of the floor, made from matchstick pieces. Then the plain white background bifurcates into green and blue, and the matches begin to patrol their shared border with a sentry keeping pace on either side, a pointed matchstick for a weapon. But the music remains lighthearted, and the border is just an arbitrary line on the ground. Nothing seems very serious. Until it does (plate 2). When one sentry accidentally knocks over a block expanding the blue territory into the green, push comes to shove very quickly—a childish squabble turns brutish when one matchstick sentry slices the other with his weapon, cutting him in two and leaving him gasping as he tries to bring his halves back together.

The sound of a man desperately choking for air, which entirely takes over the soundtrack of the film for a few stark moments, is in its way more shocking than any gunshot in a live-action movie. It had been nearly a hundred years since audiences had watched two matchsticks come alive in Leicester Square, brightly reaching out to the world to communicate. No animator could ever recapture the absolute magic of that primordial moment of visual enchantment. But there was still room for another kind of shock and surprise. What Bardin and his fellow animators were building into this film was a kind of answer to that initial moment of animism that Melbourne-Cooper effected for his audience. If Melbourne-Cooper brought his matchsticks shockingly to life, Bardin would put his just as shockingly to death—a death imbued with all the pain and suffering that embodiment entails, just as though the matchsticks had truly been alive. There is no other act that could have made Bardin's matchsticks more real or more human: he was enacting Melbourne-Cooper's conjuration in reverse.

After that initial, shocking hack to the enemy's lungs, the conflict only escalates: from matchstick duels to matchstick cavalry to matchstick machine guns to matchstick tanks. Eventually, the children's tune of the film's early minutes switches to a martial drumbeat and a cavalry horn, the trappings of military glory and parade. But the parade music does nothing to mask the slaughter: matches cut in half, trampled underfoot, punctured by machine-gun fire, each with the kind of graphic sound effects one would expect from any war film. Yet one of the short's most disturbing moments comes not from this imagery of death, which quickly becomes abundant, but from its brutally frank depiction of injury, when one of the mangled matches reappears with his wounds heavily bandaged and continues to fight alongside his comrades, laboredly and haltingly, as if in wrenching pain.

In its last act, the film becomes consumed by hopelessness: from war comes apocalypse, eventually and inevitably. Realizing they are overwhelmingly outnumbered and facing a green matchstick onslaught, the remaining blue matchsticks call upon their weapon of last resort: a matchbook missile that ignites the marching armies of the green in terrible flames. A lilting melody, Alessandro Marcello's *Oboe Concerto in D Minor*, slowly and surprisingly takes over the soundtrack as the camera pans across the flaming matchsticks. The lullaby-like tune offers no escape, underscored as it is by the distinct sounds of screaming that can still be heard beneath the music with the occasional flaming matchstick man running in terror across the foreground of the frame. Soon the conflagration spreads even to the blue sticks, as fire knows no borders and makes no political distinctions: they too share in the fate that they thought they had inflicted only on their enemies. For a moment we can even make out amidst the chaos that bandaged blue soldier engulfed in fire, briefly passing before our eyes in the foreground of the frame. The scene of devastation when the fire ultimately dies down is a tangled forest of charred and twisted matchsticks lying lifeless, the green and blue backgrounds now mixed into an end-of-the-world red. It is, in its way, as unsettling as any image of actual wartime destruction, the matchsticks turned this way and that like shriveled burn victims. It is an image of practically nothing, just a bunch of matchsticks, and yet it is instantly iconic—a *tableau mort*, as the art historians would say, imbued with everything awful from the terrible century since Melbourne-Cooper's happy matches first made their appeal: No Man's Land, fire bombings, Stalingrad, the Holocaust, Hiroshima, napalm, the imagery of nuclear annihilation. All of it is there. And also none of it. It's only matches.

BEYOND PROPAGANDA

Matches Appeal is, inescapably, propaganda. It could be trying to get you to buy war bonds. To support the troops. To enlist. Its structure would remain the same. Melbourne-Cooper clearly sees it as his mission to draw his audience's attention to one aspect of the conflict then unfolding in South Africa even as he dissolves the rest of that conflict in fantasy and historical detachment. In addition to his brush with Cavell's sense of animism, he includes a heavy dose of what film scholar Dan Torre calls animation's "irreality," its ability to keep the most harmful and disturbing aspects of the world safely at bay no matter what its subject.[5] Harnessing animation's powers of fantasy to amaze his audience toward action on one issue, Melbourne-Cooper uses that fantasy to distract them from all the other issues that might complicate the first—the war's shocking casualty count, which already in the first two months totaled over three thousand, or the rapid escalation of Britain's commitment, which increased fourfold from ten thousand to forty thousand troops between October and December of that year. (This is to say nothing of the atrocities and humiliations that were later inflicted by Britain in what would become one of the most brutal guerrilla conflicts of the colonial period, leading to as many as forty thousand civilian casualties.) What is missing from his film about the war, in other words, is *the war*. Just as what is absent from his version of embodiment is the actual lived condition of embodiment: the pain and injury and degradation that the body gives us, along with its animism and vitality and agency.

This is a model that we will see, in different ways, again and again and again in animated propaganda. One sees it in the First World War propaganda short *Britain's Effort* (1918) by famed illustrator-cum-animator Lancelot Speed, wherein the need for more munitions translates into a charming but disorienting scene where the bullets themselves literally march out of England, cross the English Channel, and swarm the European mainland to bloodlessly overwhelm the unseen enemy. One sees it again decades later in the Japanese cartoon *Sankichi the Monkey: The Storm Troopers* (1934), from the era of the Second Sino-Japanese War, wherein the invasion of China is depicted as a fun-filled, almost docile enterprise, a comical conflict between monkeys and pandas wherein the latter merely disappear when they are shot and the former suffer not a single casualty at all.

Or again this century in the computer-animated *Saudi Deterrent Force* (2017), wherein a Saudi invasion of Iran is enacted entirely without resistance and met by teeming crowds in the streets of Tehran holding posters of Saudi Crown Prince Mohammed Bin Salman and celebrating their liberation.

Taken as a whole, the annals of animated propaganda enact a profound violence on the historical record. As much as such films might urge, glorify, or justify war, they can almost never bring themselves to actually show it. Such films deliberately render war as a blank space, adamantly and often breathlessly justifying that which they refuse to depict. Along with the genre's one-sidedness, this careful act of erasure is one of the form's most consistent aspects. The story of the twentieth and twenty-first centuries as told collectively by its animated propaganda films is thus a confounding refraction of reality, one where fantasy and ideological wish fulfilment come to substitute for actual events. Watch enough of these films, and you will come to encounter some strange historical rewrites. Not just that the single greatest issue facing the British in the Second Boer War was a notable shortage of matches. But also that the Germans in World War I were overwhelmed and defeated by the ingenuity of British tanks (*What Next*, 1916). Or that the German invasion of the Soviet Union was easily repulsed at the border (*Fascist Jackboots Shall Not Trample Our Motherland*, 1941). That the Nazis' genocidal animus against Europe's Jewish population was an act of righteous self-defense (*The Troublemaker*, 1940). That Japan was brought to its knees years before the end of the Second World War (*Tokio Jokio*, 1943). That Japan was making preparations to invade the United States just months before the dropping of the atomic bomb (*Momotarō, Sacred Sailors*, 1945). That American warships were preparing to attack North Korea throughout the 1960s and 1970s (*Missile Pencils*, n.d.). That a broad coalition of Islamic forces is currently on the verge of invading Jerusalem (*Conquest of Jerusalem*, 2015). Or even that Iran once sank the entire American fleet in the waters of the Persian Gulf (*Battle of the Persian Gulf*, 2015).

It might all be amusing if it were not so overwhelmingly disturbing. It is not just the endless parade of destruction that depresses. It is that in each of these films, there is a stultifying sameness no matter the historical situation or the actual conditions of the war at hand, a standardization of outrages born of the limited template such films are willing to apply. The cumulative effect is that of a rabid echo chamber where the same claims and the same counterclaims bounce back and forth in endless succession across history, applied to different groups and different nations at different times in distressingly similar ways. The message is so often the same, taken from a very limited menu of possible narrative lines. The enemy is monstrous and is victimizing us. The enemy is weak and is helpless against us. The enemy is subhuman and shows no shred of sympathy. The enemy is subhuman and is deserving of no sympathy.

It is no wonder then that *Matches Appeal* has been subject to so much controversy among film historians, with many specialists seeing it as more likely connected to a match campaign run during the First World War then the Second Boer War—though Melbourne-Cooper, who lived until 1961, himself always claimed the earlier date. The arguments on both sides of the debate are intricate, and like many historical quandaries it may never be conclusively resolved.[6] But what is perhaps most fascinating in this otherwise arcane discussion is the degree to which Melbourne-Cooper's film *allows* itself to be removed from history in this way. In other words, there is nothing in *Matches Appeal* that firmly attaches to either the Second Boer War or the First World War per se. This, ultimately, is the condition of all propaganda—a form that is grounded in fantasy and therefore always at least partly unmoored from history.

The same cannot be said for *Conflict*, which is shot through and through with history, even to the point of overflowing. Unlike Melbourne-Cooper, Bardin is not concerned with a local issue like the Boer War supply shortage that his British predecessor sought to address. Instead, he means to deal with the broad contours of history and catastrophe in the twentieth century, the structures of war and atrocity writ large. The film's closest immediate subject is of course the Berlin Wall, both in terms of the literal line that divides the two matchstick camps and also the size disparity between the sides— the blues, like the outpost of American troops defending West Berlin during the Cold War, representing only a small garrison against the overwhelming battalions of the green, the full weight of the Soviet Army. Yet even this weighty metaphor fails to exhaust the possible meanings of Bardin's film, which instead is attuned not just to the condition of East and West Berlin in 1983 but to the entire experience of living in a moment poised perpetually on the brink of world-wide war, a moment already haunted by unshakable memories of the last worldwide war (and also the one before that), a moment whose primary experience of history was explicitly one of catastrophe, of revolution and invasion and struggle: in other words, the condition of living as a Russian and a European and a human in the fraught moments of the later twentieth century during the endgame of the Cold War.

For Bardin, the idea of living in a moment defined in its past, present, and future by the atrocities of war was not simply some abstract idea: the history embedded in *Conflict* was also very much woven into his life and family story. Bardin was born into war, birthed in 1941 while his mother was in the midst of fleeing the German bombardment of Kiev. (The devastated city after the war, a lost home that Bardin never knew, looked not unlike the final horrid images of fire and destruction seen in *Conflict*.) Bardin's father was a career officer in the Soviet Armed Forces who fought against the Nazis at Stalingrad, then served the rest of his life in the Baltic Fleet out of Latvia. Bardin too, following in his father's footsteps, served for a time in the Soviet Army before leaving to pursue his dreams of being an actor. It is in this context that we must view his work as an animator, along with the context of the immediate moment to which he was responding. *Conflict* appeared in the midst or in the aftermath of so many competing horrors: in the middle of the continued tensions in Berlin, in the wake of the more than one million casualties of the Vietnam War a decade before, near the midpoint of the Soviet Union's embroilment in Afghanistan, which had generated upward of a hundred thousand casualties already, and in the perpetual and inescapable shadow of the nuclear stakes of the Cold War. (In the very same year the film was released, there was a major malfunction in the Soviet nuclear early warning system, which for a time falsely indicated that the US had initiated a nuclear strike.) Unlike Melbourne-Cooper, who turns away from the specifics of war even as he tries to bring attention to one aspect of its suffering, Bardin tries to encompass it all, to craft a single work of art about all of that suffering all at once: Hiroshima and the Holocaust, the global Cold War and its terrible local wars, the conflicts his mother endured, the battles his father fought, the threat of annihilation faced by all. This capaciousness of content is one of animation's most unique and distinguishing properties: its ability to conjure a seemingly endless chain of succeeding images and overlapping meanings, one "which can by right continue to infinity," in the words of philosopher Gilles Deleuze.[7] As Bardin seems instinctively to sense, it is largely in its capacity toward infinitude that animation's utility resides: its ability to capture both the particular sufferings of individuals and the general terrors of the twentieth century— animation's first century, its own century. In Bardin's matchstick world, far away from Melbourne-Cooper's, lies another model for animation, one that does not turn away from history but actively turns toward it with eyes open.

Behind Bardin's work lies a simple entreaty. It is the same one you can see in the work of animators from Nepal crafting films about the nation's civil war in the early twenty-first century and American artists returning from the trenches of World War I to the country's new animation studios in the 1920s and dissidents in Eastern Europe using animation to surreptitiously critique Soviet invasion and members of the French Resistance using animation to spread messages of struggle and subversion under the noses of their Nazi occupiers and artists in the Congo using animation to illustrate children's memories of atrocities committed during military rule and Arab filmmakers trying to communicate the militarized conditions of life in the Palestinian territories and Croatian draftsmen telling the story of Sarajevo under siege and Israeli soldiers haunted by memories of past campaigns and Saudi computer artists speaking to recent military action on the Arabian peninsula and activists against the Vietnam War trying to convey the urgency of their critique. All of these animators and many, many more beyond them share one urgent appeal: the demand that animation be given a role to play in telling us the most terrible stories of our times. Animation—this fantastical engine of wonderment, this living window into the realm of fancy, this dream sanctuary—can also, these filmmakers insist, be equipped to fashion for us a view into the darkest recesses of the modern experience and to channel such atrocity into art. Animation, they insist, *can bear witness*.

To claim such a role for animation is to claim for it a place at the very heart of the lived experience of the twentieth century and its aftermath, an epoch that the French historian Annette Wieviorka has deemed "the era of the witness."[8] No longer in the twentieth century could the orderly *continuum* of sanctioned history, to use the term offered by the philosopher Walter Benjamin, sustain its pretenses of masterly explanation and clear causality. The history of the twentieth century, Benjamin warns us presciently from 1940, would be a history of the *discontinuum*, of the jagged and the unfinished, of "situations which we no longer know how to react to, in spaces which we no longer know how to describe," per Deleuze's description of the postwar condition.[9] The real work of history would quickly become the work of the witness, the experient who gives testimony to trauma and tragedy without recourse to or need for the historian's mechanisms of explanation. The language of witnessing originates among survivors of the Holocaust, a cataclysm distinguished not just by its infinite immorality but also by the efforts of its perpetrators to eliminate any record of its occurrence. The witness takes upon herself the task of giving to history that which could never otherwise be known, that which even seems unknowable. To bear witness is to engage in what the Bulgarian-French philosopher Julia Kristeva evocatively calls "the rendering of the invisible into image."[10] It is the act of representing what cannot and has not yet been represented, testifying to the spaces of experience that history deliberately hides or that have been deliberately hidden from history. "What art is possible for the invisible?" Kristeva asks. "For the unthinkable?"[11]

If, like the Soviet state censors, you think of animation primarily as a medium of broad juvenile entertainment, then the idea that the form might ever bear witness to the gravest events of recent human history seems either outlandish or perverse. What does the medium of Mickey Mouse have to tell us about napalm and the Holocaust? But the very fact of animation's detachment from reality is also part of its tremendous power. Animation is, in film scholar Scott Bukatman's reading of the form, a realm distinguished by its *illogics*: the contradictions that "allow us to escape the rigors of structured time and established habits of mind," leading to "little utopias of disorder, provisional sites of temporary resistance."[12] Which is, of course, exactly the realm of the witness. To the *continuum* of history belongs logic, with its careful order and its resplendent assurances of meaning. The realm of the witness is the realm of history's *discontinuum*: its underside of trauma, cataclysm, and oppression, its deepest layers where logic and order fail to penetrate. Voices normally do not resonate from such depths, so far are they submerged under history's master narratives. When they do break through, often they speak in a language few are equipped to understand, trying as they are to describe events that exceed description. To actually listen to history's *discontinuum*, Benjamin says, is like no other process of cogitation; rather it is "to seize hold of a memory as it flashes up at a moment of danger."[13] He does not know it, but he could be speaking about animation.

ART FOR THE INVISIBLE

For the artist tasked with bearing witness to history's near-inexpressible underside of atrocity, there is arguably no more potent medium than the animated film. Against the insanity of war, perhaps the only honest accounting can come from an art form of *illogics*. The standard *history* of war, as literary critic Elaine Scarry has brilliantly shown, is in almost all cases riddled with elision and obfuscation: the very language with which journalists, historians, and authors typically write about war is shot through with metaphors and standard turns of phrase that subtly but surely displace and hide from view the actual events and lived experience of conflict. "The written and spoken record of war over many centuries," she writes, "certifies the ease with which human powers of description break down in the presence of battle."[14] Rarely in most historical or journalistic accounts, she observes, are we given even the briefest insight into what she calls the "interior of war," the actual action of war-making known intimately to its participants and victims but for all others carefully enclosed and kept out of sight by a nearly impenetrable barrier of defensive metaphor. "Any activity that itself actually occurs in the interior of war will be much more difficult for the human mind to assess," she writes, as it will in almost all cases be carefully "redescribed and made invisible."[15] For in its actual content, that hidden "interior of war" is often too terrible to describe or comprehend.

It is not just that war destroys: that much is obvious. "War is injuring," Scarry writes. "The purpose . . . is to alter (to burn, to blast, to shell, to cut) human tissue, as well as to alter the surface, shape, and deep entirety of the objects that human beings recognize as extensions of themselves."[16] Rather, the worst truth, the one that is so often left unspoken, is that the whole interior of war is a concerted process of what Scarry calls *unmaking*—of taking apart not just buildings and bodies but also, and just as consequentially, the concepts and categories that we use to understand the world, rendering the conflict zone not just dangerous to those caught inside of it but frankly unknowable to them as well, everything familiar turned completely unrecognizable. "'The structure of war' and 'the structure of unmaking' are not two subjects but one," Scarry writes. War is "in the most literal and concrete way possible, an appropriation, aping, and reversing of the action of creating itself."[17] This is what the discourse of war endeavors most of all to keep from view—the degree to which the combatant is always involved in a process of *unmaking* that is both projected outward and also directed inward, a simultaneous unraveling of world and self.

Scarry talks about this terrible *unmaking* in broad, philosophical terms. But for Virginia Woolf it was something shockingly specific, a point best evidenced in musings from her great antiwar treatise, *Three Guineas*: "This morning's collection [of Spanish Civil War pictures] contains the photograph of what might be a man's body, or a woman's; it is so mutilated that it might, on the other hand, be the body of a pig."[18] What kind of world is it where we cannot tell the difference between a man, a woman, and a pig? A world that has lost its moorings in the normal and the comprehensible: one that is now a world apart. Philosophers might speak of this as the breakdown of the *subject-object distinction*, one of the most basic and fundamental of our cognitive approaches to the world, that which allows us to discern what is alive and what is not, what has agency and what does not. For the French philosopher Simone Weil, writing in the immediate wake of her experiences as a partisan in the Spanish Civil War, the unraveling of the subject-object distinction is the defining characteristic of the experience of war, its most basic and fundamental action. The nature of all violence, she writes, is that it "turns anybody who is subjected to it into a thing."[19] War is the ultimate extrapolation of this function: for its combatants, for its casualties, for its captives, for its bystanders and civilians. The experience of war at its core is the experience of subjects turned into objects through death. War, she writes, "turns man into a thing in the most literal sense: it makes a corpse out of him. Somebody was here, and the next minute there is nobody here at all."[20] Or else they are turned into objects in life through capture or impending execution, what she calls "the ability to turn a human being into a thing while he is still alive. He is alive; he has a soul and yet—he is a thing."[21] Even the perpetrators of violence find themselves consumed and subsumed by its power. "Force," she writes, "is as pitiless to the man who possesses it, or thinks he does, as it is to its victim; the second it crushes, the first it intoxicates."[22]

Victor, vanquished, perpetrator, victim: no one escapes war's unmaking of the most basic distinctions of our world. For Weil, as for Scarry, the collapsing of categories and shattering of distinctions is no mere byproduct of conflict: it is the soul and the purpose of war, the secret content of its interior action. "The art of war," Weil writes, "is simply the art of producing such transformations, and its equipment, its processes, even the casualties it inflicts on the enemy, are only means directed toward this end."[23]

Is there an art form better suited than animation to this incomprehensible place of perpetual transformation that is the interior world of war? Is there an art form more capable of bearing witness to a dimension where classifications no longer apply, where subject and object switch places, where one can no longer tell the difference between human and animal, man, woman, and pig? Since its inception, animation has been regarded as an artistic realm where the world may be unmade: its essence, according to Russian film theorist and filmmaker Sergei Eisenstein, lay in its "rejection of once-and-forever allotted form, freedom from ossification, the ability to dynamically assume any form."[24] Typically, such freedom is associated with fantasy and escape. Yet as much as animation is regarded as a realm of fancy, there is an unmistakable hint of violence in its assault on logic and norms—what art historian Roger Cardinal calls its tendency to "annihilate the very conditions of rationality."[25] Turning subjects into objects, objects into subjects, evacuating both through the destruction of subject and object alike—all of Weil's classifications of the interior experience of war comprise the natural and historical terrain of the animated film. It is what we might call the dark side of Cavell's reference to "drafts of the world's animism," the violence such animism visits upon our deepest notions of how the world and its inhabitants, subject and object alike, should behave. A world where simple matchsticks come alive and write messages to the audience is a world with precious little regard for the basic categories of lived experience. The same is even more profoundly true for a world where those same matchsticks, which should never have been alive in the first place, can now be injured and killed, as in Bardin's *Conflict*. It is only in the realm of animation where we can watch that which was always a dead object suddenly become a living being. Likewise, it is only in the realm of animation where suddenly that which was never alive can die—perhaps the ultimate expression of animation's fundamental *illogics*. This interplay of life and death, living and non-living, subject and object, person and thing—the same dynamics of disruption that commentators from Weil to Scarry have seen as being the crux of war's interior experience—is and always has been at the very center of the unruly work of animation. As media scholar Paul Wells once put it, "Every animation re-orders the world."[26]

PHOTOGRAPHY, DRAWING, AND ANIMATION

In this sense, the witness offered by the animated film is not just distinct from but also in many ways opposed to that of modernity's prevailing form of wartime representation: the photographic image. Before there were even modern cameras, there were photographs of war—the origins date back to Roger Fenton's daguerreotypes of the Crimean War of 1853–56, thirty-five years before George Eastman began selling his first commercial camera and forty-five years before animation arrived at the turn of the century. The result a century and a half later is a world awash in images, even of what Benjamin would regard as history's underside. "Being a spectator of calamities taking place in another country is a quintessential modern experience," Susan Sontag writes in her masterful account of the ethical difficulties of picturing violence and suffering, *Regarding the Pain of Others*.[27] For those who have not known war themselves, what they think they know of it is a measure mostly of what they know of its pictures. For that, Sontag observes, there is always "a nonstop feed: as many images of disaster and atrocity as we can make time to look at."[28]

Yet for all their ubiquity, just how much these photographs actually reveal about war's terrible "structure of unmaking" remains an open question. The basic condition of the photograph is marked by distance and remove—a detached *regarding of* more than an engrossed *entering into*. In Sontag's definition, photography is "an omnipotent, and predatory, viewing from a distance."[29] The photograph is, in her account, as much a barrier as a window, a demarcation of distance even more than a source of connection. "The whole point of photographing people is that you are not intervening in their lives—only visiting them," she writes. "The photographer . . . has no intention of entering into the horror of those images as experienced by the inhabitants of those worlds."[30] Hence the deeply problematic nature of what Sontag calls the act of "regarding the pain of others," the encounter at the heart of war photography. To commit the conditions of war to film inevitably turns us all into spectators of a drama we can hardly understand, separating us from the subjects being captured on celluloid even as the photographer tries to bring us closer to their experience.

There is no doubt that photography can uniquely capture the basic visual reality of any situation (though in the age of digital manipulation, this need not always be the case). The same is true for any form of live-action filmmaking, especially in the documentary tradition. Sontag calls it the condition of displaying "something directly stenciled off the real."[31] But the very parameters of photographic representation mean that this proximity will always remain, to some degree, illusory. To photograph is to frame, and in framing reality photographs also act to constrict and even to change it. "There is an aggression implicit in every use of the camera," Sontag warns. "In deciding how a picture should look, in preferring one exposure to another, photographers are always imposing standards on their subjects."[32] The great Civil War photographer Matthew Brady, no stranger to the battlefield, famously declared that "the camera is the eye of history."[33] But perhaps he also said too much, for the impulse of history is always toward order and explanation—toward *continuum*, per Benjamin. The problem of the photograph, according to Sontag, is that it can work to obscure even as it aims to reveal; as an instrument of interpretation and understanding, the filmic record is also part of the very apparatus that consigns so many victims to history's dark spaces, framing them out of the story and removing them from view, placing their experience into the realm of the invisible.

One response to the compromised position of the photograph has been the rise of drawing as a counterforce in historical narration. From the *manga* works of Hiroshima survivor Keiji Nakazawa to the testimonial accounts of Art Spiegelman's *Maus*, based on his father's experience as a Holocaust survivor, to the journalism of Joe Sacco detailing his work in the Palestinian territories and in Sarajevo, the graphic novel as it has evolved since the middle of the last century has repeatedly endeavored to record and to represent some of the worst horrors of the modern age. Such works embrace and radically foreground their own subjectivity, offering up in every line that is placed upon the page a personal testimonial and an act of interpretation. In this way, they stand against the seeming objectivity of the photograph and its claims to transparent truth. "What is written about a person or an event is frankly an interpretation, as are handmade visual statements, like paintings and drawings," Sontag writes. "Photographed images do not seem to be statements about the world so much as pieces of it."[34] Or, as she later adds: "Artists 'make' drawings and paintings while photographers 'take' photographs," one being openly an addition to the world, the other a kind of subtraction.[35] Yet the drawing and the photograph also, inescapably, share a common limitation. Both are bounded forms, both tethered to the fixity of the single, still image. As comics scholar Hillary Chute has observed, the graphic novel is defined by its "trafficking in the presentation of the stationary framed image" and by its "unique spatial grammar of gutters, grids, and panels suggestive of architecture."[36] As much as such works may endeavor to present their readers with the rendering of unspeakable acts, they must always organize and present those images within the boundaries of frame, page, and book: literally boxing them in and keeping them under covers.

The question of the frame is no small matter: it is in many ways the question of the historical record itself. Grounded in the material

components of the page and attuned to the private experience of reading, the graphic novel and its related forms must inevitably regulate
the material they present, offering a deliberate organization of experiences that in themselves wildly exceed such presentation. Against
the boundedness of the drawn image and the carefully controlled architecture of the graphic narrative, the medium of animation offers a
boundless, amaranthine plasticity: an entryway to the cinema's own
"states of reverie, of waking dream, of strangeness or enchantment,"
in Deleuze's words.[37] To capture the singular image—whether to
make a drawing or to take a picture—is always, inevitably, to *choose*:
to include this in the shot and not that, to shoot here and not there,
to draw this and not that. In Sontag's words, "To photograph is to
frame, and to frame is to exclude."[38] But what becomes of those left
out of the frame? "What pictures, whose cruelties, whose deaths are
not being shown?" she asks.[39] Reflecting in 2004 on the abundance of
imagery of the Iraq War, the philosopher and literary theorist Judith
Butler asks aggrievedly, "If 200,000 Iraqi children were killed during the Gulf War and its aftermath, do we have an image, a frame for
any of those lives, singly or collectively?"[40] The ethics of the frame
are deeply fraught, for what photo or even series of photos and what
drawing or even series of drawings could ever capture two hundred
thousand deaths?

But maybe one matchstick can.

THE ERA OF THE WITNESS

At its heart, animation offers not just a means of bearing witness,
marked by its capacity for illogics and its potential for unbounded
transformation. It also offers an ethics for bearing witness. The
ethical representation of real human suffering is one of the gravest
issues in the philosophy of the visual arts. "The justification of the
neighbor's pain is certainly the source of all immorality," says philosopher Emmanuel Levinas, who himself served as a prisoner of war

during World War II.[41] Insofar as the photographic image creates a *spectator* to suffering rather than a *witness* to it, the problem of its ethics remains open. The wording of Levinas's moral formula—the *justification* of the neighbor's pain—remains purposefully broad: it is not just those who enact violence that share in its moral culpability but anyone who is aware of such actions and justifies them, including those who choose to simply do nothing. How is the photographer—even with the best intentions—not part of this moral conundrum, "venturing out into the world to *collect* images that are painful," per Sontag's description?[42] In their ubiquity, in the distance they create, photographs, Sontag writes, can "make a compassionate response seem irrelevant."[43] Is this not part of what Levinas calls the justification of the neighbor's pain? It is not that we should never look upon suffering—in fact, Levinas insists that we must, declaring in one of his most famous and most enigmatic pronouncements that "*ethics is an optics*."[44] There *must* be a moral way to look: to see and to acknowledge the suffering of others. But how? What is the imagery that turns the viewer not into a spectator or even into a reader but into another witness, into what the psychoanalytic theorist and Holocaust survivor Dori Laub calls "a witness to the process of witnessing itself"?[45]

For Levinas, it must be an imagery "founded in the idea of infinity"—an idea that brings us again into close proximity to animation. Levinas's pronouncement that *ethics is an optics* is repeated throughout his book *Totality and Infinity*, and the means to creating an ethical form of imagery depends in his philosophy on the difference between the two ideas in his title. For Levinas, the idea of *totality* is something like Benjamin's idea of the *continuum*: a realm where everything is ordered and arranged, where everything has a place and meaning is already fixed. Levinas speaks of totality and history interchangeably: both are consumed by an "objectivity" that maintains that to know and to classify and to distinguish and to solidify is the beginning and ending of truth.[46] The problem with totality is that it leaves no room for excess and for change, no capacity to encounter that which is unassimilable. An ethical stance toward the world, Levinas argues, requires the perspective of infinity: an excision of limits, an openness to that which is unclassifiable, a recognition of understanding as a constantly receding horizon rather than a fixed border. "Infinity," Levinas writes, "overflows the thought that thinks it" and creates the possibility for "a situation where totality breaks up."[47] For Levinas, ethics is a way of looking at the world without the boundaries of fixed and immutable categories, of always allowing oneself to be subject to the possibility of the new, of opening ourselves to the potential for bearing witness to that which we never before imagined. If ethics is an optics, it is a way of looking at the world with an infinite openness to that which we do not already understand.

Levinas never specifies what this ethical vision might look like in practice, except to relate it to the realm of "dream and subjective abstraction" and speak of it as a kind of "overflowing"—an imagery of incessant multiplicity, not beholden to any fixed categories.[48] Maybe, once again, it is a matchstick. Not just any matchstick, of course. A matchstick that is also a man—and a borderline and a weapon and a cavalry horse and a vehicle. And also just a matchstick, an object that ignites when struck against the side of a matchbook. And also every soldier stationed in Berlin, West and East. And also every combatant in the global Cold War and its bloody local conflicts. And also any soldier ever involved in a border dispute that turned suddenly violent. And also any victim engulfed by war's flames. And also anyone ever touched by violence at all. If there is anything that might be called an art form of the infinite, unbounded by preset forms and limitless in its possibilities, it is animation. The disruption of totality is one of the organizing impulses of the medium. Where Levinas's idea of totality is committed to rigid systems of thought—this is this and that is that—animation is committed to their breakdown—this is this and also that and also something else again, as the matchsticks are. That animation has an inherent capacity for infinite invention is something that every animator knows. As Pixar animator Andrew Gordon once put it, "You can do anything in animation."[49] That this limitless capacity for invention might also serve as the ethical basis for crafting images of the most unimaginable suffering, suffering that exceeds any normal schema, is something that has been discovered time and again across history by those animators who have come face to face with the exigencies of conflict and catastrophe. A true ethical imagery, one that does not merely package the suffering of its victims into postcard images but brings the viewer into the space of that suffering to better illuminate its distorted physics of trauma, will be an imagery that remains open at all moments to an infinite world of possibility and change.

The depth of the world's need for such imagery can be measured by the sheer ubiquity of this form—in the vast number of animated films that speak to the experience of war from a position of knowledge and personal history, a position of witness. If animation allows us to uniquely glimpse the interior experience of war, then this may go a long way toward explaining the urgency with which so many of those subjected to war's vicissitudes have turned to this mode. For nearly every war fought in the proximity of a functioning animation industry, there have been animated films about that war. And since the advent of modern digital technologies and the appearance of consumer animation software, the correspondence between war and animation is approaching total parity: we may very soon reach the point where *every* war on planet Earth is rendered in animation by the artists in its vicinity. For Laub, the act of bearing witness comes always with a sense of compulsion. "There is, in each survivor, an imperative need to *tell* and thus to come to *know* one's story," he writes.[50] In the pages that follow, I aim to give an accounting of a great many of these films, to honor their imperative to tell and to ask what they help us to know, we who did not live through these same sufferings. Some are tools of resistance, undertaken under great duress in situations of occupation and oppression, while others are forms of protest meant to challenge democratic regimes engaged in immoral acts of war. Many are expressions of pacifism born from personal experience and bent on opposing the fundamental premises of war. Some are the work of memory, made by artists reconstructing their own recollections of wartime devastation. And still others are designed as living memorials to the dead, taking the testimony of those who have suffered and transforming it into new work for a new age.

As organized here, the films move from the center of the lived experience of war and atrocity, where the shorts and features all were made in the midst of wartime violence, to a point far outside war's reach, where each film's traumas exist only in inherited memories. Each of these films is touched by the actual experience of war—not the free reconstructions of artists working years or generations after the fact and not the imaginings of filmmakers who never lived through the conflicts they convey, however sincere their efforts may be. Whether as combatants or civilians, leaders or bystanders, observers or unwitting victims, the animators considered here have themselves in nearly every case experienced the traumas they depict. They have turned to the medium of animation as a tool of personal reflection and a means by which to leave a record for future generations to know, to fill out history's *discontinuum* with expressions taken from lived experience. They have turned to animation, in other words, as a means of bearing witness.

It is a process that continues. Wieviorka's *era of the witness* has not yet ended nor looks to anytime soon. Every animator who has ever tried to capture the experience of war knows this. "Does [the] unreal world of animation help to escape the reality?" an interviewer once asked Bardin, decades after *Conflict* and his many other films from the Soviet period. "Unfortunately not," he replied. "If you don't go to politics, then politics comes to you. It comes through doors, penetrates holes and it becomes impossible not to think about what is happening."[51] Bardin's words, uttered in 2014, were especially fraught given the political context of the time. That was the year when Russia forcibly annexed Crimea from Ukraine and subsequently began supporting military factions in the eastern regions of the country bent on independence. The story of bloodshed between neighbors, so much like that which Bardin had so painstakingly and achingly crafted nearly thirty years before in *Conflict*, had come to pass in his life yet again. It would be an especially profound and distressing repetition. Born in Russia to a family from Ukraine, Bardin's national and ethnic allegiances extend to both sides of the conflict. Once united under the auspices of the Soviet Union, these intertwined nations had been peaceable neighbors for decades since. In Bardin's words, reflecting on the sudden new crisis, "We turned out to be in [a] situation to which we were not ready—our nearest neighbor suddenly has become an enemy."[52] He could be describing his own film, made in another age, almost another world. But he is speaking about the present. The act of bearing witness remains as urgent as ever.

PART ONE

AT WAR

CHAPTER 1

RESISTANCE

A young architecture student named Walter Tournier is huddled in the darkroom at the Laboratory Roca, home to some of the only film development facilities in all of Uruguay. It is peaceful outside at the moment: the film lab is tucked into a quiet, residential section of Montevideo full of one-story storefronts and the occasional high-rise apartment. The trees that line the streets are all in bloom. But the calm at the moment is deceiving. It is 1973, and a guerilla war has been plaguing the city for nearly a decade. The Tupamaros National Liberation Movement, a leftist group, has been conducting kidnappings and assassinations for years alongside more flamboyant operations, robbing banks and openly distributing the money in the city's slums. American agents from the CIA have been helping the Uruguayan authorities plan their counterinsurgency operations. Political arrests are a regular part of life in the city, and torture is common.

Tournier knows this all too well. A member of the left-wing film society Cinemateca del Tercer Mundo, or C3M, he has been involved for years in organizing screenings of revolutionary cinema around the city: fictional and documentary films from Cuba and Colombia as well as a few homegrown works by local Uruguayan filmmakers. He has already been arrested once for his activities, grabbed and hooded on the street and taken to a secret location. Years later he would still vividly recall being gripped by "a brutal fear" during the ordeal.[1] By the time of his release, C3M was nearly gone, most of its members having been arrested and imprisoned or else having fled the country.

With only a few stalwarts left, Tournier and the others decide to commit to one last project before disbanding and going underground: a film they will all make together, in secret. It will take them nearly a year and a half to complete, and in the midst of their production, in June 1973, there will be a coup: President Juan María Bordaberry will dissolve the Parliament and begin to rule the country with a junta of generals, vastly increasing the pressure on the country's insurgents and dissidents. Still, Tournier and his three fellow filmmakers press on, filming and compositing and editing all on their own, with no production apparatus to speak of. Even with the crisis unfolding around them, they are desperate to complete their film: a work they are calling *In the Jungle There Is Much to Do*, a fifteen-minute animated short, a film for children.

Specifically, it is a film for one child: the three-year-old daughter of the imprisoned Uruguayan artist Mauricio Gatti. *In the Jungle* is framed as a story for her, though in truth she was already older and had already heard its story many times before. Confined to the marine barracks in Montevideo for interrogation in the early 1970s, Gatti drew his daughter pictures of animals from the jungle who had been taken off to a zoo, and he gave them to her along with some lines of verse whenever she was allowed to visit, a father's way to explain his incarceration to his child. One of Tournier's associates in C3M had the idea of turning the pictures into an animated film, one that could be shown to all the children of the country's many political prisoners. Even as their world dissolved and nearly all their friends and contacts vanished into secret prisons or unmarked graves, Tournier and three other animators labored ceaselessly on the project, crafting a complicated work of cutout animation made by layering paper figures over a colored board, which they slid over and past one another one painstaking frame at a time with needles. The final product is mesmerizing. The Uruguayan folk musician Jorge Estela sings Gatti's verses over a guitar while images taken from his drawings dance and play on screen. Set in a striking palette of primary colors, with every inch of the screen dashed in pigment, the figures move in two dimensions only, left and right, up and down, like they have commandeered the pages of a book. The story the film tells is as simple as it is poignant: the animals, once happy and free in the jungle, working and sharing and playing with their families and their friends, are rounded up by hunters from the city and put inside a zoo. A kindly girl hatches a plan with the animals who still remain in the jungle, and together they pull off a daring escape, rescuing their captured friends through a secret tunnel. The scene where the plucky little girl, her hands thrust casually into her pockets, nonchalantly leads her jungle menagerie down a busy city boulevard, much to the delight of a trolley full of screaming children in the background, is a delightful act of fancy, as perfect an example of animated whimsy as you will ever find. The film ends with the happy animal families reunited, the hunters thwarted, and the world set right again.

For Uruguay's military authorities, this simple fable—as seemingly innocuous as any Disney fare—was an unacceptable act of political subversion. Tournier and the remaining C3M members managed to organize only a single screening of the film, specifically for the relatives of political prisoners who had not yet returned. Tournier was arrested again shortly thereafter, and, after being released on a technicality, decided it was time at last to leave the country. The extensive film collection of C3M, which numbered into the hundreds, was confiscated by the police, but a few copies of In the Jungle managed to get smuggled out. The film spread across Latin America and then around the world and became a signal point for anyone facing political persecution, "a symbol of denunciation" in the words of one account.[7] Tournier would go on to become one of the preeminent animators in Latin America, decorated with numerous international awards for films both political and nonpolitical. One of his latest, Seven Seas Pirates from 2012, is an old-fashioned children's adventure story, with no particular political overtones attached.

Were the authorities in Uruguay wrong to fear In the Jungle and treat this children's tale as a deeply subversive film? From their perspective, not at all. Though its story is one that you could tell to any three-year-old, its creation was an act of defiance and its content was laced with messages of resistance against authority and solidarity for the victims of the state. The animals in Tournier's jungle live in an anarchistic utopia, unconstrained by any forces other than kinship and love and unattached to any source of authority other than themselves. Meanwhile, the hunters—evil urban-dwellers whose stark black-and-white uniforms contrast with the rainbow-tinted animals and mark them as both wardens and as unwitting prisoners themselves—possess no legitimate claim to impose their system on the coterie they capture. The mission to free the creatures in the zoo, though as charming an adventure as you will find in any child's story, is also an obvious act of insurgency: a mission planned carefully in the jungle (plate 3) and executed in the city through means of subterfuge, eventually spilling out spectacularly into the city's streets.

But there is also another, entirely different register in which the film is dangerous—not as an instance of counterpropaganda but as an act of witness to crimes that were supposed to be invisible. The images that populate Tournier's frame are taken directly from Gatti's sketches when he was confined in the marine barracks; the verses are the ones he wrote in that prison. Although they do not speak specifically to Gatti's particular condition—he shields his daughter scrupulously from any aspect of his incarceration except the cage— they speak in general terms about the *fact* of his imprisonment. They constitute what literary critic Shoshana Felman discusses as the mandate to universalism so often seen in acts of witness, "the *appointment* to bear witness" being "an appointment to transgress the confines of that isolated stance, to speak *for* others and *to* others."[3] One of the fundamental conditions of most political imprisonment is its secrecy: after the 1973 coup, conditions in Uruguay's prisons would grow far harsher and the kind of minimal communication with his daughter that Gatti was permitted back in 1971 would become completely impossible. Citizens would no longer even be arrested, as Gatti and Tournier both were—for someone who is formally arrested can still be released. Instead, the state's perceived enemies would mostly be "disappeared," taken away without notice or explanation, never to be seen or heard from again. *In the Jungle* runs counter to that policy of disappearance. It offers us a voice from someone whose voice was never supposed to be heard. The very fact of its witness, abstracted though it may be, is an act of resistance: it is exposing to international view that which the officialdom of its nation does not want to be seen. Embedded in this whimsical story of a handful of animals trapped inside a zoo is the terrible narrative of a country that before the decade's end would come to have the highest percentage of political prisoners anywhere in the world, a nation that would come to be known as "the torture chamber of Latin America."[4]

RESISTANCE AND THE PUBLIC TRANSCRIPT

In the Jungle is beautiful and powerful, but it is not unique. Where there are conditions of systemic oppression and violence—where one nation is occupied by another after war or where the levers of state are violently seized from inside and turned against a people— you will frequently find works of animation that tell the story of that ugly process and give voice to those subject people. This is the work of what I call *resistance animation*. If the work of the propagandist in times of war and conflict is to support and justify the mission of the state, then the goal of the dissident is to subvert and oppose that mission. The defining feature of this dissidence is that it is offered from within the state but in opposition to its aims, either because the state has been occupied, because it is viewed by the artist as in some way illegitimate, as in civil war, or because the state is engaged in military actions that the artist feels deeply to be an abuse of its powers. The work of resistance is in some sense the most natural political purpose to which animation can be applied. As many commentators have noted since the beginnings of the medium, animation always carries within it the potential for subversion. It is, as critic William

Kozlenko wrote in the 1930s, the only filmic form "that has freed it-self almost entirely from the restrictions of an oppressive reality."[5] We might think of this capacity as the inversion of the Pixar anima-tor's observation that "you can do anything in animation."[6] In ani-mation, you can always also *undo* anything—be they lines or charac-ters or ideologies. This ingrained capacity for critique and constant tendency toward change is a formal feature of the animated medium that the propagandist must always struggle to control, most espe-cially in times of war. For the resistance artist, the formal freedom of animation can become an embodiment of the physical or ideological freedom that they seek. In the truest possible sense, to borrow from media theorist Marshall McLuhan's famous phrase, the medium will thus become the message.

Yet that message must never be made too apparent. In other words, the work of resistance animation must always speak in a dou-ble voice, for it is always addressing two audiences at once: those in power, whom it is usually not in a position to openly offend, and those without, for whom and to whom it actually means to speak. In the one case, its message must remain opaque, lest it draw the ire of those who could prevent it from ever being seen; in the other, it must simultaneously be perfectly clear, lest its purpose as an expression of solidarity and a rallying cry for the opposition be missed by those who need it most. This is the reason that *In the Jungle* had to be told as a children's fable: it had to be innocuous enough to be shown in public and yet powerful enough to raise hopes. Within its own histor-ical moment in Uruguay during the period of the 1973 coup and the ongoing guerilla war, the film was, on these terms, a failure: Tourni-er's known status as a leftist and his affiliation with C3M marked the work as dangerous from the start, no matter its content. Every single film in C3M's possession was considered to be a threat: it was an archive understood by state and subversive alike to be a weapon. But the covert nature of the film's message, even if it was known to the authorities in Uruguay, was a major factor in its circulation and success once it passed beyond the borders of Tournier's home country, into the places where he was unknown: in Argentina during the years of the Dirty War or in Chile under the rule of General Augusto Pinochet and in so many places beyond. To the officialdom of these authoritarian states, *In the Jungle* was a children's cartoon about a zoo. To the loved ones of the disappeared, it was a revelation, a message made just for them and a witness to their suffering.

The oppressed and the marginalized, says historian James Scott in his seminal *Domination and the Arts of Resistance: Hidden Transcripts*, are always used to speaking with a double voice and listening for others who might be doing the same. It is a condition of power that it regulates the expression of those who are subject to it, and it is a condition of being subject to power that one learns to echo its dictates in public while speaking one's own truth out of earshot. With few exceptions, Scott writes, "the public performance of the subordinate will, out of prudence, fear, and the desire to curry favor, be shaped to appeal to the expectations of the powerful."[7] Scott calls the open discourse of a nation sanctioned by and acceptable to those who hold the power the *public transcript* of the historical record and observes that the material entered into this record will always exist "in close conformity with how the dominant group would wish to have things appear."[8] The often unrecorded instances of subject peoples conversing among themselves—the hushed conversations and sideways glances, the inside jokes, the unheralded songs and stories of folk culture—he calls the *hidden transcript* of an era. This is the "discourse that takes place 'offstage,' beyond direct observation by powerholders," Scott writes, and its function among the subordinates of any situation is to "contradict or inflect what appears in the public transcript."[9] Though Scott does not consider the place of animation within a nation's media and public discourse, his framework is illuminating: it reveals the utter rareness of animation's condition in situations of tremendous power imbalance, animation being that strangest of forms that can exist openly within the *public transcript* even as it contributes to a subject people's *hidden transcript*. From occupied France to the Soviet satellite states, from the screening rooms of Latin America to the authoritarian states of the Middle East, animators have again and again made work with the real or implicit approval of the same authorities whose crimes they most wish to expose. In times of crisis and in the face of authoritarian inhumanity, animation has time and again promised to conform to the record of history's *continuum*, even as it has then used that opportunity as a chance to secretly speak for its *discontinuum*, its forgotten and its silenced voices. Just as the propagandist loudly makes animation a tool of the state in times of crisis and of war, so does the resistance artist quietly make it a tool of that same state's deliberate subversion.

Which is not, it should be said, necessarily the same as bearing witness. Resistance and witness stand in an important relationship to one another, but they are neither synonymous nor interchangeable. At one extreme, the animation of resistance can become simply a form of regurgitated propaganda presented in code—this is often the case with animators working in recently occupied nations hoping to recycle the tools of war propaganda under a thin layer of allegorical cover. At the other, one may bear witness in such a way that serves to trouble the offending state not at all, layering that hidden transcript so deep under the public one that it becomes effectively unrecoverable. Thus, in situations of resistance, especially in the midst of conflicts still unfolding, the animator of conscience is faced with a powerful and perplexing dilemma: how to bear witness to the suffering of a people and then conscientiously turn that act of witness into an effective tool for change, all without the one undermining or negating the important work of the other. Or, to put it another way: how to weaponize witness. The true use of resistance animation is as a kind of weapon. But it is more the weapon of the saboteur than the soldier, more about dismantling the intellectual or moral infrastructure of the enemy regime than dehumanizing and dismissing its people. The absolute best works of resistance animation—the ones that serve an urgent political and ethical purpose in their own time and go on to assume an artistic one in ours—are powerfully motivated by this tension between efficacy and honesty, politics and witness. Many, in fact, are openly *about* this tension and the strains it inevitably puts on the artist, who may or may not have ever yearned for a political role but also may or may not currently have a choice. The situation of powerlessness that is always the condition of the resistance animator tends to have a way of forcing difficult ethical decisions. Speak up or say nothing? Serve the cause or make art? Bear witness or look away? Sometimes, confoundingly but also powerfully, the answer may actually be both.

ALLEGORY AND SYMBOLISM, OR SPIKING THE ART

To see resistance animation in its barest and most urgent form, one need look no further than the state of an occupied people. For the animator, at least through most of the twentieth century, the condition of occupation presents an unusually stark moral choice: accept the resources offered by the occupier, or do not practice your art. It is an inescapable fact of the medium that in the decades before the digital revolution making animation was by and large a time intensive, resource intensive, and capital intensive operation. Cases of animated works being made clandestinely in straightforward defiance of the state—as Tournier and his compatriots bravely did in Uruguay—are on the whole exceptionally rare, as they require some degree of access to existing resources (as in the lab where Tournier was able to secretly develop his prints) and the ability to facilitate the underground distribution and screening of the work (as Tournier had via C3M)—no easy feat in the era of giant film canisters and delicate celluloid prints. Far more common than the case of the political subversive who turns to animation is that of the establishment animator who must consider turning to political subversion, taking the enemy's money but spiking the enemy's art.

Such is the case of French animator Paul Grimault, perhaps the very archetype of the resistance animator. Prior to the Nazi invasion of France near the start of World War II, Grimault struggled constantly with the task of raising enough money to complete his work. He was one of the country's most prominent animators—the only one to run his own studio during the 1930s—but still had to spend the better part of his time searching out backers who cared to support a French-based animation house, such was the devastation of the once renowned French animation industry after the First World War and the newfound postwar dominance of American cartoons in the European markets. When the war came and France fell, Grimault found himself in the embarrassing position of seeing a significant improvement in his business. Suddenly, all the American competition was taken off the market, and the Germans were eagerly distributing money to support the creation of new animated works. Enamored of Disney's aesthetic even as they rejected other aspects of his filmmaking, including what they saw as the American appropriation of European folklore, the Nazis were determined to create a European-based and ideologically acceptable alternative to Disney, and they were not above supporting talented animators in the occupied countries while they tried to get a proper German animation studio off the ground. Having spent the better part of his career soliciting funding for his films, Grimault found himself after the invasion in the unusual position of being courted: the Nazi-appointed occupation government actually advanced Grimault the funds he needed for his next film via the Crédit National.

The question of whether or not to take the enemy's money is often inescapable for the animator in wartime, and Grimault accepted this condition as the only means to continue his work. His end of the bargain—unspoken, as the hidden transcript so often is—was that he would use these contributions to craft a message of resistance for his audiences in France, even as he rendered that message indecipherable for the officials that the Nazis had installed at the Comité d'Organisation de l'Industrie Cinématographique, charged with overseeing France's film industry during the occupation. This was not the standard approach for those animators who flourished under the Third Reich, even in the occupied nations of Europe. In France, other animators like Raymond Jeannin were crafting open works of propaganda for the Nazis, as in *Nimbus Liberated* (1944) wherein the happy family of the French comic book hero Professor Nimbus, deceived by a horribly stereotyped Jewish radio announcer, is annihilated in an Allied bombing run carried out by American cartoon heroes—Mickey Mouse, Donald Duck, Popeye, and others all manning a squadron of B-17s. Or in the occupied Netherlands where fascist animators at the newly founded Nederland Film crafted anti-Semitic fables about frolicsome animals learning to turn against dissidents and racial outsiders. Amidst this panoply of hate, Grimault's wartime magnum opus, *The Scarecrow*, released in 1943, immediately stands out. Its genius lay in its ability to seemingly give Grimault's Nazi funders exactly what they wanted while at the same time speaking to the people of the animator's home nation and the terrors of the situation that they faced.

The first step in Grimault's approach is to use the film's style as a deliberate cover for its content. The Nazis in general and Reich Minister of Propaganda Joseph Goebbels in particular were desperate to match the level of visual craftsmanship and care that defines the Disney style, with the earliest Nazi attempts like Hans Held's *The Troublemaker* in 1940 being obviously poor imitations of the form. That style, which was still in the process of formation at the time in Disney's shorts of the late 1930s, stood at the intersection of multiple artistic priorities that together were beginning to create a unique house aesthetic at the Disney Studios: a studied imitation of live-action cinematography such that the animated realm took on the qualities of an immersive world (a feature greatly aided by Disney's development of the multiplane camera, which created a sense of actual depth in animation by allowing different elements of the visual field to move at different speeds); a careful adherence to real-world physics within the animated realm, despite the medium's ability to challenge or disregard such rules; and a core conservatism and even sentimentality in the content of the films, often regarded as kitsch by Disney's detractors. Sometimes defined as "Disney realism" or "Disney formalism," the formula by which the shorts of the late 1930s were created and which was then epitomized in the studio's first feature film, *Snow White and the Seven Dwarfs* in 1937, proved enormously successful across the United States and Europe. Grimault, a practiced draftsman who was no stranger to competing with the American cartoons that had recently been dominating French markets, arguably came closer than any other European animator of the war years to matching Disney line for line. *The Scarecrow* (plate 4) is a charmingly rendered work, playful yet careful, plastic yet controlled. The color palette of yellows and oranges lends the whole film a warm glow, and the characters could easily have stepped right out of any Disney film—in fact the pair of birds whose peril is so central to the film's plot strongly evoke the family of birds in danger in the classic 1937 Disney short *The Old Mill*, one of the origin points for the studio's shift to its new realist mode. Grimault's German backers were incredibly pleased with his work, calling it "excellent and unique."[10]

Grimault's second move is to make a show of explicitly divorcing his film from politics, placing his work squarely in the realm of fable and fancy and eschewing any larger purpose. It is not just that the film involves a living scarecrow, a talking cat, and two birds. Other Nazi animated films of the period were also set amidst a kingdom of animals, like Nederland Film's *Reynard the Fox* (1943) in Holland and *The Troublemaker* in Germany. Rather, Grimault casts his central figure explicitly as a being who cares more about his own gratifications than anything else going on in the world. He is a remarkably lascivious hero, and the film devotes a surprising amount of time to establishing this fact, devoting one long scene in the beginning to the scarecrow's prurient fascination with a pinup magazine, skipping over all the text of the magazine so he can ogle its pictures—including what seems to be an article about an ongoing war, represented by a picture of a cannon with the headline "Boom!" Reporting on the outside world be damned, this comfortable scarecrow could not care less about such matters. If the film engages and plays with certain stereotypical notions of French masculinity—a relatively unusual feature in Grimault's filmmaking overall—it arguably does so as a matter of strategy. One could hardly craft a more unlikely resistance hero than a scarecrow whose major motivation seems to be the fulfillment of his own sexual prurience, the only time that he moves from his perch in the field being when the dastardly cat tries to seduce him in drag. Yet resistance hero he would be.

The path to understanding the film's coded messaging lies in following the narrative thread connected to those cute little birds lifted from Disney's *The Old Mill*. They are happy friends of the scarecrow, and the film opens with them playfully scurrying through his oversized clothing and joyfully taking up a perch under his hat. The film's peaceful, pastoral world is disturbed only when a traveling cat who has come from afar notices the birds and decides they would make an excellent snack. Failing to catch them on his own, he tries to enlist the scarecrow's help, but the happy sentry just plays dumb. As the cat tries to maneuver around the scarecrow's combination of indifference and misdirection, the hero's deft sleights of hand, moving his hat this way and that while the birds fly in and out of view from the cat, proves too swift. In another animator's hands, this game of cat and mouse—or cat and bird, more accurately—might carry some signs of resistance, but the flamboyant apathy of the scarecrow is here his greatest defense. The scarecrow does not seem to be trying to thwart the cat and delight in his defeat so much as he simply finds him an annoyance and a distraction from his solipsistic enjoyments: mostly he just wants to get back to enjoying his dirty newspaper. The cat's greatest offense is therefore not so much asking for the birds per se as it is simply disturbing the lazy scarecrow at all. Hence the final move where the cat tries to play into the scarecrow's libido and lure him off his perch with a *Looney Tunes*–style seduction trick: the scarecrow follows the voluptuous lady cat in a heartbeat, only to be ambushed and have his pumpkin head knocked off, allowing the cat at last to go after the defenseless birds. It is in response to this deception and attack more than in defense of the birds themselves that the scarecrow is finally motivated to action, repaying the cat with an equivalent knock to his head. The short ends with the scarecrow and birds happily dragging the cat off in a cage, free of his meddlesomeness at last.

Viewed outside its historical context, *The Scarecrow* looks like nothing more than a European imitation of American cartoon tropes—a carefully copied Disney-style realism paired to a *Looney Tunes*–style conflict-and-escalation structure. Inside its context, it becomes a parable of resistance and defiance made all the more urgent by the desperate situation of France's Jewish population. The scarecrow, at home in his pastoral environment, is a figure of immense freedom in the film: we learn early on that his big pumpkin head can detach and reattach with ease, and though he is primarily stuck at his one perch in the field, he is capable of turning his dressing mannequin's body into a living trunk and hustling along on its spindly legs. That is to say, he is an embodiment of the basic freedom of the animated form, and, though he seems less powerful than the clawed cat who is his adversary, this freedom gives him a special kind of strength: a resilience and a wiliness that he can use when it is called for most. And the most pressing use for that freedom as established in the film is in defense of those who are most at peril, the innocent birds that the cat wants to take for himself. Those birds are marked as both vulnerable and as unmistakably different from the scarecrow within the world of the film. Tethered to a realist stylistics and essentially borrowed from a Disney film, they have none of the scarecrow's plastic freedom or transformative power. They are from a world apart, yet the scarecrow has long made them welcome in his field. Against the cat who has come in from afar and will try every strategy to order, cajole, reward, or force the revelation of the hiding place of the birds, the scarecrow must stay strong: playing dumb when he can, outsmarting when he can, and finally fighting when he must. The scarecrow must become a figure of resistance.

Depending on how you look at it, *The Scarecrow* becomes two very different films, like an optical trick that combines two images into one. On the one hand, it is a perfectly apolitical fable about a dopey scarecrow and a nasty cat. On the other, it is a clarion call to the French people to recognize their remaining strength, to shield the nation's Jewish population at all costs, and to envision a moment when they might send their conquerors back to whence they came. Screened across France and Germany alike, *The Scarecrow* towed the line of the official public transcript by effacing its own politics even as it broadcast those same politics to anyone who knew how to decipher its hidden transcript. From a formal perspective, the basic move that Grimault manages to enact in *The Scarecrow* is akin to the distinction that Walter Benjamin makes between the *allegory* and the *symbol*. Though the two terms are often used interchangeably, Benjamin argues for a vital difference in their operations and the worldviews they support. For Benjamin, allegory is defined by its apparent complexity: it demands a process of decoding and thus does not carry its apparent meaning on its face. The realm of the allegory, Benjamin writes, is "fragmentary, untidy, and disordered," a realm wherein the use of metaphor is necessarily "incomplete and imperfect."[11] But the symbol is far different. For the symbol to be a symbol, it cannot ever be unclear. The symbol, for Benjamin, is the allegory refined to the point of transparency, a mode of representation so legible that it is as if "the concept itself has descended into our physical world, and we see it itself directly in the image."[12] To encounter an allegory is to encounter a story in need of copious acts of interpretation. To recognize the symbol is to recognize immediately what it represents: it is as if one sees the thing itself. Literature uses allegories; religion uses symbols.

And politics uses symbols too. The work of the resistance artist in the context of animation is to craft a film that reads as allegory to the oppressor and symbolism to the oppressed, masking its basic simplicity under obfuscating gestures toward complexity. It is not that Grimault's Nazi backers or German audiences did not understand *The Scarecrow* to be interpretable or were fooled into some alternate and false interpretation. It is that they were lulled into thinking it to be fundamentally apolitical and therefore subject to multiple possible decoding strategies: perhaps it was about the scarecrow overcoming his laziness or the cat not making unreasonable demands of strangers. Maybe it was about just leaving things in their place. The work of allegory always requires efforts of interpretation. The work of the symbol is immediate. The scarecrow, decadent and given to the pleasures of life but also fundamentally good, *is* the French. The cat, coming from afar and issuing demands, *is* the Germans. The birds, vulnerable and seeking a hiding place, *are* France's Jewish population. The rest of the message follows from there. The successful work of resistance animation submits to an occupied nation's *public transcript* a work of allegory divorced from politics, all the while signaling to those keyed into its *hidden transcript* a work of political symbolism of the first order and through that symbolism a message to resist.

CHILDREN'S ANIMATION AS RESISTANCE

Given these conditions, the gap between the public transcript of a work of resistance animation and the hidden transcript it contains can be quite wide indeed—so wide sometimes as to turn a simple children's story into an urgent political statement, as Tournier did in Uruguay and as others have done worldwide. Part of the appeal of children's animation for those engaged in resistance is the ready applicability of childhood stories to the resistance animator's competing demands. The typical children's fable is designed both to maintain interest and basic meaning on its face as well as to welcome the work of allegorical reading and the careful alignment of character, action, and outside meaning that such interpretation entails: children can return again and again to the story as they age and mature, discovering new layers in it each time. But the children's story can also collapse these two layers into one if seen in the proper light, folding its apparent meaning and its interpretive depths into the realm of pure symbolism. It is this process that one sees in the resistance work of a children's animator like the Czechoslovakian master Hermína

Týrlová. Starting her career in the early days of Czech animation in the 1920s, Týrlová rose to become one of the foremost animation artists in the nation, founding her own puppet animation division within the country's Zlín Film Studio. When the Nazis fully occupied Czechoslovakia in 1939 in the first of their many acts of invasion, Týrlová, like Grimault in France in the years after her, found herself in the uncomfortable position of being supported by an enemy state. Declaring most of Czechoslovakia a protectorate of Germany, the Nazis dedicated themselves to cultivating a sense of normalcy in the region, and supporting the nation's established filmmaking apparatus helped serve this goal. The Nazis generously funded various Czech animation projects until the later years of the war and countenanced the work of those operating outside the main studios in Prague, like Týrlová, so long as they remained apolitical.

As an animator specializing in works for children, Týrlová never attracted much attention from the Nazis. But if she was largely apolitical in her work before the war, she would stay so no longer during the occupation years. Her first work of puppet animation and her most important work from the period of the war, the 1944 film *Ferda the Ant*, is, like Grimault's *The Scarecrow*, a piece that combines two transcripts into one: on the one hand, a playful exercise in fantasy and escape for the children of the nation; and on the other, a fervent expression of hope for the liberation of the Czech people and a vision of a better time after the war. The basics of the film, drawn from a popular children's comic book character of the 1930s, are simple. The insects of the field enjoy a happy, festive life full of work and merriment until one day a dastardly spider entraps Ferda and his love interest in a series of webs. Calling for help, a brave snail comes from afar, slowly but surely, and rescues the ants, eventually capturing the spider and trapping him inside his hard shell. At film's end, the spider is imprisoned and put to work inside a nutlike treadmill, which is used to power a string of new contraptions in the insect land as the ants and other insects dance and sing again.

As with all of Týrlová's work, the vivacity of her puppets and the inventiveness of the world she creates are a special source of wonder.

Her wire-frame figures merrily dance, play instruments, and create elaborate lever and pulley systems for mining bits of salt and harvesting twigs. In line with the general magic of this world, one could easily interpret its simple story as an unremarkable fable, about as straightforward an application of a basic rescue narrative as one could ever find. But, of course, rescue narratives can take on a different connotation when one is actually in need of rescue, and Týrlová gives hints everywhere in her film as to the actual hidden transcript that she means for her audience to receive. The happy insects of the field at the start of the film are not just any insects but identifiably Czech ones: the character of Ferda was a Czech creation—a kind of national answer to international cartoon icons like Mickey Mouse or Felix the Cat—and a beloved figure of Czech childhood. And the capture of Ferda and his love interest is no normal instance of insects getting caught inside a spider's web. The spider lives adjacent to the ants and has engineered a semi-industrial system of webs that work on levers and pulleys—a dastardly counterpoint to the peaceable industry of the ants. The adjacent worlds of the ants and the spider seem to evoke the relative situation of Czechoslovakia and Germany, both neighbors and enemies. But the real *tell* in the film comes in a subtle bit of inventiveness in the design of the snail who comes to Freda's rescue, a snail who moves not by foot but on treads, like a tank. It is an unusual detail for the film, which otherwise makes no references to the modern outside world at all, only to the realms of folklore and tradition. Despite this minor incongruity, it seems mostly like just one more instance of whimsy in the film, which is surely how Týrlová meant for it to be read and understood by her Nazi censors. But in a world at war, a tank tread is also always a tank tread. Slow and lumbering but also giant as compared to the other insects and unmistakably powerful, the lumbering snail—friend of the ants and a happy beneficiary of their industry and harvests—resembles nothing so much as the Soviet Red Army, slowly but surely rolling its way toward Germany and the liberation of Eastern Europe. Keyed into these cues, the broad allegorical overtones of this children's fable collapse into the tight, clear structures of symbolism: the ants are the Czech people, the aggressive spider who entraps them is the Nazis, and the snail is the Soviet Army on its way to deliver liberation. (One hesitates to think what this might mean for the film's final image of the spider imprisoned and hard at work, powering the renaissance in the insect's happy field, the prevalence of labor camps being an unmistakable part of the Soviet system.) As with Grimault's *The Scarecrow*, Týrlová's *Ferda the Ant* undeniably submits a dual message to the public transcript of an occupied nation, seemingly accepting the state of occupation by denying its own political intent, all the better to smuggle its political message of solidarity, resilience, and hope into the realm of open discourse.

So powerful is the realm of fable and folklore for the dissemination of resistance messages that certain animated films based on these tales can even provide cover for filmmakers who only minimally mask their hidden transcript—sometimes even when the animators themselves are known figures of resistance. Such is the case with Wan Guchan and Wan Laiming's *Princess Iron Fan*, from 1941, the first feature-length animated work produced in China, made entirely in the midst of the Japanese invasion and occupation of Shanghai during the Second Sino-Japanese War. Like their counterparts in Europe, Grimault and Týrlová, the Wan brothers were prominent and beloved figures in their national filmmaking community prior to the outbreak of war. They were two of four brothers who effectively founded Chinese animation in the 1920s, working together to master the techniques then popular in the Fleischer Studio's *Out of the Inkwell* cartoons, which combined animation and live-action material, and producing their own version of the hybrid form with *Uproar in an Art Studio* in 1926. Yet unlike Grimault and Týrlová, whose work was entirely apolitical before the period of occupation, the Wans were well-known for their propaganda cartoons during the long lead-up to the Japanese invasion in 1937, producing close to a dozen films dealing with Chinese resistance against Japanese incursions.

This background makes it all the more remarkable that *Princess Iron Fan* ever reached completion. Moving in the early years of the war from city to city and production company to production company as each was closed in turn by the advancing Japanese forces, Wan Guchan and Wan Laiming found themselves, in 1939, at the Xinhua Film Company in Shanghai, the only film studio still operating in the city at that time, protected by its location in an area of the metropolis controlled by French colonial forces, known as the French Concession. Disney's *Snow White and the Seven Dwarfs* had premiered in China in that year, and the avowed mission of the Wan brothers' new operation at Xinhua was to produce their own feature-length animated work, which would be the first of its kind in Asia and would tell a story taken from the classic Chinese tale *Journey to the West*. It took more than two hundred artists close to three years to complete the film, and the conditions under which they worked could hardly have been more challenging. Over the long months of the film's production, most of eastern China fell to the Japanese, and by the end of this period not even the nominally independent foreign concessions in Shanghai would remain—the Japanese Army finally took control of the French Concession where the Wan brothers were finishing their film just weeks before its completion.

Astoundingly, the Japanese allowed *Princess Iron Fan* to be released, and the film played in multiple cinemas in Shanghai. It even played in Japan itself, where it was enthusiastically received by the nation's animators and filmmakers. The Wan brothers, once associated with such films as *Go to the Front!* (1938) and *Wang Lawu Became a Soldier* (1938) during the early years of the war, suddenly became artistic celebrities to the Japanese, the subject of numerous articles in the Japanese press and a specific point of inspiration for animator Mitsuyo Seo, who would just four years later helm Japan's first feature-length animated work, the war-themed propaganda film *Momotarō, Sacred Sailors*. That animators in China had been able to produce a feature-length animated film—one of the very first in the world, just a few short years after Disney had demonstrated the viability of the form—was taken as evidence of Asia's cultural independence from the West and a harbinger of artistic developments to come within the larger Japanese Empire. The Wan brothers would even help to promote such a view of their work. In an open letter to the admiring Japanese film critic Shimizu Akira published in Japan in 1942, the brothers spoke of their film in terms that emphasized its apolitical nature, speaking of it as an illustration of a "an educational Chinese legend or fairy tale" and explicitly disconnecting it from the war at hand. "The film project from beginning to completion took three years and during this period, the world had encountered many changes," they write. "During the making of the cartoon," they emphasize, "we were separated from the outside world."[13] While the idea of a nation's *public transcript* and *private transcript* are usually metaphorical, here in the Wan brothers' open letter we see an actual instance of artists submitting their work to the public transcript sanctioned by those in power, attesting to the film's adherence to the cultural standards and political agenda of the nation's occupying forces.

None of this would have been possible, and the film most likely would have been destroyed, had *Princess Iron Fan* not on its surface seemed so politically innocuous. Unlike the propaganda works that the Wan brothers completed before falling under occupation, this film drew from the realm of legend, its story being among the most famous in the long Chinese literary tradition. The turn to traditional fable—modeled on Disney's own turn to European folklore in *Snow White*—was specifically praised by the film's Japanese proponents, and the Wan brothers emphasize it in their open letter. "We always had this notion that the Eastern art of film-making should embody Eastern color and taste and it should not imitate and follow wholly the style of Hollywood," they write.[14] They go even a step further in the actual opening of the film, where a prologue plainly declares the picture to be a work for children and a vehicle for their moral education. The film's purpose, the prologue states, is aimed at "encouraging a healthy mentality for children," and the film's story is deliberately edifying: "The pilgrims' story at the Flaming Mountain represents the difficulties in life, and in order to overcome these difficulties, we have to keep our faith and work together."[15] The prologue carefully frames the film as being politically innocuous; it presents the film as an allegory—a story that invites critical interpretation so as to transpose its immediate situation to a variety of others encountered in one's life. And on one level, this holds true. The storyline of the film easily accommodates the interpretation that the prologue proposes. On a journey to recover important religious documents, the monk Tripitaka and his mythological companions, the Monkey King, a monk pig, and a friar named Sandy, reach an impassable realm of fire. Only the magical iron fan of a local princess, married to the evil Bull Demon King, will dampen its flames. One by one, the companions try to coax or steal the fan from the reluctant princess, and all of them fail in turn. Only when they finally work together at the end of the film are they able to obtain the fan and put out the fire in their path. It is, indeed, a story about learning to work together, and also a delight to behold: constructed in sober tones of black and white, the film combines a delicate artistry evocative of classical Chinese scrolls with ribald character design in the model of the comic Fleischer brothers shorts of the 1920s and 1930s, creating in total a work at once beautiful and effervescent.

And it is also entirely about the Japanese invasion of China and the absolute imperative to resist—if one is keyed into the symbolism of the film's hidden transcript. Part of the brilliance of the film as a work of resistance is the way in which it uses the extant elements of the story of *Journey to the West* to cover for its real-world referents. The Wan brothers' prologue may frame the film as a story about adversity set in purely abstract terms, but the actual obstacle faced by the characters in the film is a realm of total fire. The film's depiction of this burning realm is, in the context of the brutal razing of Shanghai and other cities at the time, absolutely devastating. The Monkey King, who goes to inspect the conflagration, does not confront merely some abstracted wall of flames: it is a whole landscape consumed by fire, a wide expanse entirely annihilated. He starts to sweat profusely as he stands and regards this realm, but the perfect droplets look not so much like perspiration as like tears. The Wan brothers in fact linger on such images, forcing the viewer to confront them. For anyone who had lived through the realities of Japan's horrific bombing raids and wholesale destruction of certain conquered territories, this great obstacle in the path of the film's character was no abstract allegorical component in need of excessive interpretation: it was China itself, in flames.

And the response to those flames, the way to put them out and allow the characters' journey to continue past such destruction, is collective revolt. It is not just the main characters who must ultimately unite and work together to defeat the evil Bull Demon King, as the opening prologue implies; it is in fact all the villagers of the land, hordes of local men together attacking the evil bull and his castle using whatever farming implements they have at hand. Whereas the central characters of the film are all rendered cartoonal to a greater or lesser degree—some by virtue of their animal identities, others in an exaggerated rendering of the human form—the villagers who participate in the final revolt are all, to a one, drawn in a photorealistic manner through a process known as rotoscoping or rotoscopy, wherein the artist traces over live-action film footage. They are, in other words, not just abstract extras in the story but the actual people of China, drawn to resemble themselves. And though they are attacking a mythical figure capable of transforming from human to bull, that figure is indelibly associated with the Japanese military—the real *tell* being not in the visual design of the bull but the sound design of the film. That is, the sound made by the Demon Bull when enraged is not an animalistic sound at all but a mechanical one, the unmistakable whirl of an airplane propeller. For a nation destroyed and demoralized by Japanese bombing runs for close to a decade—the earliest coming in a prewar air raid on Shanghai in 1932 that deliberately targeted civilians, the first of its kind in the world—the horror of that sound would be unmistakable. The Wan brothers might have claimed in their letter from 1942 that the film was disconnected from the world, and they may have insisted in the prologue of the film that it was all an abstract lesson about cooperation, but what they had actually constructed underneath the public transcript of an apolitical children's story drawn from classical legend was a powerful act of witness to the sufferings of the Chinese people, a testimony to the conditions of their devastation, and a call to arms against the occupiers who had brought such suffering—one that played in cinemas across that occupied nation with the unwitting endorsement of those occupiers themselves.

BREAKDOWNS OF RESISTANCE

The Scarecrow, *Ferda the Ant*, and *Princess Iron Fan* are powerful works, meticulously crafted statements by master animators that make the art of resistance look almost effortless. It is not. A careful balance between the realms of allegory and symbol—a balance at which Grimault, Týrlová, and the Wan brothers excelled—is not always so easily maintained or so expertly accomplished, and the long record of wartime animation is studded with works that seem to be misfires in this same basic project. It is arguably in this context that we might best understand the problematic work of the German animator Hans Fischerkoesen, a prominent commercial artist from Leipzig who specialized in advertising work in the years before the Second World War and was essentially drafted into service by the Nazis to help bolster the animation division at the country's Babelsberg Film Studio. Unlike other German animators of the Nazi era, Fischerkoesen has attracted attention from later historians and animation scholars for the apparent lack of ideological verve within his works. A far superior draftsman to his peers and a more sophisticated storyteller, Fischerkoesen's work arguably comes closer to Goebbels's ideal of building a homegrown competitor to Disney than that of any other German animator of the time. And unlike the obvious militarism in Held's work or the crystal-clear references to Nazi anti-Semitism in those of a colleague like Heinz Tischmeyer (whose most famous film from the war, *Of the Little Tree That Wished for Different Leaves*, from 1940, tells the story of a tree picked bare by a rapacious Jewish figure), Fischerkoesen's main films of the war years seem markedly free of political purpose. *The Snowman*, from 1943, tells the story of a child's wintertime creation who magically comes to life and is determined to see the summer, stowing away in an icebox until July only to realize his terrible mistake once it is too late. (Given its Nazi pedigree, the film bears an uncomfortable relationship to the snowman character Olaf in the Disney blockbuster *Frozen* [2013], who likewise dreams of finding a way to see the summer.) In his 1944 film *The Silly Goose*, meanwhile, a headstrong goose leaves its farm and is nearly kidnapped by a nefarious fox.

No one would ever mistake *The Snowman* or *The Silly Goose* for works of true radicalism. Whatever else they argue for, they seem to share a basic conservatism that demands one know one's proper place and not go adventuring where one does not belong. But if this is their message, it is one that is shared by untold numbers of fables and folktales before them. Their basic conservatism aside, it is difficult to track Fischerkoesen's films back to any kind of more specific articulation of Nazi thought. Recognizing this apparent interpretive void, many film scholars have hazarded readings that make Fischerkoesen out to be a kind of quiet artistic saboteur set down in the middle of the Nazi media apparatus, a figure of "resistance and subversion" in the description of animation scholar William Moritz.[16] For Moritz, Fischerkoesen's films evince a fine sense of critique, necessarily subtle but also unmistakable: his work, Moritz argues, "warns against being seduced by the glamor of fascism, and encourages us to think carefully about home and the city and responsibility—to realize what happens to victims and to do something about it."[17] Others, including Fischerkoesen's own son, do not see such interpretations as squaring with the actual man that they knew. "My father was completely apolitical," he told the German newspaper *Der Spiegel* for a 2013 profile. "We know that my father was not a NSDAP [Nazi Party] member. But he definitely wasn't a resistance fighter, either."[18]

Whether or not Fischerkoesen intended to offer his films as a form of subtle resistance to the Nazi program may ultimately be impossible to say. But what can be said with certainty is that if they were intended as beacons of resistance of any kind, they undoubtedly failed at that project. The very interpretive uncertainty that Fischerkoesen's films invite, evidenced most of all by the years of debate among scholars that they have provoked, places those films squarely in the realm of Benjamin's concept of the allegory, that "fragmentary, untidy, and disordered" realm where meaning is always "incomplete and imperfect."[19] Fischerkoesen's snowman may be "an average person . . . trapped in a given environment" and yearning for something better, as Moritz says; then again he may be an arrogant upstart who gets what is coming to him when he melts.[20] Such interpretive uncertainty is both common and extremely generative when it comes to works of art, but for the partisan invested in urgent political communication it is anathema. Whatever other interpretation the resistance animator's work may later sustain, the immediate exigencies of the political moment call not for allegory but for symbolism, for a clear and unmistakable transference of a thing into its representation so that it might be spoken covertly in the public record where otherwise it would be entirely forbidden. The zoo animals *are* the nation's political prisoners. The honorable scarecrow *is* the French Resistance. The powerful snail *is* the coming Soviet Army. The Demon Bull King *is* the Japanese military. But whatever the snowman is remains fundamentally unclear. If this made Fischerkoesen a poor fascist ideologue, that may or may not be to his credit. But it does not on its own make of him a figure of resistance, at least in any meaningful sense. To bury one's politics so deep that they cannot be readily uncovered is, from the perspective of the animators of resistance and protest, not to offer up those politics at all.

Of course, an animator in a situation of occupation who is used to working in the realm of propaganda may also find himself beset by the opposite of the Fischerkoesen problem. Such is the case with the rare postwar Japanese film *Cherry Blossoms*, from 1946, one of the first animated works produced in Japan after the nation's 1945 defeat. As elsewhere, the conditions of occupation in Japan after the war produced a dynamic wherein the American occupying forces sought to both control and support the nation's tradition of animation as part of their general efforts to restore a sense of normalcy after years of war, which in Japan lasted nearly a decade and a half in total. New animation studios were formed in the very first months of the occupation, and the leading Japanese film studio, Tōhō, put a new emphasis on animated film production, sponsoring a famed series of lectures for their staff by the master animator Kenzō Masaoka. One of the first works to emerge from this new postwar environment was Masaoka's own film *Cherry Blossoms*, an impressionistic and largely nonnarrative eight-minute short that in its lush aestheticism and absence of story seems to be quite carefully designed not to offend. Nearly the whole of the film consists of the travels of two diminutive nymphs, who are both born from flowers at the film's beginning and travel through the Japanese countryside observing various scenes of nature and daily human life: two dogs playing, a boat making its way downstream, people rushing this way and that with umbrellas in the rain. A misty and beautifully sketched work, which through details of shading manages to give the impression of being in color even though it is made entirely in black and white, *Cherry Blossoms* is a stunning visual meditation.

It was also never released to the Japanese public at the time, shut down by studio heads at Tōhō before ever being shown to the American occupation authorities. The problem in this seemingly neutral exposition on flowers and landscapes was the inherent symbolism that those flowers and those landscapes had taken on over the course of the war years. For Japanese audiences trained, like all wartime audiences, in the immediate recognition of nationalist symbols— think of Donald Duck kissing his model of the Statue of Liberty in *Der Fuhrer's Face*—*Cherry Blossoms* was a slow tour through the political iconography of the defeated nation, the chrysanthemum flowers that fill the frame representing Japan's imperial government, Mount Fuji standing for the Japanese nation itself, and the cherry blossoms of the film's title, known for blooming briefly, a potent symbol of the kamikaze pilots so often celebrated in Japanese wartime film. If Fischerkoesen's symbolism in works like *The Snowman* and *The Silly Goose* was submerged too deep to be accessible to audiences (if it can be said to have existed at all), that of a film like *Cherry Blossoms* was kept too close to the surface to escape the eye of those now in power. Whether this was the inevitable result of animators trained in fifteen years of wartime filmmaking trying suddenly and unsuccessfully to accommodate their skills to peacetime, or whether it was a deliberate attempt to smuggle a hidden transcript of defiant nationalist pride into the occupier's request for a new public record, the failure and subsequent disappearance of *Cherry Blossoms* from circulation was ultimately a failure of the inevitable balance that resistance animation must strike between its public mode of allegory and its hidden mode of symbolism.

What the experiences of *Cherry Blossoms*, *The Snowman*, and other works of real or possible resistance animation reveal, both in their successes and in their failures, is just how delicate political symbols are in times of war and just how pointed the stakes are in the ideological conflict that always accompanies occupation or other civil strife. The watchful censor, where there are censors, will always be compelled to spot in an animated film the kinds of subsumed details that took *Cherry Blossoms* out of circulation, the triggers to a political symbolism that opposes the governing power and that those in power will hence always want to erase. For the animator who comes of age during a period of prolonged, even lifelong occupation—not the short-lived conquests of the Nazis or the seven-year American occupation of Japan but something like the lifespan hold that the Soviet Union had over its Eastern European satellite states during the decades of the Cold War—the constant negotiation of object and symbol can become a regular, even normal part of the animation process: an endless game of catch-the-subversive-symbol with censors who may sometimes prove overeager to eliminate any hints of dissent. Such was the case with the Polish animator Stefan Schabenbeck and his 1969 entry to the International Short Film Festival at Oberhausen,

Germany, *Drought*. Likened by some commentators to such artistic masters of existential allegory as Samuel Beckett, Schabenbeck was at the time a rising star in the well-funded world of Polish animation during the Soviet era, animation being for the Soviet Union and its satellites a major generator of international prestige in the cultural battlefronts of the Cold War.[21] *Drought* is in many ways typical of Schabenbeck's much-lauded work: thematically abstract but concrete in its visual realization, deeply concerned with people's lives but set on a scale so vast in its scope as to almost be metaphysical. It is a form of visual poetry, one whose politics are buried so deep within its metaphors as to be almost indistinguishable—but not quite.

The five-minute film concerns a group of tiny, indistinguishable people—no more than a swarm of stick figures really—endeavoring to build a bridge across a gaping chasm in an abstract, largely empty landscape. Schabenbeck's rendering of this striking and quasi-apocalyptic world, expertly sketched with architectural precision, contributes to a general feeling of despair that pervades the work. Across the chasm, we see another mass of stick figures also building a bridge, but something in the bleak design of the film and the atonal music that underscores its visuals warns us not to get too hopeful about any possibilities of connection. Inevitably, the two bridges fail to link up, each built just slightly askew of the other. No matter, though: the two people-masses each build a corner into their bridges so that they can finally come together after all. But no sooner do they manage to connect than one mass of people begins to squabble with the other, and rather than connect their bridges at last they instead build a wall at the point of connection so as to keep the other mass of people out. It is a savagely cynical conclusion to the narrative, one whose despair is further compounded when the camera pulls out into an extreme wide shot revealing a landscape full of a seemingly infinite number of giant cracks, each with another group of tiny people trying to build across it a little bridge. And then it begins to rain—giant, destructive, annihilating drops that drown the ant-like world of scurrying stick figures, leaving only a clear and empty landscape.

Most of Schabenbeck's films were well received within Poland and abroad, and he was a regular presence on the international festival circuit during the 1960s, even winning first prize at the San Francisco International Film Festival. Before *Drought*, he had yet to run into trouble with the censors in Poland or elsewhere in the vast Soviet-aligned system. But there was a distinct problem with *Drought* according to those censors, the ones from East Germany specifically: it was the wall. The problem was not the film's general statement on the ways that people around the world fail to communicate, nor the despairing vision that actual connection between peoples might in fact never come to pass and perhaps we should all just give up. The issue was simply the implication that a wall—*any* wall—might have something to do with such existential problems: a proposition that might in turn raise the specter of the Berlin Wall being seen as a negative force in the world and not a necessary bulwark against Western capitalist encroachment as the Soviets always insisted. (Indeed, the Soviet animation studio Soyuzmultfilm was turning out propaganda films around the same time extolling the great virtue and wisdom of the wall, which can be seen literally blocking Western military advances in films like *A Lesson Not Learned*, from 1971.) The problem, in other words, was a problem of symbolism and of the possibility that Schabenbeck, for all his decoration, might be attacking one of the most important international symbols of the superpower state to which Poland was a client. It was enough to shut down the distribution of the animator's meticulously crafted work, which was withdrawn from that year's Oberhausen competition and shelved, and to force Schabenbeck's transfer to another animation studio inside Poland without any further explanation; he left the Polish film industry entirely a year later. Schabenbeck has insisted, even well after the demise of the Soviet Union, that he in fact meant no reference to the Berlin Wall in this case, that his act of resistance was inadvertent.[22] And it seems possible to believe him, insofar as his work always tends to the abstract and prophetic more than the immediate and political. But such is the tricky terrain of the realm between allegory and symbol, the territory in which the resistance animator always seeks to operate and which the censor always seeks to patrol. The vigilant authoritarian state must always be on the lookout for symbols being taken out of its control and reconditioned: in that rhetorical move can lay the beginnings of political action.

RESISTANCE IN A DEMOCRACY: PROTEST ANIMATION

For animators like Schabenbeck living under conditions of close political control, any unauthorized brush with symbolism, no matter how subtle, could be a step too far. Yet for those animators free to engage in open protest in democratic societies, the subtlety of most resistance animation would likely prove ineffective at best. In this way, the dynamics behind Schabenbeck's fall from grace help to illuminate the relationship between *resistance animation* and what might be best understood as *protest animation*, forms that can be seen as the authoritarian and democratic expressions of the same processes. Both are engaged in negotiating or exploiting the vulnerability of the political symbol during times of crisis and war. Yet while resistance animators live under conditions of occupation and authoritarian rule that force them to speak only in a whisper, protest animators live in a democracy where they must shout as loudly as possible to be heard, all the more so amidst the din of protest and counterprotest in divisive times of war. Thus the tendency of the protest animator to use the visual power of the animated film in as shocking a way as possible, often in a direct, frontal attack upon a beloved or respected cultural symbol—the opposite of the resistance animator's tendency to bury symbolism under layers of inoffensive misdirection.

An archetypal example of such protest work, and one of the most viscerally affecting examples of this relatively rarefied genre, is the 1969 anti-Vietnam protest film *Mickey Mouse in Vietnam* created by the painter and filmmaker Lee Savage and the legendary graphic designer Milton Glaser (creator of the "I Heart NY" logo) for a one-time showing at an antiwar event called the Angry Arts Festival. The film, just one minute long, packs a tremendous ideological punch, even if you know exactly where it is going before it even begins. Within the span of that minute, a crudely drawn version of Mickey Mouse—no doubt violating every article of American copyright law—decides to enlist in the army, travels across the Pacific by boat, and lands on the shores of Vietnam (plate 5), where he is suddenly and unceremoniously shot in the head by an unseen enemy within seconds of entering combat. Roughly drawn so as to evoke the two-dimensional quality of a young child's notebook sketches, the film switches in its last moments to a relatively ambitious top shot, forcing us to stare down upon Mickey splayed out in a rice paddy with a bullet wound in his head, blood streaming down his face.

Though its visual style is purposefully naive, the film is a sophisticated application of animation toward the purposes of antiwar protest. Told in any other format—live-action, narrative, song—the minimalist story of the film would either wither under its own simplicity or spiral into surrealism: Mickey Mouse enlists, and then he dies. And were the film to feature anything other than an iconographic cartoon character—were it, say, simply about a nameless young recruit—it could hardly expect to sustain much attention. But to watch an American cartoon icon like Mickey Mouse—a worldwide symbol of happy youth and innocence, whether one regards that status cynically or in earnest—descend upon the jungles of Vietnam and perish almost instantly is to receive in the span of a few seconds a dizzying overload of antiwar protest messages: about the terrible waste of American youth, about the idiotic fantasy of the mission itself, about the complicity of American corporations and the American media in perpetuating the war, about the literal death of American innocence. The political philosopher Hannah Arendt famously identified the Vietnam War as the world's first military conflict fought not over power but over the *image* of power: "How could they be interested in anything as real as victory when they kept the war going not for territorial gain or economic advantage . . . and not even for the reality, as distinguished from the image, of power?"[23] Another word for the image of power is the symbol, making the work of protest animation like *Mickey Mouse in Vietnam* a form of direct attack on the rhetorical heart of the American war effort.

Such instances of open war declared on an image of power are common to protest animation, which tends to move the submerged symbolism of resistance animation to the surface of the film. One sees a particularly naked example in the avant-garde protest film *The Barbarians* by the French filmmaker Jean-Gabriel Périot, whose output stands at the experimental intersection of documentary and animation, moving thousands and sometimes hundreds of thousands of still photographs over and past one another in explosive, rapid-fire montages: a process of animating not the visual content inside each photograph but the actual photographs themselves. Made in 2010 in the midst of the ongoing wars in Iraq and Afghanistan and in support of worldwide antiglobalization demonstrations underway that year, *The Barbarians* begins with an intentionally dull slideshow of posed group photos from the G8 summit and other gatherings of world powers, the heads of state smiling benignly at the camera again and again. Slowly, other group photos begin to be mixed in: weddings, sports teams, family photos. And then military units: American, French. But also militaries from the developing world, also paramilitaries and partisan groups. All smiling in what has become a near blur of terrifying, militarized banality. At a breaking point, the film then switches to images of street protest: antiglobalization demonstrations but also street actions in Latin America, in the Middle East, in the Parisian *banlieue*—rapid at first but then slower and then slower still until the street protest photos start to take on the aura and calm of the G8 photos at the start of the film. Who exactly, the film asks us, are the barbarians? The calm, poised world leaders and the unseen but omnipresent militaries behind them, both theirs and those of their client states? Or the furious protesters in the street, who are opposed to this system and are lighting up cars? What is an image of political power, and what of barbarity? The film ends with an epigraph from the radical writer Alain Brossat, exclaiming "We are scum! We are barbarian!"—refigured as a statement of pride, a source of political power. Périot's film turns on the question of the image of power—which picture makes us feel calmed, and which makes us recoil? Which represents order, and which disorder? Which picture is lying, and which one is telling the truth?

Périot's assault on images of political power in general and on the likeness of the head of state in particular bears echoes of another work of wartime protest animation, perhaps the most famous of the genre—one that takes the idea of exploding the image of the head of state far more literally than *The Barbarians*. I am referring here to a 1968 protest film called *Escalation*, an important thematic predecessor to *The Barbarians* as well as an unofficial companion piece to *Mickey Mouse in Vietnam*, insofar as it offers an answer of sorts to the question posed by *Mickey Mouse* of what Disney's work might come to mean in times of war. Visually these two Vietnam era protest films are radically unlike one another: as works of wartime iconoclasm go, *Escalation* is far more visually accomplished and also far more in line with dominant protest narratives then circulating in the culture, especially ones centered around the perceived lies and hypocrisy of the president. Here at the start of the film a giant cartoon version of President Lyndon B. Johnson's head is wheeled onto the screen as if on a parade float (plate 6). As a voice evocative of Johnson's begins to sing "The Battle Hymn of the Republic," the president's nose starts to extend like Pinocchio's, growing longer and longer until it literally explodes into a rapid-fire montage of sex-, war-, and Americana-themed photographs, directly anticipating the kind of photo-collage approach that Périot will later use. The attack on LBJ as an icon and personal representation of the lies and distortions fueling the Vietnam war effort—and likewise the phallic obsessions such warmongering was believed to represent—was certainly nothing new in America's antiwar protest culture of the time. Watching the president's nose grow longer like Pinocchio's could almost be considered unconscionably trite—were it not for the significant fact that the film was actually *made* by one of the Disney animators from *Pinocchio* (1940). That artist was legendary animator Ward Kimball, two-time Academy Award winner and one of the most important artists to work for the Walt Disney Company in its early days, part of a group of core Disney animators known by film buffs as the "Nine Old Men." Of Kimball, Disney himself said he was the "one man who works for me I am willing to call a genius."[24]

Kimball's persona and reputation hang over every moment of *Escalation*. Though not nearly so famous as Disney himself, he was for those who knew of him an icon of American animation history, and it is this iconicity that gives *Escalation* its particular political power. In the context of Kimball's prior work, *Escalation* becomes that rare work of counterculture made by a one-time gatekeeper of America's mainstream culture, a literal attack on a national symbol of American power, the president himself, made by a man who spent his career creating nationally recognized cultural symbols for American export abroad. Kimball was specifically the animator responsible for the character of Jiminy Cricket in *Pinocchio*, for the mice Jaq and Gus in *Cinderella* (1950), for Tweedledee and Tweedledum, the Mad Hatter, and the Cheshire Cat in *Alice in Wonderland* (1951). To have Kimball enter so directly the debate over America's war efforts in Vietnam is an unmistakable mark of the symbolic civil war then unfolding within American culture. When the man who created Jiminy Cricket is so moved by an issue that he makes a cartoon about blowing up the president's head, you know that you are in the highest realm of cultural crisis. *Escalation* was a signed work made by a known artist. Kimball financed it himself and presented it personally in the context of a tour of college campuses where he gave speeches against the war. It was the only independent animated film ever made by any of the original Disney animators, who otherwise did their work entirely in the context of the studio. And that personal stamp was a pivotal part of its message, a literalization of the cultural conflict predicted by *Mickey Mouse in Vietnam*. If the shock of *Mickey Mouse* was predicated on a perceived breakdown of the nation's core symbols in the context of what its animators viewed as a destructive and immoral war, then Kimball's speaking tour in support of *Escalation* was the actual manifestation of that very breakdown: Jiminy Cricket against LBJ, Mickey Mouse against the army, and a nation ideologically at war against itself, engaged in a heated struggle over the proper meaning of its central symbols.

PROPAGANDA, EX POST FACTO

In this way, the condition of the protest animator and the resistance animator can be seen as not so very different from the condition of the propaganda animator. Their work may be different, but the dilemma of that work may be in many ways the same: a war over symbols, though bloodless, can still be a violent conflict, one in which enemies are demonized, moral exclusionary zones established, and actual people erased. To be opposed to a particular state at war, whether democratic or authoritarian, is no guarantee that one is on the side of the human and humane, that one might not find cause to justify the suffering of one's neighbor. Thus may the seemingly noble figure of resistance backslide into the far less inspiring visage of the propagandist, as when today's protester in the street becomes tomorrow's ideologue in power. Faced with the drastic shifts that come with the end of war, the collapse of states, the realignments of power in a civil war, for whom and to whom will the resistance animator and the protest animator speak? Can they find the means to show war's face in the midst of their political and national commitments?

Alas, the history of animation is full of sad turns where the work of resistance feeds directly into acts of propaganda and where what seemed like arguments against dehumanization morph into rationalizations for recrimination. The annals of postwar animation are often as rife with hate and anger as any catalog of films from the jingoistic lead-up to a war. Look through the films of peoples recently freed and you will often find there full-throated expressions of their darkest revenge fantasies, examples of what I call an *ex post facto propaganda* that is no less brutal in its intents for the fact of its arriving so late. Such is the case with a short 1945 film called *Il Duce Narrates*, Greece's first-ever work of animation and a showcase of revenge fantasies enacted on the figure of Benito Mussolini, Il Duce, who initiated an invasion of Greece in 1940 that led to a joint Italian-German occupation of the nation. Specific recriminations enacted on Mussolini's figure here include, among others, crushing him inside a giant fist formed from a map of Greece until blood comes dripping out the sides of the hand or drowning him at the bottom of the Mediterranean Sea (while also impaling him on the mast of a sunken battleship) with a rock tied around his neck by a displeased Greek goddess. In the newly freed Czechoslovakia, Hermína Týrlová's delicate wartime childhood fables, imbued with their subtle political messages of hope, give way in the postwar years to openly violent fantasies of animated revenge. She makes *The Revolt of the Toys* at the close of the war in 1945, though it is not released until 1947. The film is an outcry of pent-up anger wherein a Nazi officer, played by a live-action actor, forces his way into a Czech toy shop and is attacked by an army of stop-motion dolls and figurines, whimsical beacons of childhood who collectively beat him, tie him up, and literally set him on fire. In France, Paul Grimault will follow up *The Scarecrow* with a classic and beloved postwar work, *The Little Soldier*, from 1947. Telling the story of France's postwar world by means of a toy soldier who returns injured from war to a bombed-out town where nothing, not even his beloved toy shop and ballerina doll love interest, remains the same, the film is a delicate tale of trauma and recovery refigured through the animated objects of childhood. And it also includes a particularly gruesome ending for the collaborator figure in the film, a wicked jack-in-the-box toy who stayed behind during the war and lorded his power over the other toys in the shop. Ensnared in a gin trap near the end of the film, the collaborator toy is left alone, stuck helpless and screaming in a snowy field as hungry birds of prey begin to circle and to swoop. For an occupied people suddenly liberated, the subtle whispers of resistance animation can turn in a moment into the angry but empty shouts of a strange form of propaganda that has come too late, a symbolic war waged most aggressively against those who have already decisively lost.

For some animators working in the resistance tradition, the very tension of the line dividing resistance and propaganda becomes itself one of their most important subjects: engaging with this difficulty and admitting to the darker possibilities of their form serves as a powerful, even vital, check on the political and moral lassitude that always threatens to undermine such work. In the case of *The General's Boot*, a stunning 2008 work by the self-taught Syrian animator Akram Agha, the necessity of such checks even becomes a part of the message of protest itself. Born and raised in Syria under the dictatorship of the Assad family, first Hafez al-Assad until 2000 and then Bashar al-Assad after, Agha began making short computer-animated films after relocating to Saudi Arabia, eventually attracting attention online and on the international animation festival circuit. *The General's Boot* is both a reflection on his experiences living under the Assad regime and a testament to the sad universality of those conditions. The film—fourteen minutes long and rendered in the boxy, early computer graphics style of 1990s era videogames, a condition of Agha's limited equipment—is premised on the visual conceit that the only part of a human being made visible will be their footwear: city streets teem with high heels and sneakers, children's shoes and old man's loafers all walking this way and that. In this world, a general—invisible to us except for his black military boots—rises to power, calling others in identical boots to follow him in perpetuating acts of violence against the citizenry, securing his rule (plate 7).

Visually limited as it is, what sets Agha's work apart is the inventiveness with which he deploys the controlling trope of the visible footwear and the invisible human: there are propaganda posters lionizing boots, grand statutes of boots, a flag with a swastika-like symbol made only of boots. In one of the most impressive scenes, a battalion of boots disperses a gathering of citizens seen only by their footwear in a manner that directly evokes the famous Odessa Steps sequence from Sergei Eisenstein's legendary Soviet film *Battleship Potemkin*, the marching boots trampling the shoes of men, women, and children as they mercilessly chase the innocents down a staircase. The degree of pathos that Agha can evoke with only a pair of shoes is remarkable, and the film's most gruesome images are as harrowing as those in any live-action film: rows of executed prisoners seen only by the pairs of shoes dangling below a hangman's platform, a firing squad wherein a row of boots stands before a single pair of shoes, the wall behind it suddenly splashed red with blood as the shoes turn on their sides.

The General's Boot, for all the brutality it depicts, seems to end with a ray of hope. After the Odessa Steps incident, protests finally break out against the regime of the boots, represented by a spinning ball of civilian shoes that grows larger and larger as it makes its way through the city, eventually overwhelming even the columns of military boots and knocking down their military base. From the statues of boots around the city emerge statues of actual people, the human form finally made real through the political acts of protest and revolt. As a result of this uprising, the general's boots are finally overthrown, their occupant still invisible: the last time we see the boots they are standing calmly in an otherwise empty jail cell. Now actual people can for the first time be seen in the world of the film: we witness a politician giving a speech to supporters in the street, with actual men, women, and children cheering him on—the human form emblematic of the coming of democracy at last. Agha created *The General's Boot* in 2008, when Bashar al-Assad's hold on Syria still seemed strong. But he first posted it online three years later in 2011, after the emergence of the Arab Spring protests in Tunisia and in Egypt and just days before the first protests against Assad in Syria.[25] For many at the time, the film became a statement on the Arab Spring, a prediction of its power and a call to further acts of protest and resistance across the Middle East. And the film no doubt works in this vein and achingly shares these sympathies. The world of authoritarianism, it shows, is a world without people, an uncanny realm of invisible humans and walking symbols: a world where the totems of power are more powerful and more meaningful than the actual people affected by those totems and that power. It is the grand statue of boots in the city's central square that makes this point most clearly—the statue is not of the invisible general wearing his boots, it is just of the boots themselves, a giant pair of marble boots enlarged and towering over the nation's people, the symbolic overwhelming and dominating the human.

But Agha also attaches an important caveat to such readings at the very end of his film, in its very last scene. We see the leader of the protest movement alone now, in a fine state room that seems to be the presidential palace. He has taken his shoes off and is staring at a safe in which are kept a pair of shiny black military boots. He stares at them, clearly agonized, struggling not to put them on. On one level, it is a statement as to the perpetual temptations of power and the hold it can take even on those who rise to such positions only with the best intentions. But it is also, vitally, a statement about the nature of political symbols themselves and the erasure of the human experience they entail. It is a statement about resistance *and* about propaganda. The main world of the film is a world of pure symbols: the military boot, the lady's high heels. As Benjamin says of the symbol, we do not need to guess at what it represents, its meaning is condensed and transparent: it functions as if "the concept itself has descended into our physical world, and we see it itself directly in the image."[26] In literary terms, the iconography of Agha's film uses a specific form of symbol called the *synecdoche*, wherein the part stands in for the whole, the boots for the man. But dwell in that realm of discourse too long, Agha warns, and the part can *become* the whole, the symbol can take the place of the thing it represents, the statue of the general may actually just be of his boots. Insofar as artists working in the mode of resistance or protest deal only in symbols, they risk falling into the same line of thinking as the autocrat and the totalitarian: a world in which ideas of power matter more than the people subject to that power, who become almost totally erased. The animator of conscience must fill in those erased people even in the midst of his or her political commitments, *especially* in the midst of those political commitments.

THE HAND

In this vein, Agha's work echoes what is perhaps the single most renowned work of resistance animation ever put to film and one that is frequently considered among the greatest animated films ever made: Jiří Trnka's *The Hand*. Like *The General's Boot*, which clearly drew inspiration from Trnka's work, *The Hand* recognizes the condition of the artist in situations of totalitarian control as being one of constant struggle with the question of the symbol. The genius of Trnka's film derives in part from the fact that it takes this very struggle as its subject, brilliantly turning a story of the artist's dilemma under totalitarianism into a statement of resistance against that totalitarianism. That Trnka would be the one to issue this protest makes it all the more compelling and all the more urgent. Prior to making *The Hand* in 1965, Trnka was already one of the most celebrated artists in all of Eastern Europe, adored in his native Czechoslovakia and showered with resources by that nation's Soviet controllers: they gave him the run of his own animation division within the national film studio Krátký Film Praha and provided him with every tool an animator might need. He was even named a "National Artist" in 1963, two years before *The Hand*. It was a situation faced before by many a prominent animator under conditions of occupation, but unlike Paul Grimault in France in the 1940s or his fellow Czech animator Hermína Týrlová during the Nazi occupation of Czechoslovakia, Trnka never showed any signs of dissenting from or subverting the mission of his Soviet backers. He made enchanting, wondrous, richly realized puppet animations telling stories from Czech folklore, and he was beloved for it. Many called him the "Walt Disney of Eastern Europe," and there was even talk of him using his prominence to start a career in the United States.[27] But in a show of loyalty to his Soviet backers and to his homeland, Trnka always denied such rumors: "I cannot make little cowboys; I know how to make Czech peasants, and nobody in America is interested in those. I am local."[28]

So it was all the more shocking when in 1965 Trnka, without warning, delivered a scathing indictment of the entire system on which he had built his career, using his legendary skills as a puppet animator to craft a fable-like work about a happy artisan puppet who is forced into the service of an authoritarian hand, who literally makes a puppet of him. On one level, Trnka's Soviet backers should perhaps have seen this moment of open dissent coming, as he had done something similar once before at the very start of his animation career, not against the Soviets but against the Nazis. That work, *Springman and the SS*, which Trnka made in 1945 as a hand-drawn animated film before he later turned to puppet animation, was one of the first films he ever worked on, having started his animation career in the immediate aftermath of the Nazi occupation. It is not a work of resistance exactly but rather another instance of ex post facto propaganda, a scathing indictment of Nazi rule made only after it had already ended. But it is also something more than that. Unlike almost every other animated work that falls into this virulent genre of post-occupation catharsis, *Springman* is actually interested in considering the possibilities of animation as a potent vehicle for bearing witness and not just for creating a fantasy realm of revenge. It is interested in being a work of (belated) resistance and also something more.

The film's overall story undoubtedly serves a cathartic purpose, even if it is somewhat less violent than works like *Il Duce Narrates* or *The Revolt of the Toys*. Trnka's *Springman* is one of the first media representations of a figure of Czech urban legend known as Pérák, the Spring Man of Prague, a mysterious chimney sweep who attaches couch springs to the soles of his shoes so that he can attack and thwart the occupying Germans and then bounce away to safety—a figure who would go on to assume a kind of superhero status in Czech culture in later years. True to his hero's spring-enabled superpower, the second half of Trnka's film is all buoyant, cartoonal vengeance on the Nazis occupying Prague as Pérák frees the prisoners of the state and humiliates the SS soldiers who try to catch him, defacing their flag along the way. But the first half of the *Springman* film is remarkably different in tone, in part because it involves Springman not at all. Instead of outlandish heroic antics, Trnka quietly explores the strange conditions of everyday life under totalitarian occupation, using the anarchic freedom of animation as a means of representing such inherently absurd conditions. The story starts in the apartment of a Nazi collaborator, a man who salutes his framed picture of Hitler at every turn and spends most of his time spying on his neighbors through a telescope, taking notes on their behavior. For the collaborator, everything around him is suspect, and nothing is as it seems: a street sign advertising tools for sale is suspect for its resemblance to the hammer and sickle, a man slipping on a banana peel is eerily reminiscent of a Cossack performing a Russian dance, a man eating his dinner is put under suspicion for somehow having more food than even the collaborator himself. Eventually, the collaborator can take it no longer and calls the SS, who not only gather outside a suspected neighbor's apartment but also manifest inside it as well, appearing spontaneously from behind pictures on the wall and from inside his kitchen stove. The collaborator has the soldiers arrest a pet bird for whistling "Yankee Doodle," a kitchen pot for daring to fall off the stove while the soldiers are saluting a statue of Hitler, and his neighbor for in fact being a subversive (it turns out to be true, though not for any reason that the conspirator suspected). The image of the SS parading down the street with three captives in tow—a pet bird, a kitchen pot, and the bound neighbor—is an absurdist picture of the first order, the neighbor turned enemy, the countryman turned foreign agent, the object turned animate, the human turned object, and the figures of authority unable to tell any difference at all between any of them. Though it is as silly and as plastic as any *Looney*

Tunes cartoon, it is also a profound application of the transformative powers of animation used as a tool to represent the transformation of normal life and common sense under conditions of oppression and surveillance. It is an attempt to use animation, in other words, to offer up truths of everyday life under occupation in a way that no other form could possibly convey.

The impulse to speak to the true conditions of life under occupation would stay with Trnka for the rest of his career, as would the struggle between the first and second half of *Springman*—the struggle between animation as a tool of truth-telling and of witness and animation in thrall to the political symbol and questions of political power. Those two forces are the same ones that will collide in the fever dream that is *The Hand*, where art and power, the organic and the symbolic, will come into an existential conflict that proves in the end unresolvable. On its surface, the story of *The Hand*, eighteen minutes long and entirely wordless, is devastatingly simple, like a tale out of folklore; and like such a tale, its simplicity hides vast layers of depth. The film tells the story of a humble potter who lives alone happily making his pots until one day his world is changed when a white-gloved hand appears urging the potter to make a statue of the hand. The potter refuses, but the hand persists: pleading, cajoling, offering money and rewards. When the hand returns again with a television set as a lure—clearly a luxury in this simple, folkloric world—we begin to suspect that this may not be just any hand; indeed, it is quite literally the hand of the state, as he next appears not in white but in black and orders the potter to do his bidding, actually turning him into a puppet and forcing him into service. The potter is moved to a golden cage where he is showered with laurels and pinned with awards, all while he is forced to work night and day on a giant statue of the hand (plate 8). Exhausted, overwhelmed, and broken, the potter manages one last rush of strength and escapes, discarding his pins and medals as he goes and returning to his simple apartment. He is pursued, and he dies. In a final twist of irony, the potter is pinned with medals again and given a lavish funeral by the hand, solidifying his unwanted status as a hero of the state.

The story of *The Hand* is clearly, painfully autobiographical. It is that rare work of resistance animation that discards the level of the allegory almost entirely in favor of a near-naked symbolism, speaking loudly into the nation's public transcript that which is only supposed to be whispered into its hidden transcript. Given Trnka's context, it is almost suicidal in its transparency. Trnka *is* the potter, the esteemed artisan who just wants to be left alone to make his art. The hand *is* the Soviet state, which has lavished all manner of resources and special favors on its special potter. His career *is* the experience of the gilded cage, making the art that the state wants him to make and being richly rewarded for it even as he dies inside. And, reflexively, *this* film *is* the potter's act of escape, where he breaks from the golden cage, tosses away his medals, and makes a mad dash back to the art that he most wants to make. *The Hand* is Trnka's bold declaration that the famed puppeteer will himself be a puppet no longer. The Soviets, masters of political symbolism themselves, of course knew exactly what they were dealing with when they first saw *The Hand*. But in a move that was diabolical in its cynicism, they handled their puppet's sudden act of resistance in the only way that would deny him the sense of voice he most desired: not by suppressing the work but by refusing to react to it at all. Unlike Stefan Schabenbeck's *Drought* in Poland just a few years later, *The Hand* was released internationally and garnered numerous prizes abroad, including the coveted Jury Special Prize at the 1965 Annecy International Animation Festival in France. By refusing to react to the audacity of what Trnka had just submitted to the state-sanctioned public transcript of Czech culture, the censors at the ideological commission of the Central Committee of the Czechoslovak Communist Party effectively forced *The Hand*'s obvious public transcript back into the status of a secret hidden transcript: the film could not possibly mean what it plainly seemed to mean if the censors had failed to catch that meaning at all, so clearly its true meaning had to lie elsewhere. Holding fast to a scene where the hand makes a Nazi salute and another where it evokes the Statue of Liberty—Trnka's two concessions toward obscuring the obvious symbolism of the film's true referents—the official party line at the time was that the film was a perfectly welcome and ideologically acceptable antifascist and anticapitalist statement from a celebrated animator, what Moritz describes as nothing more than "a protest against foreign domination."[29] In a twist of irony befitting nothing so much as the plot of The Hand itself, Trnka was even given a state funeral by the Communist Party when he passed away just four years later, definitive and final proof of his standing as a true believer. And then just four months after he was buried, The Hand was entirely removed from circulation by the ŠtB, the Czechoslovak Communist Party's secret police, who confiscated every known copy of the film and removed any reference to it from all retrospectives on Trnka's work through the 1980s. For anyone living in Czechoslovakia after 1969, the very existence of The Hand was entirely erased.

Were this all there was to the story of The Hand, it would be enough. It is, as Paul Wells calls it, "a triumph of resistance," and the story of its ability to unsettle and disturb Czechoslovakia's Soviet overseers is one of history's only tales of a work of resistance animation actually affecting its targets in a tangible way.[30] But part of the genius of The Hand lies in the degree to which it is also far more than Trnka's personal statement of rebellion and the story of the fallout therefrom. A great part of the power of the film also derives from its discourse on the relationship of art and witness in a period of occupation and on the nature and dangers of the political symbol for the artist of any stripe. Even if The Hand had somehow managed to bury its political purposes deeper in its story so that the Soviets could never tell, it would still be a monumental testament to the lived experience of life under the totalitarian gaze and a courageous act of witness. The very fact that The Hand is a work of puppet animation is a fundamental part of this act of witness, for it renders both Trnka's hero and every single other implied person in his world immediately and perpetually vulnerable to the whims of the hands of the state. Trnka's hand asks, cajoles, and bribes to try to get what he wants: but in the end, if need be, he only has to get out the strings and the potter will be forced to act on his bidding. Like all puppet animation, Trnka's constructed world shares the lived space of the actual world even as it transforms that space into one of fantasy. As animation scholar Suzanne Buchan notes, "Puppet animation is a photographic representation of objects in space," always set in a real domain that is "three-dimensional and extant and has more corre-spondences with our own perception, expectation, and experience of space."[31] The imagined world of *The Hand* actually *is* the real world of Czechoslovakia under Soviet rule insofar as the space in which it was filmed is one and the same. Likewise, the dangers it presents are those faced by Trnka and his fellow citizens. The basic condition of life in a totalitarian state is one of profound vulnerability, one where people's agency can be entirely taken away at any time and their ac-tions turned into the forced performance demanded by the hand of the state. This is not just a matter for artists but for all those living under such rule, where personhood and agency exist only so long as the state decides to allow them.

In this way, *The Hand* carries the distinct echoes of those first few, affecting scenes from *Springman and the SS*, the ones that showed life under occupation as a series of absurd transfers between personhood and objecthood managed by uncaring enforcers who saw no real dif-ference between the two states: person, object, bird, pot—it was all the same to them. In *The Hand* too, the difference between person, object, agent, and puppet is vanishingly thin and always subject to revision: it is a world that allows precious little room for true per-sonhood. Likewise, it offers precious little room for privacy or any kind of life outside the literal reach of the state. One of the running gags of Trnka's film—which, it should be said, is also shockingly funny despite its weighty subject matter—is the way in which the potter can never quite anticipate exactly where the hand will come from next: through the door, through the window, even from inside a box that mysteriously appears in his home. The hand comes in at all times of day through any manner by which the potter might access the outer world. The hand even appears on every channel of the tele-vision that he gives to the potter as a gift, meaning there is not any single point of connection between the potter and the outside world that the hand does not ultimately control. The irony of this situation is that it breeds in its subjects, the potter most especially, a fundamental paranoia that is no less destructive for the fact that it is also entirely correct: twitching and turning by film's end, the potter worries that he is being watched from every side. And the truth is that he *is*, which does not make the sensation of such paranoia any less crushing. It is one of the finer and more brilliant details of the film that in the end the potter is not killed by the hand but by his own fear of the hand. Having boarded himself into his little room after escaping from the cage, the potter worries that the hand will somehow find a way to enter through his armoire, and so he tries to board it up as well, in the process causing one of his beloved pots to fall and hit him on the head. It seems like a moment of absolutely tragic absurdity—the potter driven so mad that he thinks the hand can enter through the armoire—until a few moments later when the hand actually enters through the wall of the apartment and then through another wall and then through the ceiling, dissolving all boundaries of interior and exterior, public and private, and forcing us to realize that the tragically absurd is also just the natural state of affairs in a life under totalitarian rule.

All of this speaks to what is arguably the most central and the most powerful concern of the film: not the relationship between the individual and the state but between the artist and the symbol, the latter relationship being a special subcategory of the former. On one level, the hand is merely asking for a self-portrait—in fact early in the film, if you have not seen it before, it can even seem like this is actually part of the plot. But of course the symbol *is* the self-portrait of the state. What the hand is asking for is a monumental symbol of its own power, akin to the head of LBJ in *Escalation*, the heads of state in the G8 photos from *The Barbarians*, even, in a different vein, Mickey Mouse in *Mickey Mouse in Vietnam*. The hand is asking the artist to devote his art to the level of the symbol—the concrete representation of the idea of a single, unchanging truth. Yet the symbol stands in overwhelming contrast to the work that the potter actually wants to pursue: not just making pots but making pots for his tiny plants, which grow and twist their green shoots from inside his structures. The potter is quite literally interested in making art that will capture and encompass the organic, that will contain life itself. The symbol, being merely an image, is empty, gargantuan, unalive. The pots are small, but they contain life, and as such they are capable of growing and changing over time—they are capable of transformation, true *animation*. The symbol, in contrast, is always dead. To work on it is a form of penury and an entrapment; to work on it is to be put inside a cage.

Of course, the great irony here is that the hand, which asks for an art that is dead, is represented in the film by *a live-action hand*—in fact, *Trnka's* actual hand—and thus is in fact alive. The potter, played by a puppet, is just *a thing*, yet it strives for an art that is organic and alive. No other form besides animation could ever convey this dichotomy, which is essential to the film. The state in Trnka's story is not a dead force at all: it is alive, it is organic, it is flexible, it is *human*. But it has committed itself to a way of thinking and a form of representation that is dead and made of stone. It has committed itself to the symbol. The potter, in contrast, is just an object, not a subject—a recipient of power rather than an agent, like any member of the citizenry in a totalitarian state. Yet he yearns for life, for the same organic condition that the hand of state already has; he yearns for the agency that the state has monopolized and also squandered. Trnka is a master animator and a master puppeteer, and *The Hand* would not be feasible were he not both. In his hands, the potter seems to actually come alive, never mind the fact that he cannot move his face or eyes at all, that he only moves at the joints, that he is clearly made of wood. The way that Trnka turns the potter's body just so, the timing of his actions and reactions, the anxious glances that he makes around the room as his paranoia begins to grow—all of these imbue the dead wood of the puppet with a furtive life that makes the conflict between hand and puppet so powerful and the final submission of the puppet so painful. The hand does not know how or care to use well the immense power of agency that it has, while the puppet strives desperately for that same freedom.

In this way, *The Hand* is both a statement of resistance and also an artistic manifesto. As much as it is a pained howl of protest, it is also a somber reflection on the proper duties and responsibilities of the artist. Fundamentally, the terrible equation that it draws and then resists between the state and the symbol works in both directions within the film. To make art solely on behalf of the state is always to be forced to etch and to elaborate the symbol, to be caged into that process and to become dead. And also, we may surmise, to work at the level of the symbol is to put oneself in thrall to the state whether one knows it or not, to function within a discourse that the state always controls and always supervises, to put oneself inside that golden cage of meaning. If you devote your art only to working at the level of the symbol, in other words, you should not be surprised to find yourself entrapped, nor should you have any delusions that the work you are doing is alive or in any way serves the living. *The Hand* is that absolute rarity among works of protest and resistance: a piece that fights an ideological battle on the level of political symbolism more effectively than almost any other work of animated film before or since, as evidenced by its utter erasure from Soviet memory at the hands of the censors, *and* a film that calls desperately for artists to recognize the restrictions of such statement making.

FROM NEAR-PROTEST TO POST-PROTEST

In the wake of Trnka's reflections on the limitations of resistance, how might the animator maintain artistic integrity while still making work that stands in the face of authority? This question is one that animates the oeuvre of one of Trnka's most lauded and internationally decorated successors, the Czech animator Jan Švankmajer, who made his first film just one year before Trnka made his last.

Švankmajer has always been a problematic figure in the vein of resistance and protest, as despite making most of his career under the
same general conditions of Soviet-influenced restriction as Trnka did
a generation earlier—and far more so in the immediate aftermath of
the 1968 Soviet-led invasion following the Prague Spring—he never
spoke against those conditions as clearly or forcefully as Trnka ultimately did. Švankmajer was even banned from making films by the
Czech authorities for seven years in the 1970s—but more for the intentional vagaries of his work than for any political specificity. (The
film that resulted in the ban, a combined animation and live-action
short subject called *Castle of Otranto*, was one in which he created a
fake historical documentary but refused the censor's orders to make
it a comedy so that audiences would not become confused.) Surely,
there is a sense in which Švankmajer *seems* sympathetic to critiques
of the Soviet system, but it is hard to pin down the nature of any particular criticism. Like his near contemporary Stefan Schabenbeck in
Poland, Švankmajer's animated work tends to operate at a fairly high
level of abstraction, such that attaching any one symbolic meaning
to its ephemeral shades of interpretation seems like a betrayal. For
instance, there is the Claymation woman in the thirty-second film
Flora, from 1989, who is tied to a bed with a glass of water just out
of reach, her whole body made of fruits and vegetables that rapidly
decay as police sirens are heard in the distance. The basic surrealism
of the work and its harsh juxtapositions of images and signs fights
against any attempt to attach a straightforward symbolism to the
piece, even as the combination of the constrained human form and
the decay of organic growth *seems* to point toward a critique of political repression.

One can see the same near-protest at work in one of Švankmajer's
most famous pieces, *Dimensions of Dialogue: Exhaustive Discussion*,
the final three-minute segment in a longer, multipart film from 1982
about conversations that involve some form of surrealistic conceit.
Here, two disconcertingly realistic clay heads stare at one another
across an empty table, both belonging to heavyset middle-aged men

and possessed of deeply expressive eyes. Out of the mouth of one head shoots a toothbrush instead of a tongue; from the other comes a roll of toothpaste. Next comes a piece of bread, countered by a knife with butter. Then a shoe and a shoelace, a pencil and an eraser. But quickly the pairings go awry: bread and toothpaste, toothbrush and sharpener, shoe and butter, and so on with greater and greater fervor (plate 9) until both heads are so exasperated with their argument-in-objects that they crumble into heaps of unformed clay. The difficulty of deciding what to make of Švankmajer's bizarre scene is part of the very power of the piece. Is it a commentary on the state of political conversation in the Soviet sphere during the late Cold War? A testament to the difficulty of communication under a state of permanent surveillance? A reflection on the universal problems of communication and meaning, which are limited to no political party or system? Švankmajer's work touches on each of these and denies none of them, and the degree of its multivalence can be seen in the bizarre series of responses it produced among Communist Party censors and international festival judges alike. Initially passed by the censors as ideologically acceptable when it was completed in 1982, the film went on to win the Golden Bear Award at the Berlin International Film Festival—at which point the party officials back in Czechoslovakia, reconsidering the ideological implications of the film, protested and demanded that the film stock be returned. Instead, the Berlin festival judges sent the film to the Annecy International Animation Festival, where it was awarded the top prize, which resulted back home in Švankmajer being banned from filmmaking yet again. Was the film political or not? Even the Communist Party censors could not entirely say—in the end they censured Švankmajer not for his politics but for what they called his "pessimism."[32]

For Švankmajer himself, his works are always subversive in their way—just in a way that is common to animation itself and even to any sustained work of imagination, which he sees as always being in opposition to the fixed, settled, and total. "Imagination is subversive because it puts the possible against the real," he claims. "That's why you should always use your wildest imagination. Imagination is the biggest gift humanity has received. Imagination makes people human."[33] In this vein, Švankmajer is in his own way following the mandate set out by Trnka, for more than anything else his work is a study in deferring, defeating, or deflating any hint of obvious symbolism and the restrictions of meaning such ways of thinking impose. It is in this sense a kind of anti-protest act of protest, a position Švankmajer more or less lays bare in one of his most supremely surrealistic works and one of his most important. Called *The Death of Stalinism in Bohemia: A Work of Agitprop*, the 1991 film fits temporally into the realm of ex post facto propaganda, having been composed in the immediate wake of the 1989 Velvet Revolution that ended Communist rule in Czechoslovakia. But *The Death of Stalinism* is no simple celebration of oppression's end; rather, it is more of a warning about the ways systems of oppression perpetuate themselves even when they seem to disappear. The idea that we might ever actually see a "death of Stalinism"—defined not as a specific ideology but as the fact of ideology itself—is the title's first dark joke. The idea that this piece is an act of *agitprop*, or a protest work combining *agitation* and *propaganda*, is of course the title's second.

What *The Death of Stalinism in Bohemia* actually *is* is a near-uninterpretable montage of imagery specific to twentieth-century Czech history and Czech politics combined with utterly disconcerting scenes set in a kind of birth room of political discourse, where one set of ideologies gives birth to another. The film uses the idea of animation in strange and literal ways, oftentimes by merely adopting the kind of symbolism and synecdoche one might see in an animated film and applying to live-action images. In one scene, for example, we see a series of kitchen rolling pins of various size barrel down a Czech street—the kind of image that, were it to be traditionally animated and shown in the context of all the film's other references to Czech history and politics, would surely be evocative of the Soviet-led invasion of the country in 1968, when tanks rolled down the streets of Prague to stamp out a student uprising. As it is, however, they just look like rolling pins rolling down a street: and the very absurdity and inconsequentialness of this image is a significant part of Švankmajer's point. To think that any play of symbols, whether abstract or concrete, political or apolitical, could ever capture the reality of something like the 1968 experience is for him a conceit of the first order, and a dangerous one at that. For the artist to get too caught up in politics is just an invitation, he argues, to help perpetuate the system, regardless of one's stance toward it. Hence the supremely disturbing imagery that repeats throughout the film wherein a white alabaster bust of Stalin's head is rushed into a hospital delivery room— the inanimate treated as animate and the object treated as subject, as in traditional animation—whereupon doctors desperately open up the fake statue, revealing a real pulsating mass of organs and tissues inside, from which they produce another white alabaster statue, first of Klement Gottwald, the Communist Party chairman installed as president of Czechoslovakia by the Soviets in 1948, and then in the second instance of the scene a figure that we cannot see but whose birth cries we can hear. Švankmajer thus shows us the space where ideology is born, a secret chamber wherein one set of dead symbols gives birth to another set of dead symbols by way of the organic processes of living beings. The symbol for Švankmajer, as for Trnka, is always a cover and a substitute for the real, and we will never be able to pry organic meaning out of its inorganic form whether it is new or old (if there is even a real difference between those two). The *agitprop* in *The Death of Stalinism* is thus an *agitprop against agitprop*, a protest against protest, a call for the artist to recognize the absurdity of trying to intervene in the political play of symbols and to redefine the artist's scope of work accordingly. It is a message very much in line with Trnka's ultimate conclusions in *The Hand*, even if it is far darker and more cynical in its articulation.

But then what is the animator of conscience to do? Must the animator only be an artist when sometimes the world calls equally, or more loudly, for an activist? The answer to that question is one that the Canadian artist and filmmaker Pierre Hébert has been trying to probe in collaboration with composer Bob Ostertag since 2001. In that year, Hébert and Ostertag performed the first of what they have come to call Living Cinema performances, special live sessions in which they combine activism and animation in search of an ethical form of political protest art—"live commentary, on the razor blade, of the world situation," in their words.[34] The core of their performances consists of a projection of filmic images related to various international instances of war, atrocity, and trauma: the September 11 attacks in *Between Science and Garbage*, the war in Iraq in *Endangered Species*, the 2006 Israeli invasion of Lebanon in *Special Forces*, and others. Drawing on a rich tradition of avant-garde animation in which drawings are made directly onto filmstrips, often in highly abstract, nonfigural forms involving meditations on only shape or color, Hébert takes the war-related films projected in his performances and draws directly over those images as they are projected on screen—nonfigural images that highlight shapes seen amidst the wreckage and carnage of war, tracings of faces and bodies. The result is an unstable hybrid of the filmed and the animated, the live and the recorded, with each of Hébert's performance pieces standing at the nexus of those terms. They are part performance art, part animation, and part protest action. But what they are most of all are acts of witness, attempts to recover the actual imagery of war so often overlooked in times of war and to literally *mark* them as being seen. They are instances of witness as a form of protest—or what we might perhaps call *post-protest*, insofar as they enact the processes of protest absent the engagement with symbols that protest typically entails.

And in this sense their very existence is subversive. Works like Hébert's Living Cinema are an attempt to take a step toward giving recognition to the specific instances of death and destruction so often ignored or abstracted in our discussions of war and to expose the gaping silence of the political leaders who cannot and will not acknowledge such images, in words or in policy. Hence the fact of Hébert marking the images on screen as they are played. It is those markings—abstract, impressionistic, connoting nothing in particular—that literally perform the act of witness. They mark that the filmic images have been seen. They declare that those horrific experiences captured on film have been witnessed, and they confirm that they will not be ignored. Hébert, drawing abstract shapes and images on film stock of some of the most terrible events of our time, does not necessarily expect to change anything in the larger politics of his moment. But he expects to act as witness, and to bring his audience along in that experience of witness as well. For Emmanuel Levinas, this act alone is one of the origin points of ethics. "The witness testifies to what has been said through him," he writes. "Because the witness has said 'here I am' before the other."[35] If anything might move us beyond war, it is this.

CHAPTER 2: PACIFISM

In the dead of night on July 15, 2015, a new Facebook page appears online. It is public, and it is anonymous. It includes only a single phrase, written in Arabic, repeated in multiple places: "Extremism Kills." It is the name of the page, the name of the user profile, a hashtag ready for posting on Twitter. The page, though largely blank, does not appear in a vacuum. In February of that year, Houthi rebels in Yemen, who were largely Shia Muslims, seized control of the nation after an eleven-year insurgency. One month later, a coalition of Sunni nations led by Saudi Arabia began bombing the country and established a naval blockade; Saudi advisors were believed to be on the ground helping to coordinate local resistance. The Houthis, in turn, seemed to be receiving arms in secret shipments from Iran, and there were reports of uniformed Iranian military advisers operating in the country. By the middle of July, when the Facebook page appeared, Human Rights Watch was reporting abuses on both sides of the conflict, with civilian casualties already reaching into the hundreds; those numbers would soon grow into the thousands.

For a few moments that early morning in July, the Extremism Kills Facebook page remains empty. And then, just before 2 a.m., a single posting: a video lasting just over a minute and a half. It will be the only activity on the site that its anonymous creator or creators ever undertake, but it will be enough. The video will quickly go viral. Within days, there will be hundreds and then thousands of comments on the otherwise empty Facebook page. "Likes" will start adding up, eventually reaching into the tens of thousands. Entertainers and public figures from Egypt to Oman will begin using the hashtag and linking to the video. It will be reposted on YouTube by users around the world. Requests will start pouring in, all posted in Arabic to the largely vacant Facebook page: inquiries from media outlets in the Middle East, an invitation from the Philadelphia Independent Film Festival. All of them will go unanswered. The creator or creators of the page will not reveal themselves. The video will have to speak for itself. Soon, its total views on Facebook will stand at just under a million, with another half a million more watching on its various global YouTube postings. All of this will be over a cartoon.[1]

The anonymous video, posted under a title that roughly translates to *The Extremists' Game Destroys the Innocent*, is either the work of a seasoned animator or an incredibly talented savant. Rendered with the finesse and attention to detail that one expects from a Pixar short, it begins in an ambitious overhead shot of a chess board set in the middle of a desolate, bombed-out landscape, then zooms in to pan across the figures lined up on either side of the board: nervous, breathing, *human* pieces, though distinctly sculptural and clearly carved from wood—you can see the rich veins of the grain and the polished sheen of the lacquering on their skin and on their clothes. On one side, the figures appear to be Sunni militants—some clad in the turbans and flowing robes of Afghan-style *mujahideen* and others in civilian clothes, with the men wearing head coverings and the women in burqas as is more common in Sunni nations; they are armed with AK-47s and led by a spindly figurehead evocative of Osama bin Laden. On the other side, uniformed soldiers who appear to be Shia fighters, some wearing the green fatigues and insignias of the Iranian military as well as civilians in the green-and-red headbands of Shia militias. Save for the leaders in the back, nearly all the pieces are beset by an obvious and crippling fear, their eyes set wide as they stare at one another across the board (plate 10).

That fear is well placed, for what erupts once the first pawn is literally kicked into action by the Sunni leader behind him is a cavalcade of graphically rendered violence. The panic-stricken Sunni pawn clad in civilian clothes and trembling as he holds his AK-47 quickly perishes in a confrontation marked by head-shattering bullets, explosive suicide vests, the blast of a rocket launcher attack. The chess pieces, more wood than flesh, splinter and shatter with each new injury, but their hard materiality and obvious objecthood makes them seem no less human. The pure visual spectacle of the violence aside, the most enthralling aspect of the short is the microdrama of watching each chess piece navigate a conflicting flood of emotions: abject terror at the prospect of death with each new move; renewed commitment to their cause at the prompting of their leaders; pity, sorrow, and anger at the loss of their comrades in front of them. The only ones who seem unaffected by the slaughter, both physically and emotionally, are the two king pieces, the tall Sunni *mujahid* and the portly Shia general, who both laugh villainously as the battle unfolds. At the very end of the fight, when the Sunni commander suddenly faces the prospect of death himself with a Shia pawn shakily pointing a pistol at him, he is immediately saved—not by his brethren Sunni fighters, who have all been killed, but by the Shia general, who shoots his own soldier rather than allow a fellow leader to be shot. The two kingpins cackle and embrace, put away their weapons, and step off of the chess board together and into the war-torn landscape, walking arm in arm: the only two figures left alive, and the only ones, we now realize, who were not merely objects trapped on the board at all and who were in fact always free to leave or stop the fight. The short ends with a message in Arabic cast starkly against a black screen, the same as the video's title: "the extremists' game destroys the innocent."

In a region where animation is frequently deployed as an inflammatory partisan tool, *The Extremists' Game* is unique. The regional proxy war in Yemen has unleashed a torrent of animated fantasy confrontations in which Saudi Arabia and Iran fight one another directly, the victory of course entirely predetermined by the nationality of the animation studio. There is the 2017 video *Saudi Deterrent Force*, released anonymously online by animators in Saudi Arabia, in which Saudi forces decimate Iranian defenses and invade Tehran. The Iranian animation studio Fatimat az-Zahra Animation Group responded by releasing plans for an animated counterstrike, a film called *Conquest of Mecca* in which "the Muslim nations join Iran and liberate Mecca from Saudis," as the animator Farhad Azima told the *Tehran Times*. Safely ensconced (for now) in the realm of computer animation, the region's religious and political tensions play out in breathtakingly direct form in these online videos, each side always convinced of its total domination of the other. Meanwhile, in the conflict unfolding in Yemen offline in the real world, more than ten thousand people have been killed within the first two years and more than three million displaced.[2]

Those ten thousand dead—including more than five thousand civilians—are the true subject of *The Extremists' Game*, which, for all its obvious fantasy and playful intermingling of the object and the human, is more closely bound to real life than anything you might see in the graphically accurate and ostensibly realistic world of *Saudi Deterrent Force* or *Conquest of Mecca*. The video's overarching metaphor of war as chess board and soldiers as pawns—tired though no less resonant for its overuse—is arguably the least interesting and least important aspect of the short. What ultimately matters most in the video is not the metaphor of the game but the furtive glances of the pawns as they look to see if their turn is next, the mix of trepidation and anger that stirs them as they shoulder their weapons and enter the fight, the fear when they recognize the moment of their own death in the barrel of a raised gun or the jerking trigger finger of a suicide bomber. The video is an attempt to bear witness to the experiential realities of sectarian strife by way of the animator's favored tools of metaphor and abstraction—and *through* that act of witness to make a larger point about the violence and warfare in the region. It is not a point about who is right and who is wrong, who is strong and who is weak, but a universal and total denunciation of the conflict itself. It is not a statement against *this* war in the region but *all* war in the region.

Can an animated film actually stop a war? Certainly not in any immediate sense, but the long and venerable tradition of what I call *pacifist animation* of which *The Extremists' Game* is but one part has often tried to use the form to help shape public discourse on armed conflict, aspiring toward the kind of impact that the anonymous *Extremists' Game* video has already had. Like *The Extremists' Game*, such films often arise in the midst of a specific armed conflict—often in its early days, as here—but like that video their target is also far larger: not just a protest against one specific war but an impassioned call against the fundamental act of war-making itself. The act of witness—so frequently marginalized in the propaganda animation that supports and encourages war and even in much resistance and protest animation, bound as such films often are to one or another side of an ongoing struggle—is here a fundamental part of the animator's approach. The open exposure of war's terrible and omnidirectional violence is part of the very raison d'être of the pacifist film, and this mission frequently calls on animators to look unflinchingly at the lived experience of the conflicts unfolding around them and to broadcast that experience to their viewers.

At bottom, the pacifist animator seeks to expose what is already known but often left unsaid about the condition of war, that which Elaine Scarry identifies as the center of its terrible interior experience: "Reciprocal injury is the obsessive content of war."[3] Any wartime photograph might try to do the same, of course. Eddie Adams's famous Vietnam War photograph of South Vietnamese General Nguyen Ngoc Loan executing a suspected Viet Cong member, Nguyen Van Lem, or Robert Capa's iconic picture of a Spanish Republican soldier, Federico Borrell García, taken at the moment he was shot also try to lay bare Scarry's *interior content* of war.[4] But as Susan Sontag reminds us, the wartime photograph is a dangerous and ultimately unreliable rhetorical tool—a tool that can easily become a kind of weapon of its own. "To photographic corroboration of the atrocities committed by one's own side," she writes, "the standard response is that the pictures are a fabrication, that no such atrocity ever took place . . . or that, yes, it happened and it was the other side who did it, to themselves."[5] The job of the pacifist animator is to evade this repurposing and redirection by emphasizing not just war's violence or war's suffering but its indelible *reciprocity*: its condition of blanket, universal suffering that always afflicts both sides. Frequently the work of the pacifist animator is to reduce the depiction of war to the depiction of reciprocity itself, something that few photographs could ever achieve. Hence the utility of the chess metaphor in *The Extremists' Game*, which renders strike and counterstrike in rapid succession until victor and victim can no longer be distinguished. The job of the pacifist animator, in other words, is to explode the layers of misdirection and obfuscation and distancing that so often cloud the rhetoric of war—what Scarry calls the many "paths by which injuring disappears from view"— leaving behind after the dust settles only the act of witness, in all its unavoidable immediacy.[6]

"LOOK! LOOK AGAIN!": PROTO-PACIFIST ANIMATION OF THE 1920S

Arguably, the origins of pacifist animation lie in certain early acts of witness that appeared in the immediate aftermath of war—specifically in a number of cartoons that came out of the experience of the First World War. It is not that these cartoons are themselves committed to a pacifist vision, though such viewpoints were widespread during the epoch after that terrible conflict. Rather, they handle the explosive material of wartime experience with a degree of unguardedness that cannot help but raise questions as to war's purpose, whether such vexing questions were intentional or not. Made by animators with direct knowledge of the front, these films had not yet learned to constrain or conceal the act of witness at their core. They are what we might call *proto-pacifist* films—works that anticipate the approaches of pacifist animation even if they do not openly embrace such politics—and they were among the most popular animated films of their moment, made by some of the most important animators of the day.

The first and most important of these precursors is an animated short called *Felix Turns the Tide*, from 1922. Felix the Cat, one of the first major figures in animation's long history of anthropomorphic everyman types and a direct forerunner to Mickey Mouse, is remembered today largely through the television reboot of the character in the 1950s, which still has a following among animation aficionados. But during the heyday of the original Felix film series in the 1920s, his cartoon stardom was second to none. Felix mania reached heights that can only be measured against the crazes inspired by certain other titans of twentieth-century global media, figures like Charlie Chaplin or the Beatles. "It is almost incredible," wrote one industry observer in a trade journal in 1924, "but the most popular outstanding figure in the film trade at this moment . . . is Felix the Cat. Never in my short but eventful life in the Film Industry have I ever seen anything to equal Felix's popularity, prestige, and general screen personality. Honestly, our stars in the flesh are unknown in comparison."[7] Even the king and queen of England were at one point seen carrying Felix dolls. Fixed to no particular time or place, Felix had many different kinds of adventures over the course of the nearly two hundred films he starred in between 1917 and 1930. But no doubt one of the strangest of those adventures, and certainly the most harrowing, comes in *Felix Turns the Tide*, wherein the most beloved animated hero in the world at that time ventures not into some adventurous jungle or exotic new city but onto the battlefields of the First World War, battlefields that are depicted in horrifyingly gruesome detail replete with heavy machine-gun fire, high explosives, and staggering mass casualties—heaps and heaps of lifeless cartoon corpses piled up on screen.

Animated depictions of the First World War were nothing new to American audiences by the time that Felix short premiered in 1922. Almost as soon as the conflict in Europe began in 1914, American animators mined it for material: the *Heeza Liar* films from Bray Studios, the first true animated series from one of the first modern animation studios, started featuring its bombastic hero on animated

European battlefields within months of the first shots being fired. And of course American screens featured animated propaganda films during the years of the country's direct involvement in the war, starting in 1917—martial-minded shorts like *How Charlie Captured the Kaiser* or *Our Four Days in Germany* where known cartoon heroes like Charlie Chaplin's animated alter ego or comic strip icons Mutt and Jeff sallied forth to defeat the German enemy and did so single-handedly and with ease. But none of the animators behind those early films had any idea of what the combat experience of World War I was really like: by definition those wartime films were made by artists who remained on the home front. Never would those anima-tors know the almost apocalyptic experience that Walter Benjamin evokes in his classic description of the epistemological shock encoun-tered by the young men who went to serve in that very first modern war: "A generation that had gone to school on a horse-drawn street-car now stood under the open sky in a countryside in which noth-ing remained unchanged but the clouds, and beneath those clouds, in a field of force of destructive torrents and explosions, was the tiny, fragile human body."[8]

The situation would be vastly different with a postwar film like *Felix Turns the Tide* where the "destructive torrents and explosions" and the "tiny, fragile human body" that Benjamin evokes haunt every frame of the short. Otto Messmer, the creator of the Felix char-acter, was himself a combat veteran of the war. Deploying with the 104th Field Signal Corps out of Newark, New Jersey, in the spring of 1917, he spent about half a year in the trenches: a relatively short time, but an impactful one. His division suffered more than six thousand casualties in only five months of total combat, most of them in terri-ble close quarters fighting amid the woods and ridges of the Lorraine region in northeastern France. Born to German immigrant parents in West Hoboken, New Jersey, and himself conversant in German, Messmer was perhaps more sensitive than most to the absurdity and reciprocal horrors of a conflict in which he was sent to fight against the soldiers of his ancestral home. He would in fact speak of this very aspect of the war a lifetime later in interviews from the 1970s, where he recalled, in the words of his interviewer, "a German sniper shot out of a tree, who conversed with Messmer in German as he lay dying. The man showed the American soldiers pictures of his wife and children and offered them cigarettes and candies."[9]

Messmer's sense of the war as being an unmitigated disaster for all involved is everywhere apparent in a short like *Felix Turns the Tide*. After a series of brief opening scenes in which Messmer dutifully positions the war as being both just and honorable—the rats have made an unprovoked attack on the cats in what is billed as "World War One and a Half," and Felix heroically comes to the defense of his beset species after securing permissions from his employer and proposing to his sweetheart—the tone of the film dramatically and unalterably shifts. The early scenes in *Felix Turns the Tide*, like most scenes in the Felix shorts, are rendered in simple ink on white paper with a level of outline and abstraction that more closely resembles a newspaper comic strip than the detailed drawn worlds of later cartoon heroes. In contrast to these early scenes' sparse visual aesthetic, however, the first scenes of battle are positively teeming with activity and action in every section of the frame, all of it calculated to shock. Instead of finding himself deployed into a fantasy realm of wish fulfillment where the enemy crumbles instantly, Felix stumbles into a cartoon version of actual combat, a realm of unmasked atrocities marked by a pervasive sense of hopelessness. No sooner does our hero arrive at the front with his fellow recruits then we are confronted with unsettling depictions of those same enlisted cats being shot and blown up by the well-fortified rats, who easily defeat multiple waves of assaults using nested artillery. Literally everyone with whom Felix entered the war is killed within the first few seconds of combat, their bodies seen exploding into the air.

The unavoidable persistence of the dead cartoon bodies is one of the most visually disturbing aspects of the film, a far cry from those more common animated worlds where vanquished figures simply fall out of view or disappear. To actually be dead is to actually have been alive, and Messmer never lets his viewers forget the carnage that is the actual work of war. In fact, he explicitly demands that we pay attention. "Look!!" the feline general commands Felix after their numerous attempts at attack have been defeated; he directs the hero's gaze to a field strewn with the slumped and crumpled bodies of dead cats. "Look again!!" he says in the next moment, directing Felix to look at yet another field, yet more corpses—hundreds of little identical Felixes, all dead (plate 11). Realism was one of Messmer's primary goals. He alternated black and white backgrounds between frames to create a disorienting flicker reminiscent of bomb blasts, and for explosion effects he poured white salt onto a special black card under the animation camera to create the illusion of smoke and debris. The pockmarked landscape and, most of all, the rows upon rows of dead bodies stand as a stark statement against the kind of bodily elasticity and physical impunity one typically associates with cartoons, Felix's especially. Offering his viewers very little aesthetic protection against the graphicness of his images, Messmer forces them to gaze upon what the war has wrought: he is literally commanding them all to look, demanding that they bear witness to a version of what he himself had seen four years before in the trenches of France.

It is a visually shocking series of moments. But what is perhaps even more remarkable within the short is the narrative breakdown that Messmer allows around these images, the degree to which he lets Felix's entire enterprise come extremely close to failure. "We're licked unless we get re-enforcements!" the feline general informs Felix: the entire cat army has been killed, only the general and Felix are left. All those dreams of heroism by all those enlisted cats have led to nothing but slaughter. The rescuers must now themselves be rescued, a humiliating and desperate position. Felix does in the end succeed, but his titular tide-turning is accomplished via a deus-ex-sausage that is so unexpected—and so outlandish, even within the already gonzo world of the short—that it essentially begs not to be taken seriously as a point of narrative resolution. Unable to take the rat's great citadel, Felix's battlefield innovation is to call for backup from the butcher shop where he used to work. He telegraphs his old boss back on the home front, who wires over a brigade of sausages that manages at last to take the hill. As historian of animation John Canemaker writes of the scene, "The sight of Felix leading a battle charge on an enemy fortress followed by hundreds of wiener warriors ranks as one of cinema's great Absurdist images."[10] And the absurdity only deepens when one considers that the battalions Felix has enlisted to ensure his final success are made up of the very foodstuffs it is his job to butcher and sell back home—that they are literally made up of dead meat, things once living that have already been killed. It is a dark commentary indeed on the nature of being a soldier, a kind of backward literalization of the common metaphor by which a combat situation is likened to being a sausage grinder. Felix wins the day by literally reanimating an army of the already dead. Inevitably, the sausages' battlefield success generates even more piles of casualties: instead of fields full of dead cats, we now see another field overflowing with rat corpses. The sausages seem to suffer not a single loss in their grand offensive. But they don't need to: their very personages embody the bloody and chopped-up status of the expendable combat soldier. Felix hasn't exactly won the battle; he has merely managed to replace his own side's literal losses with a potent metaphor for that same carnage.

Felix Turns the Tide never ventures into overt pacifism. Metaphors aside, Felix ultimately triumphs, and the short ends with him at the head of a grand parade, one that evokes the "Spirit of '76" iconography of the American Revolution, a flag-bearer, a drummer, and a flutist all marching down the center of the street. The ostensible message is that Felix is a hero and has bravely done his duty even under the most trying of circumstances. Of course, whether the outcome was worth the carnage remains an open question that Messmer's film introduces but never resolves. The film's powerful act of witness, metaphorically invoking the vast scope of the horrors that Messmer himself encountered on the battlefield via a world of cats, rats, and sausages all vulnerable to mechanized mass casualty, is in a sense too weighty for the rather flip preparatory and concluding segments of the film. What is a parade compared to a slaughter? And what is the word *hero*, which flickers above Felix's head as he talks about enlisting, compared to the masses of dead comrades on the actual battlefields of that war—comrades who all look identical to Felix himself and who likely all had those same thoughts of heroism as they patriotically joined in the cause. *Felix Turns the Tide* ends with no thesis statement, no message of intent like the one at the end of *The Extremists' Game*—but the latter's solemn warning about war destroying the innocent would certainly fit right into the dark world of Messmer's film.

That world of suffering and unanswered moral quandaries would grow darker still in the several imitation films that *Felix Turns the Tide* spawned in the later 1920s—in particular, one made by another animator with direct experience of the front whose later fame would far exceed Messmer's own: a young draftsman out of Kansas City, Missouri, by the name of Walt Disney. Nine years Messmer's junior and too young to be drafted during America's brief time in the war, Disney, idealistic and yearning for experience, actively sought out the war in any way that he could. After failing to gain entry to several different branches of the armed forces by trying to hide his age, he joined the Red Cross as an ambulance driver in September of 1918, deploying just after the signing of the Armistice that November as part of a small team of volunteers tasked with helping in the postwar recovery. Disney's encounter with the realities of postwar France must have made him glad to have missed the supposedly glorious fight he was once so eager to join. Though he worked mainly as a chauffeur for visiting officers during his time overseas, he also had extended bouts of service in other, far more wrenching capacities: tending to the wounded at the Evacuation Hospital No. 5 in Auteuil, where the injured were laid out up and down the Longchamps racecourse; managing a garbage detail made up of beleaguered German prisoners of war; ferrying supplies back and forth across the decimated cities and ruined landscapes of the former battle zones. Disney's evenings were spent bunked in an unheated chateau where he had to cover himself with newspapers to try to stay warm, shivering through the night. His time in France added up to "a lifetime of experience in one package," he later mused.[11]

As with Messmer's short, the lingering memory of those experiences can be seen in the more nihilistic moments of the film Disney made to compete with *Felix Turns the Tide*. That film, called *Great Guns* and released in 1927, starred not Mickey Mouse but an earlier one of Disney's cartoon creations, a Mickey prototype called Oswald the Lucky Rabbit—a character clearly designed to capture some of the Felix magic, both by directly lifting aspects of the cat's iconic black-and-white design and also by sending this not-quite-Felix hero on notably similar adventures, though usually with some sort of tweak. Thus Disney's version of the war, contra Messmer's, is not a matter of grand battalions lost or saved but of small one-on-one conflicts that punctuate the narrative—which makes Disney's film no less bloody or shocking than Messmer's and no less imbued with his own wartime experience. At the center of its gruesomeness lies the admission of war as a reciprocal act, one in which victor and vanquished alike are damaged and destroyed, if one can even manage to tell the difference between the two. In one grisly scene from the short, for instance, two soldiers fire simultaneously from opposite trenches and shoot each other dead, both falling back in mirror images of one another. Elsewhere in the film, Oswald stands in a grimy trench in the middle of the pouring rain desperately hugging a picture of his sweetheart back home as the trench floor fills with dirty rainwater and bombs fall all around him: when a heart rises above his head to visualize his loving thoughts, that heart is immediately shot with a bullet and explodes. Part of the reason that Disney's short never reaches the levels of carnage of Messmer's work is that Disney insists on personalizing the war that he depicts in scenes like this, sometimes literally so. In one alarming shot, we see a massive battlefield cannon point directly at the audience and fire, bringing us immediately into the action. In a very different moment of personal conflict, Oswald takes to the skies and enters a dogfight with an enemy airplane only to find that the planes themselves begin punching one another; soon the pilots have jumped out of their cockpits and started punching each other mid-air as well before realizing they need to jump back into their aircraft.

Though it lowers the staggering body count of Messmer's film, the young Disney's approach in *Great Guns* makes his hero Oswald no safer from casualty than Felix. In a shocking twist, the short nearly ends in Oswald's death and total disintegration into ash when he is hit by an ordinance shell. Only cartoon fantasy can resurrect the destroyed hero, a sentimental deus-ex-fiancée that is no more convincing or reassuring than the absurdist deus-ex-sausage in Messmer's work. Dressed as a battlefield nurse, Oswald's loyal girlfriend sneaks onto the field and takes her beau's disintegrated remains to an absolutely chilling battlefield hospital—basically a demolished building with a sign that reads "Hospital," a lone saw hanging ominously on the wall, and a machete perched near a cot in the corner (plate 12). (One wonders what exactly Disney saw during those months with the Red Cross.) Here, in the relative sanctity of the hospital structure, Oswald's girlfriend reconstitutes her beloved out of the pile of ashes he has become. Though Oswald's revivification affords Disney the chance for a happy ending and a late-in-the-game gesture toward the transcendent power of love, the absurdity of the resurrection also renders the ending somewhat hopeless. Not by accident does Oswald's girlfriend bring him back to life using questionable tools: she places his ashes in a martini shaker, mixes, and pours him back to health, offering a wry commentary on the role that alcohol often played in sustaining many veterans after the war, helping them to drown the very memories that imbue every aspect of *Great Guns*.

No one would ever accuse Disney of being a pacifist. (Indeed, in addition to overseeing numerous propaganda films for the US Office of War Information during the next world war, he also conceived and produced the hybrid animation–live-action film *Victory through Air Power*, from 1943, which helped lay out a specific war strategy that he hoped the Allies would employ.) By the same token, Messmer himself never expressed any openly pacifist views during his time animating the Felix shorts. He in fact wasn't even known as Felix's creator at the time, as his producer and boss Pat Sullivan took most of the creative credit for the series despite having little creative input into the films. But *Felix Turns the Tide* and *Great Guns*, drawing heavily on the wartime memories and experiences of their creators, both exist in a space that constitutes the primary territory of the pacifist film—a space that acknowledges and gives testament to the universal destructiveness of wartime conditions, from which no one is safe regardless of cause or country. The fundamental aesthetic of the propaganda film is exactly that of an asymmetrical vulnerability: the victor will always conquer the vanquished; the victim will always be subject to the villain. The fundamental condition of pacifist animation is something close to the opposite stance: no one who enters the fray is safe; all will suffer. The pacifist vision originates in a recognition of shared vulnerability, which is a first step toward shared humanity. Messmer and Disney, having both witnessed to different degrees the reality of war as an unrelenting exercise in "reciprocal injury," per Scarry's description, translate this sense of shared vulnerability directly into their films. To show war so unflinchingly becomes in itself *almost* an argument against it, no matter the patriotic parades and loving fiancées who buttress and bookend those horrific scenes.

Disney himself would on some level recognize the proto-pacifist implications of his work and quickly endeavor to course-correct, essentially remaking *Great Guns* just two years later with his new animated hero, Mickey Mouse. Titled *Barnyard Battle* and released in 1929, the film is awash in much of the same basic imagery as *Great Guns*—trenches, barbed wire, a landscape pockmarked from artillery fire, plus an unforgettable image of Mickey gleefully and indiscriminately firing a Gatling gun out a barnyard window (plate 13). (When he runs out of ammo, he happily turns the keys of the piano behind him into bullets.) Yet for all the iconography of war that Disney here recycles, something drastic and important has changed. Though Mickey and his barnyard cohort face numerous perils within the film, there is not one instance where they are shown to be actually vulnerable to that danger, where they actually suffer harm. Only the cat invaders who dare to threaten the peace of Mickey's barnyard home suffer any injury, and even then such violence is carefully redirected away from the actual imagery of death. The short ends with a pile of bodies—a direct invocation of Messmer's earlier imagery—but they are *all* from the enemy side. And they are also decidedly *not dead*, which Mickey proves by purposefully stabbing one with a flagpole, causing him to scream in pain and run around the yard. There is cruelty in the short and there is violence, but there are also strenuous efforts to constrain both elements. Fundamentally, whatever violence *Barnyard Battle* includes, it is decidedly *not* the reciprocal violence of war, a violence to which all are subjected equally. Disney manages to sanitize the memory of the First World War as it appears within his work, to turn it into an iconography—some trenches, some barbed wire, a machine gun—without acknowledging or engaging with any of its experiential realities. It is, to use a slight anachronism in the trajectory of Disney's career, a kind of theme park ride version of the First World War: an engagement with its visual tropes where one is never truly in danger of being touched in any way by its unpleasantries. In the place of the vivid witness of a short like *Great Guns* or that of its predecessor *Felix*, *Barnyard Battle* offers only dim recollections of the front stripped of their meaning and used as decoration: wartime imagery without a war and violence that exists without shared vulnerability.

NEIGHBOURS

Disney's attempts at erasure in *Barnyard Battle* were an effort to rescue his animation from his own act of witness two years prior and to forestall the proto-pacifism of that earlier short. But even if he managed to erase those traces of personal witness from his animated work moving forward, that erasure did nothing to stop other anima-

tors with explicitly pacifist intentions from adapting and expanding on the conditions of reciprocity, vulnerability, and witness that
make up the ethical matrix of the proto-pacifist films that came out
of the First World War. From *Felix Turns the Tide* and its inheritors
would emerge a template that animators seeking to send a message
against war would return to again and again across the remainder of
the war-torn twentieth century and into the war-torn first decades of
the twenty-first: emphasize the disparity between the justifications
for war and its costs, demonstrate a condition of shared vulnerability
across all those involved in the conflict, and recognize unflinchingly,
even obsessively, the basic reciprocity of injury and death that is the
fundamental work of war.

Those principles might together be taken as a kind of mission
statement for one of the most famous pacifist animated films of all
time, the Scottish Canadian animator Norman McLaren's masterpiece *Neighbours*, released by Canada's acclaimed National Film Board,
or NFB, in 1952 (plate 14). Arresting, frustrating, and unforgettable, it
sets a bar that every pacifist film to come after it would need to address
and struggle to exceed. Part of the film's impact comes from its utter,
unabashed simplicity, like a dark children's bedtime story for adults.
Two neighbors who live next door to one another get into a fight over
a dandelion that grows between their two properties. The fight escalates, and they both die. What is missing in that summary is the uncanny quality of McLaren's visual realm. Though the film appears at
first to be live-action (it technically is not), it has a disconcerting cartoonal quality: the neighbors, though played by different actors, look
so alike as to have been easily traced from the same model sheet, or
the blueprint used to ensure character consistency in large, multiani-
mator projects; the bright-green grass on which they sit is as mono-
chromatic and regular as the looping background on a cheaply made
cartoon; the suburban homes behind them are literally drawn on paper and merely propped up in the background. It is in part this visual
quality of the lived cartoon—an aesthetic whose only real parallel is
in certain segments of children's television—that makes the latter

portions of the film so shocking and upsetting. What starts as a simple spat between neighbors with just a little cartoonal exaggeration for effect—a shove here, a playful duel with two fence posts there—very quickly devolves into utter savagery and murder, inclusive of each neighbor knocking down the paper house in the background, killing the woman sitting behind it, and savagely beating to death the baby she was holding.

Each of the main elements of the pacifist film, those same elements we saw in nascent form in the cartoons that came after the First World War, is here in just about the most refined and schematic mode possible. The justification for the conflict between neighbors could not be weaker—the dandelion over which they fight isn't even very pretty—yet the stakes of the lethal conflict that ensues could not be higher; all six figures in the film are subject to a totalizing vulnerability, with none of them exempt from violence, not even the two babes in arms; and the actual action of the film consists of little more than an obsessive working through of the condition of reciprocal injury even up to the point of death, each character mirroring the actions and the offenses of the other. But even that accounting still does not quite do justice to the film's most deeply disconcerting quality, which has nothing to do with actual violence per se and yet everything to do with the idea of violence more generally. I am speaking here of the unique mode of animation that McLaren used to make his seemingly live-action work, a process known as pixilation. Standing on the avant-garde fringe of animation, pixilation is a process that entails posing the actor for individual frames with incremental changes to the pose each time, as one would photograph a puppet or an object in traditional stop-motion animation. The visual imprint left by this effect can run the gamut from indecipherable to entirely unreal, and McLaren skillfully and slowly increases the obviousness of the technique over the course of the film: a few unusual movements by the dandelion to start with, escalating eventually into scenes where the neighbors fall down and seem to be carried along across the grass without any obvious movement on their parts at all or where they command the appearance and disappearance of fence posts seemingly at will. It is these sorts of deeply uncanny moments that speak to the tremendous emotional impact of the pixilation technique. For at the heart of pixilation is the literal objectification of the human body, the treatment of a human being as no different than a stop-motion puppet. To move without moving oneself is to *be* moved, to be treated as an object, to be turned into a thing. And a *thing*, as literary theorist Bill Brown observes, is an object that has lost all connection to its purpose or utility, that has been wholly divorced from its original meaning. "We begin to confront the thingness of objects," he writes, "when they stop working for us: when the drill breaks, when the car stalls, when the windows get filthy, when their flow within the circuits of production and distribution, consumption and exhibition, has been arrested."[12] The *thing* emerges, Brown adds, in "the before and after of the object"—when it is no longer meaningful; perhaps, we might say, when it is dead.[13]

And a *thing*, of course, is exactly what violence makes of us all. In this way, what is most unsettling about *Neighbours* is how absolutely *inhuman* it is. There are *people* on screen, to be sure—two of them, primarily—but there is not a single *human* at any point. They are both objects of each other's violence and—more than that—objects of their own unrelenting obsessions with marshaling force, with projecting an agency that they manifestly do not possess. This is really the heart of the film's pacifist message. Not that all war is as simple as two nearly identical men pounding each other over the head—it is not. But violence is. War involves strategy, calculation, tactics—all in the service of enacting violence, as Scarry is at pains to remind us. "Injury," she writes, "is the thing every exhausting piece of strategy and every single weapon is designed to bring into being: it is not something inadvertently produced on the way to producing something else but is the relentless object of all military activity."[14] And violence, no matter the type, is nothing more and nothing less than the act of turning a subject into an object, of turning a person into a thing. Pixilation is a violent form of animation when considered in

light of its effect on the human form. *Neighbours* is about such violence, and thus it is about all violence. It is *not* about how we are all
the same, all neighbors in a kind of universal community. It is about
how we are all *made the same* by violence—for any object detached
from its purpose and turned into a *thing* is really just the same as any
other *thing*, all of them lifeless. The single most disconcerting part
of watching *Neighbours* lies in the sensation of watching two seemingly living human figures and coming to realize, slowly, that they are
already dead.

When *Neighbours* was first released seven years after the end of
World War II, the world was at war yet again: North Korea, South
Korea, the United States, China, and the Soviet Union were all em-
broiled in the Korean War, the first of many Cold War entanglements
to come. With two world wars completed and what looked like the
possible beginnings of a third underway, it seemed at the midpoint
of the century that global war was to be a basic and perennial fact of
modernity. For McLaren, this was not just an abstract idea—it was
something that he saw up close. In 1949, he was invited by the United
Nations Educational, Scientific and Cultural Organization, UNESCO,
to travel to rural China to teach local artists the basics of animation.
The violent civil war between China's communists and nationalists that followed the end of World War II was still ongoing, but
fighting seemed to be centered in the north of the country, far from
the southern province to which McLaren was assigned. "P.S. The
fighting is nowhere near this place," he wrote in one letter home to
his mother.[15] That all changed when the nearly defeated nationalists
made a desperate retreat through the southern reaches of the country
en route to Taiwan, and McLaren's work effectively stopped as the
village he was staying in endured wave and counterwave of nationalist and communist troops passing through, the locals trying to sup-
portively welcome each new brigade so as not to suffer reprisals—
"Only if we are careful will we be left alone," the village's mayor told
the animator.[16] The evidence of China's long years of suffering was
everywhere around McLaren during the trip, and he speaks of the

abandoned battlefields in his letters home. Now the evidence of new fighting was passing right in front of him, each band of soldiers welcomed with a smiling face from locals who were absolutely terrified. McLaren finally left China in May of 1950, one month before the start of the Korean War, with the world erupting into conflict yet again just as he returned home. This is the context in which *Neighbours* was made. As distant and clinical as the film seems in its stylistics—as befits a film based on the total evacuation of its human subjects—the short is truly an anguished, emotional cry against cycles of violence that seemed already to have taken hold worldwide, endlessly perhaps. We should beware the world that perpetual war makes, McLaren cautions, for in the end no one will be exempt from its consequences. If, as Emanuel Levinas would write some forty years later, "the justification of the neighbor's pain is certainly the source of all immorality," McLaren's short in its condition of universal dehumanization and blanket objectification adds a vital rider to that sentiment—that the suffering of our neighbor is also ultimately our own.[17]

OUT OF THE ART HOUSE

Like *Felix Turns the Tide* before it, *Neighbours* would inspire a host of similarly themed works that pay tribute to its influence even as they try to extend its reach. One of the most ambitious would also be one of the closest to it temporally—a thinly veiled adaptation of the short from 1965 called *Pink Panzer*, part of the Pink Panther series of theatrical shorts that ran in American movie theaters between 1964 and 1977. *Pink Panzer*, relatively forgotten today, is a minor six-minute short that ran briefly in movie theaters before feature presentations in 1965 and then was recycled on television as part of the Saturday morning *Pink Panther Show* starting in 1969. Though it is best known for its association with legendary American animator Friz Freleng, who helped create the character and produced the series, it is in its own right an absolutely tremendous specimen of pacifist animation insofar as it aims to take the art-house avant-gardism of McLaren's film and bring it to the American mainstream, infiltrating local movie theaters and even broadcasting such messages directly into millions of American living rooms.

At the time of *Pink Panzer*'s release, McLaren's film still had only found a relatively limited audience in the United States—this despite having won an Oscar in 1952 (perplexingly, in the Documentary [Short Subject] category, a sign of pixilation's liminal place between the worlds of animation and live-action). The short had gained a great deal of notoriety in Europe, where it garnered thousands of theatrical bookings. But its original run in the United States was limited to just one theater in New York City; most cinemas did not want to play the strange and disturbing piece. McLaren even agreed to a cut suggested by an American educational distributor that removed the beating and murder of the wife and child figures in hopes of garnering more bookings outside of commercial theaters, though with the escalation of the Vietnam War in the 1960s he insisted that those scenes be put back in starting in 1967.[18] In light of all the difficulty McLaren was facing with his work, it is all the more remarkable that Freleng—an icon of American animation, renowned for creating or developing characters from Porky Pig to Bugs Bunny—made the decision with his collaborators to take the basics of this odd Canadian antiwar film and insert them directly into his work.

Of course, *Pink Panzer* is never quite as disturbing as *Neighbours* itself. It stars a friendly, near-fluorescent anthropomorphic panther, after all. There are no wives or infants to be murdered, and the familiar stylings of the short—a 1960s era update on Freleng's classic *Looney Tunes* aesthetic—are the visual equivalent of comfort food compared to the haute cuisine of McLaren's pixilation method. But even with these changes, the basics of McLaren's work come through. As in McLaren's short, the piece revolves entirely around two once-friendly neighbors living side by side, the Pink Panther himself on one end and a cheerful, bumbling middle-aged man named Harry on the other. And as in McLaren's short, the conflict that arises between them is utterly inconsequential—in this case, a matter of unreturned gardening tools—and entirely out of proportion to the rapidly escalating pattern of responses. If the violence in *Pink Panzer* never reaches the truly brutal fever pitch of McLaren's work—no one is visibly hurt at all in the short, in fact—the scale of the neighborly confrontation and the direct connection drawn to international militarism is far greater. Here, a battle that first consists of aggressive acts of lawn maintenance that breach the dividing line of their two properties soon turns into an all-out suburban war, with the Pink Panther and his neighbor each bringing out heavier and heavier military hardware—a machine gun, field artillery, a tank (plate 15)—with flashes of actual documentary footage of those same weapons being used in acts of war-making.

The shock of those images in that moment cannot be overstated. The Vietnam War was then in the midst of the large-scale escalation that followed the Gulf of Tonkin incident the previous year; by the time the *Pink Panzer* short premiered in late 1965, there were over one hundred thousand US troops in the country and a massive bombing campaign in North Vietnam was underway. Images of the war were suddenly becoming a regular part of nightly news broadcasts—in fact, 1965 generally marks the start of what television critic Michael J. Arlen has famously called the "living room war," the world's first conflict to unfold in real time on home television screens.[19] The photographic imagery in *Pink Panzer* is nothing so intense as what the nightly news was broadcasting and ultimately all rather staid, just weapons firing into the void mostly, but the degree of visual equivalency being drawn between news imagery and cartoon imagery is remarkable in itself: here too was an important wartime commentary to be made, the short announces. *Pink Panzer* never references Vietnam directly, but its stance on the escalation of that war in particular and the entire enterprise of the Cold War more generally could not be clearer. Throughout the short, a mysterious narrator's voice— unusual for the series—has been goading on both the Pink Panther and his bumbling neighbor, reminding them of the tools that are in dispute, urging them on to acts of greater and greater retaliation. At the very end of the short, just as the Pink Panther begins to fire from his tank and Harry opens fire with his field artillery piece, we finally see the source of that voice—literally the devil himself, red horns and pointed tail, cackling at the chaos he has sewn. Such warfare literally does the devil's work.

Violence in American cartoons has long been widespread, and war imagery is common. Conditions of actual reciprocity, where both sides suffer proportionally at the other's hands, are, however, exceptionally rare in the victor-victim world of most American animation; to tie that reciprocity directly to images of war even rarer still. Not since the strange brew of the immediate postwar cartoons of the 1920s had most American audiences seen a popular animated work so open about the reciprocal dangers of war-making, and hardly ever had they seen a cartoon so explicit in its message against unthinking militarism, saying quite literally that we should see the devil in those actions. The *panzer*, it must be remembered, is the famous Nazi tank, technically an entire class of armored tanks from early in the war. To link that machine to the titular hero of the cartoon series— the opening credits showing the tank itself, which the Pink Panther later drives into battle against his neighbor—offers an ominous juxtaposition. The panzer is a villainous tank, the weaponry of an evil adversary. Yet the Pink Panther is no villain, just a 1960s era update to the venerable everyman tradition of American cartoon heroes, a lineage that runs back through figures like Bugs Bunny and Mickey Mouse all the way to Felix himself. To be caught up in the militaristic escalation of the Cold War mindset, the short proposes, is literally to make our heroes no different than our adversaries, to become that which we should most condemn. The same individuals who might never think to visit the kind of art-house cinema where they would encounter an even more unsettling film like McLaren's *Neighbours* could easily find themselves watching a cartoon explicitly telling them and their children that Cold War militarism and Vietnam War escalation was turning their culture toward evil.

PLATE 1. *Matches Appeal* (UK, 1899)

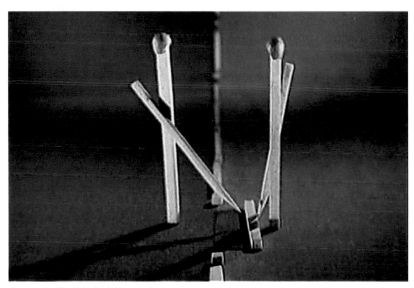

PLATE 2. *Conflict* (USSR, 1983)

PLATE 3. *In the Jungle There Is Much to Do* (Uruguay, 1973)

PLATE 4. *The Scarecrow* (France, 1943)

PLATE 5. *Mickey Mouse in Vietnam* (USA, 1969)

PLATE 6. *Escalation* (USA, 1968)

PLATE 7. *The General's Boot* (Syria/Saudi Arabia, 2008)

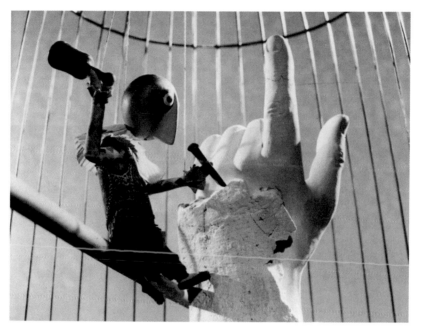

PLATE 8. *The Hand* (Czechoslovakia, 1965)

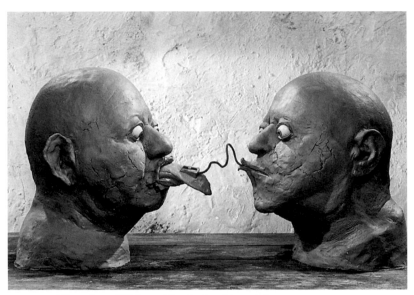

PLATE 9. *Dimensions of Dialogue* (Czechoslovakia, 1982)

PLATE 10. *The Extremists' Game Destroys the Innocent* (country unknown, 2015)

PLATE 11. *Felix Turns the Tide* (USA, 1922)

PLATE 12. *Great Guns* (USA, 1927)

PLATE 13. *Barnyard Battle* (USA, 1929)

PLATE 14. *Neighbours* (Canada, 1952)

PLATE 15. *Pink Panzer* (USA, 1965)

PLATE 16. *Tolerantia* (Bosnia and Herzegovina, 2008)

PLATE 17. *The Cake* (Croatia, 1997)

PLATE 18. *The Hat* (USA, 1964)

PLATE 19. *Bosko the Doughboy* (USA, 1931)

PLATE 20. *Peace on Earth* (USA, 1939)

NEIGHBORS AT WAR

For animators like McLaren and Freleng, such messages—whether evocatively implied in the manner of the avant-garde or explicitly broadcast in the form of the mainstream American cartoon—are ultimately metaphorical, grave and important as they may be. Though both films were made in response to ongoing warfare happening at the time, that fighting was still a world away; there were no actual neighbors who were literally going to war with one another in Canada or the United States within the twentieth century. But McLaren's approach to pacifist animation in general and the influence of *Neighbours* specifically takes on a new level of urgency in situations where neighbor has in fact turned on neighbor. Such is the case with a 2008 variation on *Neighbours* from Bosnia and Herzegovina called *Tolerantia*, created by first-time animator Ivan Ramadan. Born in Yugoslavia in 1985, Ramadan made the film explicitly in response to the ethnic and religious wars that marked the disintegration of that nation and the formation of its successor states between 1991 and 1999, wars that claimed over one hundred thousand lives when he was a child and adolescent.

Ramadan calls out this connection at the very start of his film but also distances himself from it: according to the text on screen, the setting of his film is "central Bosnia . . . the end of the last ice age," and at its start we see only an empty, snowy field, the camera eventually panning to reveal a single, cartoonal caveman frozen solid in a block of ice. The playful visual style of the computer-animated film seems to keep the darker history it evokes safely at bay. The short is richly detailed in its specifics but also rendered abstract by the sheer emptiness of its locale, all white snow and gray stones. The comic, grotesque figure of the caveman might as well be walking on a blank page when he finally thaws out of the ice. At first it seems that the film might be the story of this caveman's struggle to build the first rudiments of civilization, filling in the whiteness of the empty snow (and by extension the blank page) with the hard work of creation, comically rendered. Laboring to build a huge ziggurat structure single-handedly out of gargantuan stones, the caveman eventually succeeds: standing atop the pyramid next to a crowning wooden edifice he has created that looks vaguely like a mosque's minaret, he opens his arms and stares at the sun, an act of both worship and rest.

It is only then that the full narrative of the short becomes clear, as a rock suddenly hits the caveman in the back of the head interrupting his act of worship. In a classic comic reveal, the camera pulls back to show us that there are in fact *two* ziggurats that have been built next to one another, the seemingly empty field being actually not so empty after all. Atop the other ziggurat is another caveman, only he has built a different wooden edifice, one that more closely resembles the angular dimensions of the Christian cross, though its actual structure is closer to that of a football goalpost. He chides his neighbor's more circular edifice design in grunts and groans and proceeds to show him how to properly worship the sun with his rectangular structure. Of course, theological debates are difficult when one exists in a time before language; simply throwing rocks is much easier. The rectangular neighbor's initial volley is inevitably met with another rock thrown by the first caveman with the circular religious structure. The resulting volleys of strike and counterstrike quickly take on the tempo and mayhem of a classic *Looney Tunes*–style short. In fact, the *Looney Tunes* series includes numerous films in which adversaries battle from atop adjacent forts, as in *Bunker Hill Bunny* from 1950 or *Assault and Peppered* from 1965. As the comical cavemen grunt and groan their way through volley after volley of stone and ice, Ramadan creates a latter-day successor to those works.

But there is a notable difference between the *Looney Tunes* mayhem and Ramadan's depictions. In those classic shorts, the violence is ultimately one-sided: Bugs Bunny as an American patriot is the unscathed victor in the former; Daffy Duck as a villainous aristocrat is the utterly defeated loser in the second. But in the world of *Tolerantia*, the scenario of dueling neighbors is ultimately more McLaren than *Looney Tunes*. In a devastating extreme long shot, Ramadan pulls his camera back to force us to watch the seemingly comic proceedings from a great distance: as rocks hurl back and forth causing small explosions of dust and ice, we recognize that each caveman is tragically taking apart his own structure in order to inflict damage on the other (plate 16). The violence of the short is entirely that described by Scarry as being the fundamental violence of war, which destroys target and aggressor alike. It is a literal *unmaking of the world*, and as such it "does not simply entail the possibility of injuring but is itself injuring."[20] Such destruction, Scarry reminds us, is always a human destruction, always an unmaking of that which makes us civilized—"a deconstruction not only of a particular ideology but of the primary evidence of the capacity for self-extension itself: one does not in bombing Berlin destroy only objects, gestures, and thoughts that are culturally stipulated but objects, gestures, and thoughts that are human, not Dresden buildings or German architecture but human shelter."[21] Ramadan captures this perspective to devastating effect, showing us in metaphor how wars of religion actually unmake those very religions themselves. Both cavemen perish in this fight, simultaneously hit by rocks in a particularly bloody instance of cinematic cross-cutting: the inherent reciprocity of war made literal and direct. And after that: nothing, for centuries. Ramadan returns to his extreme long shot as the sun sets on the ice age structures and the screen fades to black. It then fades back up for the ending credits, the world now green and verdant, the two temples in ruins and covered in grass. There are no people at all to be seen.

For an animator like Ramadan living in the wake of crippling civil conflicts and unchecked atrocity, the stakes of the pacifist stance could not be any higher. Ramadan watched as a child, from the ages of six to fourteen, as neighbor turned on neighbor and an entire civil society came crumbling down in the midst of that conflict. Those destroyed and abandoned temples at the end of *Tolerantia* are not merely metaphors of some ancient, endless human story: they are also emblems of far more recent and remembered strife. The question that lingers in the mind as one stares at the wreckage and all the real-world suffering it represents is, What can be done to make things different? How can we avoid the whispering voice of the devil, as Freleng would have it, urging us to turn our neighbor into our enemy, reminding us of past slights and goading us on to escalate our conflicts until nothing is left but ruins? The attempt to reckon directly with such questions lies behind another branch of the pacifist tradition in animation, one that does not so much replicate the structure and violence of a work like *Neighbours* but instead engages with the question of how to stop the escalation that McLaren, Freleng, Ramadan, and others so potently expose. One of the most affecting works in this tradition is the short film *The Cake* by the Croatian animator Daniel Šuljić, who, like Ramadan, knew too well the terrible violence that followed the disintegration of Yugoslavia. Šuljić was an art student at the Academy of Fine Arts Zagreb when fighting began between Serbs and Croats in his native Croatia. *The Cake* was made as a direct response to those and other overlapping conflicts and released just as they were ending, appearing in festivals in 1997 in a brief respite between the end of the horrific Bosnian War in 1995 and the start of the Kosovo War in 1999. It is a reflection on the causes of that conflict and a tentative diagnostic of the steps that might be taken to avoid such strife in the future.

Of course, on its surface it is nothing of the sort: it is ostensibly a cartoon about a birthday party. Rendered in strikingly minimalist terms—the persons assembled on screen little more than black stick figures set against a plain white background—the film seems at first like it is about nothing at all. The eight anonymous figures finish their dinner and cheer the arrival of a giant cake (plate 17), a boisterous but indistinguishable soundtrack of party conversation layered over the scene. But a problem quickly emerges: while some of the figures receive giant pieces of cake, others get far smaller pieces, and a few get next to nothing at all, almost a joke of a slice. The conversation is so buoyant and the party is so festive that it takes a while for the figures to notice: those with the smallest slices catch on first, some of those with the largest are oblivious throughout, or at least want to appear that way. Yet even once the discrepancy is observed—one intrepid figure even traces a series of lines on the plate to show just how unjustly the desert was divided—the will to fashion a change never quite arrives. In the absence of a negotiated solution, certain members of the party start to take matters into their own hands. Distracting fellow dinner guests by dropping forks or pulling out their chairs, they try to surreptitiously switch the plates when the others are not looking. Even an attempt to organize a vote simply results in one of the figure's cake being stolen. Inevitably, the situation erupts into violence: minimally at first, just a kick to the shins and some pushing. But when one party guest hits his head on the table as he falls backward from a punch, landing motionless and dead on the floor, the barrier to lethal violence has been breached. Knives and forks become weapons, the implements of civilization and fellowship turned into tools of war. Šuljić is never sentimental about the scenario he creates: there is no moment when the party guests all stop and recognize their madness. Instead, the brawling serves to eliminate just enough guests—their bodies slumped against the table— that the vicious few who remain can more effectively divide up what is left. All the pieces of cake, big and small alike, have been destroyed in the fray. But no matter. The survivors gather up the crumbs and divide them into piles that they place upon the dinner plates. The action makes a mockery of the civilized party they once had. And even this semblance of civility cannot last for long. Inevitably, some of the survivors recognize that the crumbs have not been divided evenly, and the party erupts into chaos yet again.

Fundamentally, *The Cake* is a film about politics—and specifically about that desperately thin line that divides political conflict and outright armed struggle. The civilized dinner table is always on the cusp of barbarity, while barbarity will often try to approximate the conditions of the civilized table. Though there is not a single image of war in the film, it is a deeply pacifist work, displaying all the tropes of the form. The conflict on which it centers is out of all proportion to the violence that it causes, while the anonymous figures Šuljić features—entirely indistinguishable from one another at every point in the film—all share the same degree of vulnerability to the chaos that ensues. The violence of the film is fundamentally reciprocal, passed from figure to figure rather than directed at one group of victims or one single scapegoat; more than that, though, it is also *transposable*—an assault on one figure might lead not to a counterstrike against the aggressor but a new assault on some other figure nearby, the former victim now turned into the instigator of violence. There is no such thing as victor or victim in Šuljić's film, just a faceless blur of omnidirectional aggression; the abstracted visual construction and indistinguishability of the stick figures makes it impossible to keep track of grievances and wrongs, only to recognize the horror of this war of all against all. There was a time when the initial wrongs could have been righted, but that time belonged to the era of politics: when the cake was first cut, when the sizes were first noticed. By the time the cutlery is weaponized, there is no longer any way to keep track of wrong and right. In this way, the film echoes Scarry's argument against the famous expression that "war is the continuation of politics by other means," which originates with the Prussian military theorist Carl von Clausewitz. Such dictums, Scarry argues, treat the violence of war as "the extension or continuation of something else that is itself benign."[22] War is not another form of politics, though its origins may lie in the political realm. War is war. And war is hell. For politicians to think they have any ability to control the act of war once it has begun is perhaps the quintessential act of hubris.

The very aesthetic composition of *The Cake* offers a kind of memorial to the absolute destruction that can be wrought by such multiparty acts of violence, aggression, and hubris—destruction that, once started, no politics can fix. Šuljić created the film using a simple oil on glass technique, rendering a minimalist visual world that seems initially abstract and clean. For animation aficionados, the combination of Šuljić's country of origin and minimalist manner of drawing is immediately evocative of the former Yugoslavia's legendary output in the realm of animation, marked by a distinct aesthetic of visually simple yet artistically sophisticated work known as the Zagreb school of animation. Zagreb school animation was born of both a specific production house—the Studio for Animated Film, founded in 1956 within Zagreb Film, the Croatian national film company—and a general approach to the animated form, an open rejection of the realism and visual density epitomized by Disney. Its ethos attempted to relink animation to its predecessor forms in the graphic arts, where clean lines and suggestive visuals could do as much work as detailed renderings or photographic exactitude. In the words of one manifesto from the group, their aim was "to give life and soul to a design."[23] The Zagreb school was extraordinarily influential in twentieth-century animation, regularly winning international awards and inspiring untold numbers of animators around the world. And it is a school and style of animation that all but perished in the fighting that consumed Croatia as the former Yugoslavia fell into civil war. With state funding gone and war raging in the streets, Zagreb Film entirely ceased production in 1991. When it reopened under the auspices of the City of Zagreb four years later, it was a different company, in a different world. "The Zagreb School of Animation had disappeared," writes the animation historian Giannalberto Bendazzi. "Almost all the old masters had retired or died. For the Croats of 1995, what had existed just four years before belonged to the distant past."[24] Šuljić's film is haunted by the memories of a venerable artistic tradition now lost, a lineage now broken. Though it might be emulated, as here, it cannot be resurrected: like so many things that are lost in war, it can never be brought back. As the fighting in *The Cake* grows worse and the party begins to descend into chaos, Šuljić begins more and more to smudge the lines that are so clean at the outset of the film, until in the worst moments the screen is nearly just a blur of gray streaks. It is almost as though the film itself is being covered over, scribbled out, destroyed—which is always the work of war.

THE ART OF CONVERSATION

But what if there were a way to stop the madness and return to the political realm? What if there were a way not to fight but to *talk*? This is the fantasy that lies at the heart of John and Faith Hubley's 1964 film *The Hat*, perhaps the only optimistic entry in the entire canon of pacifist animated films. (Surely, that optimism can be credited in part to the fact that the film was funded by an organization committed to nuclear disarmament, the Institute for International Order.) Created just over a decade after *Neighbours* was released, *The Hat* is a kind of answer to that film: an answer that does not deny any of the fundamental principles on which McLaren's work is based nor the absolute difficulty of transcending those conditions through dialogue as Šuljić's darkly explores. It merely wonders what might happen if we tried, recognizing this prospect as being at least partly grounded in fantasy—in fact the film literally stages a conversation that happens after a nuclear attack has been launched but then put on pause, the warheads simply hanging motionless in midair in defiance of all forms of gravity: military, political, and physical. The improbability of that moment crystalizes the improbability of the entire scenario. But animation is the medium of the improbable, even the impossible. Recognizing every danger that McLaren invokes and every challenge that Šuljić explores, the Hubleys, a husband and wife team, use the art of animation to defiantly envision that most impossible scenario of all: an honest conversation between sworn enemies.

Of course, those enemies are really enemies in name and national affiliation only. They are border guards, dutifully and silently patrolling a literal dotted line that divides their two nations. When one guard accidentally drops his hat on the other side of the border, a national emergency is triggered (plate 18). The first guard cannot continue without his hat; the other cannot allow him to reach across the dotted line to reclaim it. Both dutiful, both armed, and both stuck, the guards seem to have no choice but to escalate. Within minutes of issuing threats and demands back and forth they have come to the brink of nuclear war, each one pulling out a launch button and sending rockets up into the air. To this point, the film seems quite directly like an inheritor of *Neighbours*: two individuals on either side of a dividing line prompted by the most inconsequential of reasons to leverage the most extreme forms of violence, forms to which they

are both equally vulnerable and which they engage with equal feroc-
ity, creating a tit-for-tat reciprocity that escalates from a scenario of
my-demands-against-yours to my-missiles-against-yours. "You are
not the only one that has guns," the hatless guard warns when his
counterpart threatens to shoot at him. And yet, all of the action that
links *The Hat* to the standard tropes of pacifist animation in general
and to the conditions of *Neighbours* in particular elapse within the
first four minutes of the film. The short is eighteen minutes long. The
remainder of those minutes are devoted to an alternate scenario, one
where the missiles are paused and the guns put down. One where the
supposed enemies just *talk*.

Perhaps the most radical aspect of what follows in those remaining fourteen minutes of the film is just how *boring* it all is. The Hubleys were pioneers in the use of improvised dialogue in animated film.
They even won an Oscar in 1960 for a film, *Moonbird*, based entirely
off recordings of their children's playtime banter. Though the Hubleys
are both credited as writers for *The Hat*, the material in its long con-
versational segment was largely improvised in the recording studio by
the unlikely combination of actors that the Hubleys brought together
to give voice to the two guards: jazz legend Dizzy Gillespie and British
comic actor Dudley Moore. Yes, the inventor of bebop and the future
star of *Arthur* are featured here in a fourteen-minute discussion about
alternatives to nuclear armament. (They also collaborated on a jazz
soundtrack for the film, with Gillespie on the trumpet and Moore, who
got his start in film as a musician and composer, on the piano.) The
pairing has a kind of mad juxtapositional genius, but the Hubleys are
not merely going for a madcap matching of wits. In casting these two
particular individuals, they are looking for two figures who are entirely
out of their elements with the topic at hand, thus engineering in their
conversation a kind of limit case for what an actual discussion about
the crisis of war might broadly look like between two actual people.

The result is about as enlightening as you might expect. Gillespie
and Moore are clearly confounded trying to figure things out, constrained as they are by the rules of this world where no one can cross
the line and everyone has guns, and their conversation starts and

stops multiple times throughout the film and wanders off into digressions. They talk about how cold it is. They reminisce about their childhoods. Gillespie's character pulls out pictures of his kids. Yet they persist in the conversation. This alone gives their talk a kind of nobility, meandering as that talk may be. Gillespie goes on a long digression about war and human history, asking how we think our civilization can survive being so militaristic if so many others perished in war. Moore considers the legal impediments to nonviolent crisis resolution and wonders about an international police force. They talk past one another, over one another, and around one another again and again and again. But they try. Ultimately, *The Hat* is an act of witness not to the experience of war but to the ongoing conversation about ending it—an *actual* conversation, with all the awkwardness that that implies. It is an absolutely, vitally necessary conversation, uncomfortable as it may be. Gillespie and Moore keep talking because they have to: not just because of the imaginative rules of the film, but because of the dire state of the world beyond the film. "War to settle disputes now is obsolete," Gillespie says at one point, the armed nuclear missiles still hovering over his animated character as he says it.

The style of *The Hat*, like its dialogue, is disjointed—literally so, in the sense that the Hubleys' character design for both guards entirely eliminates all of their joints. Instead their basic body parts—forearms, hands, shoulders, torso, and so forth—all just hover in air next to one another, like a puppet strung on wires and yet to be finished. The two guards could not be more physically distinct: in their skin color, their height, their weight and body shape. Yet neither is a full figure, just a collection of parts hanging together with no points of connection, just empty space. They cohere, and yet they don't—which makes them especially human. In that, they are both the same. Each of them is quite literally a construction, a series of parts held together by invisible forces and then given a name and an identity that they must try to fulfill. The all-important line that divides them—that great border line between their enemy nations—is likewise just a collection of dots, an actual dotted line as on a map yet laid out through the landscape. It has only the power it is given and no actual materiality of its own. As the two guards endlessly debate what to do about the hat that has fallen across the line, a series of animals scamper back and forth across the border right in front of them. The composition of the line is as utterly artificial as the guards—which is not to say they do not *seem* real, at least to themselves. That sense of actuality is something they need to learn to see beyond, not unlike the sense of inevitability of the kinds of conflict they are trying to talk their way through.

John Hubley in particular knew something about the impact of imaginary things on real life, even more than most animators. Originally an animator at Disney and then at United Productions of America, or UPA, where he created the character of Mr. Magoo, he was called before the House Un-American Activities Committee in 1956 and accused of participating in meetings of the Communist Party. He denied the accusations and refused to assist the committee's investigations, and for that act of defiance he was blacklisted and rendered unhireable. Only by taking on anonymous advertising work was he able to survive. Caught up in the height of Cold War hysteria, Hubley was accused of aiding and abetting a national enemy—the people on the other side of the line, the neighbor across the picket fence. The abstract mindset of *us versus them* from which a film like *Neighbours* springs was tragically all too real for him. Likewise, the ways in which a perceived truth—the charge that he had any involvement with the Communists, which he always denied—can take on great power in the real world regardless of its veracity, enough to change a person's life. Overcoming the sense that your perceived enemy is really your enemy, that an arbitrary dotted line is actually a meaningful border, that you yourself are only one thing and not any other despite the fact that there are truly no joints holding you together: all of these are dangerous and difficult propositions. Overcoming those presumptions will take work. But it is absolutely necessary, the Hubleys argue. "There is no other alternative," as Gillespie says about disarmament in the film. The difficult conversation with the enemy is the conversation we must have, before it is too late.

Wisely, the Hubleys make no promises that such dialogue will work. The long conversation in *The Hat* decidedly does not go anywhere: it ends unremarkably with Gillespie arguing for the establishment of an international authority to resolve disputes, the second time he has brought up the point. But the Hubleys insist that such dialogues must continue. In a closing gesture of solidarity, the second guard throws his hat across the line so that now both guards have lost their hats, establishing a condition of radical equality between them—the flip side of the dangerous reciprocity that is usually at work in pacifist films. They both pull their ponchos up to cover their heads and ward off the winter cold, and they continue on their patrol, side by side, still talking. They have to. Those paused nuclear weapons are still hanging in the air. In the real world, in 1964, they were as well. The stakes could not have been higher. To have the *wrong* conversation at that time or to have no conversation at all could potentially be catastrophic. In *The Hole*, which the Hubleys made two years before *The Hat*, in 1962, and for which they won an Oscar, the animators dramatize this condition. Here another character voiced by Gillespie holds forth in a long conversation about the dangers of nuclear war with the American character actor George Mathews, both of them playing construction workers far underground in the sewers. To talk about the dangers of nuclear war is all well and good, but it is not the same as opening a dialogue with your enemy. *The Hat* ends in continued conversation; *The Hole* ends in a nuclear holocaust, the two construction workers emerging from their manhole to realize that the world has actually been destroyed while they were down below discussing the dangers of it being destroyed. There is no room for the wrong conversation when the fate of the world is at stake.

FROM BOSKO TO THE ROTOSCOPE

In this way, the Hubleys' work touches on the last great trope of the pacifist animation tradition: the prospect of complete annihilation.

It is a prospect that is rendered metaphorically in the dual deaths at the end of *Neighbours*, the ruined temples in *Tolerantia*, the ongoing fighting in *The Cake*, even the war-torn empty landscape that surrounds the chess board in *The Extremists' Game*. In those films, as in *The Hole*, it is a point of conclusion, the ultimate end-stop of the pacifist argument. But in some of the most affecting works in the pacifist tradition, the possibility of humanity's total destruction is not an ending point but a beginning. In what we might call the *apocalyptic* branch of pacifist animation, the work of the animator is to use the medium's capacity for envisioning the impossible to show us a world beyond human witness, a posthuman world of our own making, and so to terrorize us with the possible consequences of a historical trajectory where war is left unchecked. Though the tradition takes on special resonance with the development of nuclear weapons in the 1940s, it both predates that development and sometimes makes no reference to it at all. The prospect of annihilation is not about any particular technology of war, ultimately. It is about the act of war-making itself as one that always aspires to total destruction, to Scarry's total *unmaking* of the world. Here, the pacifist argument is no longer primarily an ethical one but simply a practical one, chilling as it may be. The question of "the justification of the neighbor's pain," from Levinas, is rendered disturbingly moot if there are no more neighbors at all, nor anyone else, not even us. Justify the suffering of the neighbor long enough, these films imply, and you will inevitably, inescapably, ensure your own suffering as well, even to the point of oblivion.

Such is the condition of what may be the single most famous work of pacifist animation, the 1939 film *Peace on Earth*. Frequently ranked as one of the greatest animated films of all time, nominated for an Oscar, and supposedly even nominated for the Nobel Peace Prize—*Daily Variety* reported on MGM's intention to nominate the film for that most august honor in December 1939, though the prizes subsequently were suspended during the war—*Peace on Earth* is for some the epitome of the pacifist message as expressed in animation: a

religiously inspired, Christmas-themed meditation on the importance of Christian morality, "a cartoon with a message" as one adver-
tisement put it at the time.[25] It is also an absolutely nightmarish work
of cinema, truly horrifying in its implications. The *peace* of *Peace on
Earth*, though it derives from the Christmas carol sung throughout
the film, is actually the peace of death. There is peace on Earth at last
in the film because there are no more humans; they have all killed
each other in war. It is peace of the most literal kind, peace as simply the absence of war. Though few reviewers at the time seemed to
catch this aspect, the film may be the single bloodiest ever made to
that time: not for what it shows but for what it implies, a condition of
mass casualty taken to the absolute extreme.

For anyone familiar with the work of the film's creator, the animator Hugh Harman, the nightmarishness of this scenario should
not come as any surprise. Harman and his longtime partner Rudolf
Ising, best known as the original creative team behind the creation of
the *Looney Tunes* franchise, were also the animators behind one of the
last, and by far one of the most gruesome, imitation films stemming
from Messmer's *Felix Turns the Tide* and the wave of proto-pacifist
films that followed. Titled *Bosko the Doughboy* and released in 1931,
nine years after Messmer's work and thirteen years after the end of
the First World War, the film partly has the feeling of being a necessary step in the introduction of a new cartoon everyman hero, Bosko
being yet another contestant in the sweepstakes to replace Felix as the
pinnacle in cartoon popularity in the time before Mickey Mouse was
crowned champion of that contest. Felix went to war, Oswald went
to war, Mickey went to war, and so now Bosko must go to war. From
today's perspective, the largely forgotten Bosko, who never went on
to much success after the short, is undoubtedly a deeply troubling
figure. Originally designed in the late 1920s to resemble a character
in blackface, his appearance morphed over his first several films to
become a more bland and abstracted figurehead for the new *Looney
Tunes* series. It is this version of Bosko who appears in *Doughboy*, a
kind of pure cartoon creation with no clear anthropomorphic refer-

ent, the broad white and black blotches of Felix, Oswald, and Mickey alike here turned into a kind of cartoonal species of their own. (Indeed, it is precisely this idea of a kind of purified cartoon corporeality that the Warner Bros. Studio meant to reference in openly recycling the Bosko figure as a model for the design of the main characters in their 1990s animated series *Animaniacs*, where Bosko appears in several episodes as an ancestor to the new series' stars.) In a sense, Bosko's freedom from any clear corporeality on account of his confusing design—he is neither human nor animal, neither comic nor serious—helps to give his version of wartime experience a special license for violent extremity. For though Harman and Ising's short is rather late in the game of imitating the wartime themes of *Felix Turns the Tide*, it is no less impactful for that delay.

If anything, in fact, it is by far the most gruesome of those 1920s and 1930s era First World War cartoons, a film so nihilistic in its depiction of war that it can at times be painful to watch. Here there is no attempt whatsoever to position war as possibly necessary or justified, however compromised such ideals might be by the film's end. Whereas *Felix Turns the Tide* opens with declarations of Felix's heroism and *Great Guns* depicts Oswald saying good-bye to the true love who will ultimately save him, *Bosko the Doughboy* simply opens with the imagery of war: a vista of bullets streaming over tangled barbed wire as bombs fall in the background. There is not a character to be found, just the imagery of war itself. This is followed by realistic depictions of dark cannons firing against a smoky sky and bullets soaring over pockmarked land, more images of war without people. It is the utter absence of any sense of cause that is most disturbing here. The war does not seem to stem from anything; it is just happening—it is reality itself, the baseline state for the entire rest of the film. And so when the characters suffer, we never get to know why they suffer or glimpse any part of their lives before the war that might in some small way alleviate or justify that suffering.

And suffer they do: the film is ultimately a kind of étude on the conditions of wartime suffering. It is cartoonal suffering, to be sure.

As a rule, the Bosko shorts in the early days of the *Looney Tunes* series were defined by their figural and environmental elasticity—a feature that would soon become an important part of the Warner Bros. house style, cementing its difference from the competition at Disney. But if such morphism was a prominent visual feature in *Bosko the Doughboy*, it would offer no defense against the calamities of war. At one point in the short, an ostrich who tries to lead an assault against the enemy is shot through the stomach: he pokes his head through the hole in his center, realizes his grim situation, then salutes and falls face-first into a watery grave. Later, a bird capable of transforming into a fighter plane becomes fatally engulfed in flames when Bosko returns a bomb he attempted to drop in his trench. In fact, just as the anthropomorphic characters are not protected by their bodies, neither are the inanimate weapons of war protected by their objecthood. Early in the feature, a bomb lands on an artillery piece firing at the enemy, causing the cannon, the barrel of which has morphed into a mouth, to heave several times and then collapse. The universalized carnage of the cartoon essentially cancels out any issues of the body whatsoever. Elastic or not, animate or not, all participants in Bosko's war are subject to violence and death. There is no attempt at all to distinguish between *people* and *things*: everyone and everything in the film is in exactly the same situation—capable of morphing, capable of attacking, and capable of dying. Indeed, the relatively simple death of the first cannon early in the film is topped by the elaborate killing of a second: Bosko uses a pair of pajamas on a stick to catch a bomb, causing the pajamas to become animated, walk toward the cannon that fired the bomb, unbutton the panel on the backside of the garment, and defecate the bomb back onto the enemy cannon. Death is omnipresent in this vision of war, so omnipresent and omnidirectional that even things that are not truly alive can still die. Bosko's may be a fantasy realm, but it is one that contains the apparatuses of war and the hard logic of death, against which even elasticity is no sure defense.

For all the death and destruction made terribly explicit in the Bosko short, however, what is arguably most chilling about the piece is the utter lack of narrative movement. Bosko is thrust into the middle of an active world war that is given not only no beginning but also no sense of any end. Not only is there no heroic mission to organize Bosko's adventure a la Felix or Oswald, there is no narrative movement in the short whatsoever. Bosko begins trying to survive and ends trying to survive. Whether he has been fighting for weeks or months or years, we cannot know; whether the war will ever end at all remains unclear. The true horror of Bosko's experience seems to be that there is no way out of this insanity and neither is there an obvious way through. In Harman and Ising's vision of the conflict, war is a condition that aspires to a hellish and totalizing permanence. The malleability of the body that defines the Bosko franchise makes this condition at least somewhat tolerable, for him and for us. Even as some characters in Bosko's world perish despite their elasticity, others are saved by it. Toward the end of the piece, Bosko's commander swallows a cannonball that was fired at him and falls down, preparing to die. Bosko saves him by unzipping the commander's stomach from the navel up and taking the bomb out with his own hands, an exaggerated account of battlefield surgery. Elsewhere in the short, a friend who has joined Bosko on a charge is shot in half by a rain of machine-gun fire (plate 19). With his midsection eliminated, his torso falls directly onto his legs, and he manages to waddle away. Through elasticity, death and deformity are at least tempered, if not eliminated. Even those condemned to die because of their injuries are afforded a measure of dignity through the ability to delay the moment of death: the characters in the short are always aware of their impending death and able to take some last decisive action such as a final salute or maintaining a stoic disposition. But if these elastic graces render the animated violence of the film tolerable, it is only just barely so. Ultimately, Bosko the Doughboy is seven minutes of pure death and injury, over and over and over again.

The violence in Bosko the Doughboy, unlike that in Felix Turns the Tide or Great Guns, is not born of witness, harrowing though it may be. Neither of Bosko's cocreators were veterans of the conflict depicted here—they were both just fourteen when America joined the First World War. Yet Harman in particular had an unusual relationship to the war. An idealistic young man eager for adventure, much like Disney before him, Harman had joined the National Guard at the age of fifteen in 1918 and had at one point hoped for a deployment to the front should the war last long enough for him to reach enlistment age. He even briefly entered US Army officer training after high school in 1922 but left for a career in animation at Disney's earliest venture, the Kansas City–based Laugh-O-Gram Studios, where Ising also worked. The two were surrounded in their early employment by war veterans at a time when the conflict was only a few years in the past, among them fellow animator Lorey Tague and the company's business manager, Jack Kloepper, as well as Disney himself in his capacity with the Red Cross.[26] Harman and Ising both came of age as animators in an environment where the war was in the realm of immediate living memory and at a time when the war was entering the animated lexicon, *Felix Turns the Tide* being released in the same year Harman joined army officer training. One cannot help but imagine that he heard something of the actual experiences he had yearned for but missed over on the battlefields of Europe. Just as one cannot help but feel that he may have grappled with some sense of guilt over those youthful ideals, or else a feeling of betrayal over the glorious vision of war he was sold as a kid compared to the reality he learned of as an adult. Something was being worked through in his films, because the barbarity in *Bosko the Doughboy* is unbridled.

In *Peace on Earth*, it is even more so. In fact, for all the talk in early reviews of the film's good message and holiday spirit, the short opens almost as a kind of sequel to *Doughboy*, offering a direct continuation of the ongoing, purposeless warfare of that film. We see the silhouettes of soldiers—human this time, not animal—running through a war-torn cityscape as the title *Peace on Earth* appears on screen. From the ruins of a bombed-out cathedral, we pan to a scene that could have been lifted straight out of the opening of Bosko: a twisted mess of barbed wire over a deserted landscape, helmets and guns strewn everywhere. It is quiet, though, and snowing. The helmet featured prominently in the foreground of the frame with a bullet hole in the temple gives us some inkling as to why. It is at this point that the film passes through some aesthetic gateway into a parallel dimension that is both its most effective rhetorical move and its most disturbing gambit. As the camera continues to pan, we see that the helmets strewn across the battlefield have been turned into homes by tiny woodland creatures: beneath each helmet roof are little windows all aglow with lighted hearths within. At the center of this graveyard-cum-village, we discover the origins of the Christmas carol playing over the opening pan with its invocations to "peace on Earth" and "good will to men": three adorable anthropomorphic squirrels are caroling on a street corner, a Christmas wreath decorating the window behind them.

What Harman is affecting here is a chilling reversal of the basic assumptions of the Disney aesthetic, of the worlds where loveable cartoon animals function more or less like surrogate people inhabiting an adorable surrogate world. We accept these animated worlds and show them to our children because we fundamentally understand them as metaphorical: not a claim that animals actually behave this way but a window into our own behavior through the vehicle of this animal transposition. Harman is depicting something else: not animals as metaphorical human substitutes but animals as our *actual evolutionary replacements*. It is Disney-style storytelling rendered not as children's entertainment but as horror. Part of what makes the move so effective is the total finesse with which it is pulled off. Harman began his career under Disney's tutelage, and though he left for other opportunities long before the coalescence of the studio's house style, he proved himself a master imitator of the form. The family of squirrels that form the central characters in *Peace on Earth* could have been lifted out of any later Disney film—in fact they seem to specifically anticipate the small woodland heroes Chip and Dale that Disney Studios will develop in the 1940s. And the animated animal world has all the right details, those tokens of sentimental domesticity that mark the Disney ideal: the wreath in the window, the fire in the hearth, the tea set, the doily on the wall. What makes this visual appropriation so subversive and disturbing is the degree to which Harman actually acknowledges the style as a cover, a means of excluding and forgetting and *erasing* all the aspects of the world that do not fit into its sentimental vision.

Astoundingly, Harman *enacts* this process of forgetting in the very story of the film, seeking to remedy it through an act of remembrance and recovery. "What are men, grandpa?" asks one of the adorable little squirrels as he snuggles on a comfy chair in the living room of his helmet-home. The question springs from the phrase "good will to men" in the Christmas carol they are singing, but it also springs from the total occlusion of all real-world history in the carefully controlled and ideologically managed world of the typical realist animated film. Harman's adorable woodland anthropomorph actually admits here that he has no concept whatsoever of history or context, of the very chronology that led up to and enabled the exact moment in which he is living, the very house in which he dwells. That is, he acknowledges the degree to which his world—the perfect, ideal world of the charming Christmas cartoon—is built fundamentally on the act of forgetting, the total escape from history, the abandonment of witness. The only remedy, Harman proposes, is the act of witness itself. In a move that is probably unique in the history of American commercial animation, the entire story turns on an actual instance of wartime witness enacted within the narrative of the film: the squirrel's aging grandfather sits down and tells his grandchildren of his memories of the war that led to the world they now inhabit. "There ain't no men in the world no more, sonnies," he says, beginning to act out his recollections. "As I remember the critters, they were like monsters."

Here the visual style of the film changes entirely again, returning to the kind of imagery we saw and left behind in the opening frames of the film. In the chilling scenes of the grandfather's recollections, we encounter a realism of a very different sort: not the aestheticized quasi-realism of the Disney style. Rather, we encounter something approaching the condition of actual realism, literalizing what Sontag calls in reference to photographs "something directly stenciled off the real."[27] It is not just that these animated images of combat are realistically rendered; it is that they are *actually real*. Specifically, in technical terms, they are *rotoscoped*, created using the process invented by the animator Max Fleischer in the 1910s whereby live-action film footage is traced and turned into an animated image. (This is the same process that would be used just a few years later by Wan Guchan and Wan Laiming for the combat scenes in *Princess Iron Fan*, made in the midst of the Second World War.) Thus, when we look at images in the grandfather squirrel's flashback—airplanes flying overhead, soldiers marching in formation, machine gunners peering out from their turret with gas masks on, a bayonet on an advancing soldier gleaming in the light (plate 20)—what we are *actually* seeing is live-action footage outlined and animated. It is as if we are looking at war itself.[28]

Yet the fact that this is not just newsreel-style footage of war but the rotoscoped version of that footage is powerful and important. The photograph, Sontag says, possesses a unique form of "transparency," such that "there is always a presumption that something exists, or did exist, which is like what's in the picture." And the film captures this, even if one does not know the background of the technique: the images are strikingly, arrestingly realistic, perfectly capturing the fluidity of human movement and all the more chilling for the tremendous contrast that they draw with the happy anthropomorphs on the other side of the framing device. But they also capture something else, what Sontag calls the "synthesis" of the drawing or painting, the claim that "things *like* this happened"—or, we might say, *could* happen.[29] Paintings and drawings cannot help but interpret, Sontag says, and in the case of these rotoscoped scenes that inevitability of interpretation is vitally important. The interpretation being layered here is an urgent one: while there had yet to be a war capable of wiping out all of human civilization, Harman's warning—like that of all animators in the pacifist tradition—is that there could very well be.

The war that the grandfather squirrel describes in the film and the one shown to us through his flashbacks has all the hallmarks of war as it is typically depicted in pacifist animation. It is started over nothing, over causes that do not in any way justify the disproportionately violent responses they create. "They was always a fightin'," says the grandfather. "They'd no sooner get one argument settled then they'd find something else to fuss about. If it wasn't one darn thing, it was another. When they couldn't think of nothin' else to wrangle over . . . the vegetarians began to fight the meat-eatin' people, and you couldn't make heads or tail of it." It is defined by a sense of universal vulnerability, both sides entirely indistinguishable in their suffering: there are no uniforms we can identify, no way to keep track of who is who. There is only a blanket application of war's powers of death and ultimate destruction. And there is at the center of the war flashback a profound sense of reciprocity, of a total equality of action between the two sides.

It is here that the necessity of rotoscopy becomes most apparent. Seldom if ever can a single photographic image capture the fundamental reciprocity that is war's basic action, the immediate trading of injury and death. But a composite image can, and a narrative can. At the end of the grandfather's story, he tells of how "they fought and they fought and they fought until there was only two of them left." Here we see first a single soldier in helmet and gas mask raise his rifle from a trench; then another across the way do the same from his own trench. The situation depicted here dramatically is essentially the same as that rendered darkly comic in Disney's *Great Guns* short, where two enemies rise up from opposite trenches and shoot each other dead simultaneously. It is an absurd image, but war has a way of turning the absurd into the normal, and animation has the means to capture that. Harman's gripping, terrible flashback ends in the image of each solider rising out of the water and muck of his trench and pointing his gun at his opponent, firing on him and being fired upon in turn. We only see one soldier die, but we do not need to see more: we already understand war's basic action as reciprocal, its ultimate goal total death. To watch one soldier die, slowly and agonizingly, is to watch them all.

Peace on Earth is a deeply angry work of art, a film that is full of indictments: of war, of the causes that send men to battle, and of a culture so quick to forget what actually transpires on those battlefields. But perhaps its greatest invective is saved for the medium of animation itself. The stunning accuracy with which Harman replicates the Disney style—itself still relatively new at that point, in 1939—should do nothing to hide the fact that the filmmakers seem sickened by the way that style is used to cover over and erase the actual conditions of history. Insofar as animation can ever be used as a tool of serious social commentary—and Harman was adamant throughout his life that his role in demonstrating the serious purposes to which commercial animation could be put would be the cornerstone of his legacy—it needs to be a tool of remembering, not forgetting.[30] It needs to show real experience, with the goal of making that which is most terrible seem not farther away but closer. It needs to bring the stories of humankind's greatest follies directly into the hearth of every home, the same process that is literalized here. All the fine words and hymns in the world, Harman contends, offer little compared to the ability to see, to actually look upon the betrayal of those values that humans enact on one another time and time again. If we look away and if we forget, we do so at our peril. If we do not witness now, there may one day be no one left who can.

ANIMATING THE END OF THE WORLD

The idea of a war so total that it wiped out every living being and every possible witness must have seemed far-fetched in 1939, more a kind of metaphor than an actual proposition, no matter how Harman actually meant it. And surely the timing of his pacifist message—which arguably goes back to 1931 at least, when he was first working on Bosko the Doughboy—seems poorly thought out in retrospect, given the horrors of the fascist regimes confronted in the war that started the same year *Peace on Earth* was released. Yet within just a few years, with the dropping of atomic bombs on Hiroshima and Nagasaki, the idea that a war might ferment the actual end of humanity no longer seemed so remote. The metaphor had become shockingly real, and a pacifist message originally born out of the century's first great conflict became newly relevant and newly expansive in the immediate wake of its second. So relevant, in fact, that Metro-Goldwyn-Mayer, or MGM, the production company behind *Peace on Earth*, took the unusual step of remaking and rereleasing the film sixteen years after its initial premier, in 1955. That second film, called *Good Will to Men*, from the second line of the Christmas carol that permeates the soundtrack, would not be the work of Harman himself. Famous for running over budget, he had long since departed MGM, as had his former partner Ising; the producer of the original film, Fred Quimby, would be the one who commissioned its remake at the hands of Harman and Ising's replacements, the animation team of William Hanna and Joseph Barbera, of *Flintstones* and *Jetsons* fame.

For all its structural similarities, *Good Will to Men* would be a very different film than its predecessor, from a very different time. Rendered in CinemaScope, the brand-new wide-angle film stock of epic filmmaking, it would use the same basic structure and conceit of its predecessor film with only a few tweaks: the curious rodents are mice this time, not squirrels, and they are members of a church choir asking questions in a bombed-out cathedral, not in front of their fireplace at home. It would recycle much of the same dialogue, though it would lean heavier on the Bible and on quotations from the New Testament in particular. But something vitally important is gone: the actual act of witness exactingly rendered. When the grandfather figure, now the choirmaster, launches into his story of the war that ended all the humans, the images we see are updated to the technologies of the Second World War, but they are marked by some of the limited animation techniques that were mainstays of Hanna and Barbera's work. Ever conscious of budgets, Hanna and Barbera were always alert to ways in which they could reduce the labor and techni-

cal costs of their productions: abstracted backgrounds, limited movement, and regular reuse of frames and cells all became the norm in
their work. Though their imagery in *Good Will to Men* is more carefully executed than in most of their films, its flashback scenes pale in
comparison to the vivid rotoscopy in *Peace on Earth*, giving the film a
flat, lifeless quality. There is far less visual shock when we move from
happy anthropomorphic mice to faceless human soldiers. It feels
more like a *story* than a disruptive act of witness; hamstringed by
certain visual choices, it seems ultimately no more real than the mice
themselves.

Yet this penchant for abstraction in one way serves the film ex-
ceedingly well: its visual emptiness helps to emphasize the absolute
annihilation of all human life on planet Earth that marks the finale
of the film, the end of history and witness alike. This final erasure of
humanity, astoundingly, is a moment that the film shows in full in
a terrible symphony of color, shape, and movement that is arguably
far more affecting than even those two rotoscoped soldiers targeting
one another across the trenches in *Peace on Earth*. Here the act of final
reciprocity is not one of bullets but of bombs. "Each one of them built
the biggest, the most awfulest bomb ever," the choirmaster mouse ex
plains. "And while one of them was dropping a bomb over here, the
other one was dropping a bomb over there." Horrifyingly, Hanna and
Barbera show both acts of nuclear destruction: two cities, both leveled
in scenes of mirrored decimation. For once, their tendency toward abstraction, broad color schemes, and the evacuation of detail all serve
the film brilliantly. In a vision of unsettling grace and superb composition, Hanna and Barbera then dissolve into the most extreme of
long shots: so far back that we can see the curve of the earth and the
moon out in space beyond the stratosphere—this years before the first
true satellite images were ever taken of the planet. (Instead, the scene
evokes the framing and perspective of the first suborbital images
ever taken of the earth, from the late 1940s.) Here the world is literally destroyed before our eyes. From one hemisphere of the globe, we
see the red radioactive cloud of one bomb begin to expand; from the
other, a green cloud expands in equal proportion. Slowly, beautifully,

and appallingly, they come together, overlapping like a Venn diagram wherein the central coinciding portion, rendered pure white, expands and expands until it washes over the entire screen, the radius of mutual destruction becoming the greatest radius of all. No one is wrong or right here. Such terms are meaningless when there is literally no ground on which to make them. Pacifists had long been warning that war might kill us all: *Good Will to Men* is likely the first film ever to actually show such a prospect—not in metaphor, not in synecdoche, not in a montage of individual images, but in a single extreme long shot imagining the entire annihilation of the world.

Good Will to Men is unmistakably a product of the Cold War, and its vision of apocalypse is historically situated in the fears and nightmares of that moment. Those nuclear fears are with us still, though now they are also joined by others. In our new age of drones and autonomous weapons systems, we cannot be so sure that it might not be bullets instead of bombs that will do the work of fulfilling war's drive to total destruction, even if there will not be any humans pulling the trigger. This is the theme of a pair of animated videos posted online in 2013 and 2016 by the independent Russian animator Dima Fedotov, a teacher in Saint Petersburg. The conceit of Fedotov's films, which are part of a longer series he is developing under the title *Dead Hand*, is that of a postapocalyptic, posthuman world where two nations' autonomous weapons systems continue to target one another decades after they have already succeeded in killing every human left on Earth, the actual work of war having been made entirely independent of the humans who began the conflicts. Fedotov's work shares elements in common with any number of science-fiction films, though in most cinematic tales of machine warfare the robots have turned on their human creators, a move that conveniently collapses difference and strife between those humans and utopically unites them against their would-be machine overlords. Here, however, those machines have no autonomy or intelligence of their own and continue to follow the programming set by the humans who created them, not realizing those humans are all long gone. Fedotov's work thus builds more on certain traditions of Russian animation and its overlap with science

fiction than on traditional Hollywood storytelling. Specifically, Fedotov's work recalls Cold War era animated films like Anatoly
Petrov's 1977 film *Firing Range*, wherein a mourning father builds an
autonomous tank to murder the generals who ordered his son into
battle, or a 1984 animated film from Uzbekistan, Dmitri Ivanov's
There Will Come Soft Rains, which adapts a Ray Bradbury short story
about an autonomous house built inside a nuclear fallout shelter that
continues trying to serve its family long after they have all been disintegrated by a nuclear blast.

Like other Russians of his generation, Fedotov came of age after
the heightened nuclear fears of the Cold War, during a period of pe-
ripheral, but perpetual, war: Russia's bloody Chechen campaigns of
the early 2000s, the country's flash war with Georgia later that decade, and then, as he was creating his films, the annexation of Crimea
and subsequent military intervention in Ukraine. The entries in Fedotov's *Dead Hand* series—so far *Fortress*, from 2013, and *The Last
Day of War*, from 2016—are new works of pacifist animation designed
for a new era and its new nightmares. And like much pacifist animation before them, one of their most devastating weapons is beauty.
Fedotov is an amateur animator, using commercially available com
puter software to create his films largely on his own. Yet the visual
quality of his work is astounding: as achingly photorealistic as any
Hollywood production and richly realized in the mechanical detail
of the world he creates. Fedotov's points of reference are clearly World
War II era armaments: in *Fortress* his camera lingers over an updated version of the giant B-17 flying fortress bombers, here gliding
over a totally silent city that has clearly been bombed over and over
and over again, its rubbled streets resembling footage of Warsaw or
Stalingrad from after the war. The cinematic stylization of Fedotov's
films render war-making as art, all form and no function. The total
absence of humanity means that there can no longer be any meaning in war, if there ever was, but also no suffering—just the abstract
shape of bombshell blasts rising up above depopulated streets. There
are people in these films, of a sort: human skeletons still strapped
lifelessly into pilots' seats as their planes fly themselves for years on

end. The machines treat them like people, giving them updates and providing them with data readouts, but they are just objects, less alive than the machines themselves. As realistic as Fedotov's work is, it still engages in the quintessential transposition of animation, turning subjects into objects and objects into subjects.

There is life in Fedotov's work, but it is not human life. In the most poetic images of his films, nature begins to reclaim what humans have left behind: a shaft of grass breaking through the broken concrete on the bombed-out city floor, cranes gliding gracefully alongside the autonomous flying bombers, a small tree bursting with bright-red blooms against a cracked fortification wall. Fedotov's imagery of nature slowly reclaiming what war has destroyed after humans are gone recalls that of the American writer Sara Teasdale in her poem "There Will Come Soft Rains," published in the midst of World War I in July 1918—the very same poem that Bradbury used for the title of his postapocalyptic short story in 1950 and that the animators at Uzbekfilm reused in their animated adaptation of the same:

> There will come soft rains and the smell of the ground,
> And swallows circling with their shimmering sound;
>
> And frogs in the pools singing at night,
> And wild plum trees in tremulous white,
>
> Robins will wear their feathery fire
> Whistling their whims on a low fence-wire;
>
> And not one will know of the war, not one
> Will care at last when it is done.
>
> Not one would mind, neither bird nor tree
> If mankind perished utterly

War will not end everything. The world will be reborn—but not necessarily with us. The ethic of pacifism, warns Fedotov along with the many like-minded animators who came before him, is nothing less than the ethic of survival itself.

PART TWO

AFTER WAR

CHAPTER 3: MEMORY

Jean Michel Kibushi's house in Kinshasa, the capital of the country then known as Zaire, is full of children. It is autumn of 1991, and Kibushi, an artist and filmmaker, lives in the bustling Lemba district, a residential area near the center of the city, just south of the Congo River. The noisy streets are lined with rows of single-story houses, most of them hidden behind tall concrete walls surrounding modest courtyards and gardens. In Kibushi's home that day, the children are everywhere: inside, outside, any space where they can find a flat surface to lay down their paper and their chalk. They are all drawing, all diligently at work, but the mood is tense. The government of Zaire's longtime dictator Mobutu Sese Seko, for years supported by the United States during the heyday of the Cold War but now abandoned, is all but bankrupt; the nation's currency is close to worthless, its soldiers have not been paid in months, and the country is in chaos. That September, just a few weeks earlier, close to three thousand paratroopers garrisoned near Lemba went marauding through the district: looting stores, breaking into homes, stopping vehicles in the streets, and sometimes shooting civilians on sight. The anarchy continued for nearly a week until contingents of French and Belgian soldiers arrived to restore order. The atmosphere since then has been just as heavy, with everyone sensing that the peace might not last long. Five years later a full-blown civil war will erupt, at the end of which Zaire will become the Democratic Republic of the Congo. A second civil war will begin less than a year after the first one ends. Not until 2003 will the fighting begin to subside, with the death toll in the country reaching into the millions.

For the children of Lemba, Kibushi's home is a place of sanctuary and a space for expression. It is also an archive of their memories. Trained as a cinematographer at the National Institute of the Arts in Kinshasa, Kibushi began working with the Belgian animation studio Atelier Graphoui during the 1980s; he received training in animation techniques, and with those new skills founded his own studio in Zaire with Atelier Graphoui's support—the first such venture in his nation's history and one of only a few local animation studios in all of Africa at the time. He called it Studio Malembe Maa, meaning "slowly but surely," and his goal was to spread training in animation to others throughout central Africa—to foster and grow a local community of animators where before there was none. When chaos began to engulf his corner of Kinshasa just a few years after starting his studio, Kibushi responded by opening the doors to his home, inviting twelve local schoolchildren to come to his house to draw pictures of what they had seen.[1] In animation, these local children would find a means to show the wider world the horrors to which they had been witness.

The resulting film, titled *Kinshasa, Black September* and released in 1992 by Atelier Graphoui, is punishing. To see a child's drawing of a traumatic experience is painful; to see those drawings come alive and move—to watch the dotted-line bullets suddenly come out of the soldier's gun (plate 21)—is to be placed inside the child's perspective in a way that can be absolutely wrenching. Kibushi's blunt and unsentimental construction of the film is masterful. Giving each child identical black paper and identical white chalk, he creates a shared aesthetic field that gives visual continuity to the disjointed stories and varied drawing styles. Interspersing his own hand-drawn imagery and narrating the film himself to give context to the scenes and to the country's terrible situation, he carefully layers music and sound effects over the images in sharp and arresting ways: buoyant music to accompany the early images of normal, vibrant street life, then a shocking audio rupture when the soldiers' mutiny begins—a baby crying, a car alarm, muffled gunfire coming from the distance. The vast gulf between the unsparing reality of the audio track and the childlike style of the imagery places the film in a troubling and uneasy relationship to the actual events depicted. We cannot forget for a moment that the horrible scenes rendered here in unskilled two-dimensional outlines all correspond to incidents actually experienced and remembered by the children wielding the chalk. We cannot forget for a moment that this film is an act of *witness*. Every house raided for food, every car pulled over at gunpoint, every figure shot with their hands outstretched in the air—all of the motifs that circle through the film again and again and again in different drawing styles with different points of emphasis with different levels of skill—every single line of the film comes from an experience turned into a memory turned into a drawing. The children who helped make the film, all unnamed, are entirely present in its imagery. To watch *Kinshasa, Black September* is to be transported to that time and that place in a far more vivid way than any news report or photo essay could ever hope to achieve. Watching the film is like being invited to step inside of a child's memory. We do not just see the events they want to show. We see *them*.

Kinshasa, Black September is a particularly harrowing example of an especially harrowing genre of wartime animation, that which I call the *memory film*. Often reticent to foreground their politics and generally unconnected to the film production apparatuses of the state, such films perform the act of witness in its most direct and unmasked form. Whether made in the immediate aftermath of war and conflict, as here, or sometimes decades later, they are an attempt on the part of their animators—sometimes working mostly alone, sometimes with large teams of collaborators—to convey on film some aspect of what they themselves saw and experienced in wartime. It is not so straightforward a task as it may sound. Such memory films, even when trying to give voice to only a single animator's experience, are nearly always riven by internal conflicts or contradictions, a battle between different voices and perspectives. The great variety of drawing styles in Kibushi's deliberately patchwork film is emblematic of the form, as is the tension between the cohesion that Kibushi's narration tries to convey and the scattered, episodic nature of the scenes depicted. Memory—even recent memory, the recollection of events transpired just days before—is always a collaged and contradictory affair, frequently resistant to the dictates of coherence and story. The memory film is not so much a presentation of memory as a grappling with it, a grappling made all the more fearsome and urgent by the terrible and lingering effects of war, even wars long past that live on only in sorrow and nightmares.

It is in part this persistent degree of internal conflict and uncertainty that can make the memory film such a troubled form. Many of these films—*Kinshasa, Black September* included—are often considered in terms of the standards of documentary filmmaking, as they are in many cases quite literally engaged in documenting events that have occurred in war. But the genre of animated documentary is a vexing one, for how exactly can a drawn picture—a child's picture even—actually document reality? What exactly are we supposed to learn from a child's drawing of a man with a gun taking a box from a store that tells us *more* than what actual footage of military looting in Kinshasa might do? As Susan Sontag observes, there is an assumption of a basic *transparency* in photography that does not apply to drawings, paintings, and other artistic media.[2] To draw or sketch an event rather than to photograph it is to interlace it with perception and therefore with the perceiver. The problem, in technical terms, is what film scholars call the issue of *indexicality*. Photographic images and film seem at least to promise a one-to-one relationship between what they show us and what the photographer or filmmaker actually saw: a perfect *index* of image to reality. The artist's image, with its powers of compression, omission, substitution, and abstraction, offers no such reassurances, even in its most realistic forms. They do not show us the world, they show us the artist's *vision* of the world, which is to say what they actually show us in the end is *the artist*.

As Sontag writes, "artists 'make' drawings and paintings while photographers 'take' photographs"—the one an extension of the self, the other a transaction with the world.[3]

In the case of the animated memory film, this exposure of the self over and above the events depicted is in fact exactly the point. The animator seeking to recount or reconstruct his or her wartime memories is not doing so as a means to document specific events but to grapple with the reverberation of those events in front of us, to give voice to the struggle of representation itself when it comes to matters of war and atrocity, among the most incommunicable of human experiences. The memory film does not and cannot seek to add to the record of history's *continuum*—its official, sanctioned stories and reported explanations—nor does it generally seek to promote specific counternarratives to that continuum; its purpose is neither propaganda nor resistance nor even acts of protest, and though it shows war's worst aspects up close it generally does not make any explicit statement of pacifism. Its material is the *discontinuum* of history only, all the messy detail and all the unheralded voices that challenge official narratives of all stripes and render any easy explanation impossible. Hence the disunity of so many of these films, the open fraying of narrative or message or visual structure. In some ways, it is far harder to see or try to come to understand the experience of war from these films than from the more coherent and comprehensible pictures of conflict presented in other traditions of wartime animation, be they propagandistic or pacifist—and this confusion is exactly the point. The memory film takes as a given the conclusion come to by the famed Polish war journalist Ryszard Kapuściński after a lifetime covering nearly thirty revolutions, wars, and coups around the globe. "The image of war is not communicable—not by the pen, or the voice, or the camera," he wrote, deeming the documentary project to which he devoted his life to be in some sense a failure.[4]

Of course, the task of expressing the inexpressible is always the work that falls to the witness. *Kinshasa, Black September* is not a report on events that happened in the Lemba district of Kinshasa during the days of the military mutiny and the breakdown of civil order. It is a transcription of fragmented, individual memories into artistic form. Kibushi's film is an attempt to capture the experience of those September days, to remember and convey their confusion and their terror and their madness after the fact, to find a visual form that can do that work—"to seize hold of a memory as it flashes up at a moment of danger," in Walter Benjamin's words.[5] As such, the film, like all memory films, performs the two essential actions that Julia Kristeva says are always requisite of the witness: "to begin with, the act of looking truth in the face and, simultaneously, the translation of this vision into meaning."[6] Yet meaning should not be taken as definitive here. As a form of animation, the memory film is not about finding final meanings any more than it is about documenting specific events. It is about presenting the artist's struggle with the attempt to represent that which cannot be represented and the effort to *give* meaning to that which unmakes all meaning—recognizing that the solidity of that meaning, like the stability of memory itself, will always remain out of reach.

MEMORY AND NARRATIVE

How can we bring ourselves to remember that which we most desperately want to forget? That is the question that all animators who have lived through war and who believe in their art as an instrument for expressing that experience must at one or another point confront. For some animators, narrative can be powerful a tool for capturing memory, enclosing one's individual knowledge of war inside a fictionalized tale of wartime experience. Story is not a requisite component of the memory film: some will eschew it all together, as *Kinshasa, Black September* does, while others will present their narrative in broken, unfinished fragments only. This makes the memory film distinct from most other works of wartime animation, the basic coherence of a film's story being a necessary part of the political apparatus of the propagandist, the pacifist, or the resistance artist in most cases. Even when it is used, narrative functions differently for the animator grappling with the memory of war than for most animators in these other traditions; here, narrative can be admitted to be an imperfect tool, and the stories told in most memory films tend to close in on themselves and, at some point, deliberately fall into contradiction. Even in the most straightforward narrative works in the memory film tradition, the coherence or supposed symbolic weight of the film's story will be in some way challenged—an acknowledgment of the ultimate inadequacy of any narrative to fully capture the uncapturable experience of war, even for those films that view narrative as a useful, if insufficient, device.

Such is the case with Stjepan Mihaljevica's 1995 film *November 1992 Sarajevo*, released in Europe just as the multiyear siege that it depicts was finally coming to an end in a negotiated ceasefire. The film is in many ways a kind of historical companion piece to *Kinshasa, Black September*, both of them being created and distributed under the auspices of Atelier Graphoui. Mihaljevica's work and Kibushi's are alike in numerous ways—in the urgency of their creation, in their insistence on announcing their connection to a specific time and place set in the very recent past, in their attempt to record the conditions of civilian life in a metropolis made unrecognizable by war—but they diverge, pivotally, in their approach to the question of narrative. *Kinshasa, Black September*, though it includes Kibushi's explanatory narration, makes no attempt to tell a story set within Kinshasa's devolution; instead it tells a vast multiplicity of stories, the micronarratives of each child's imagery of a store being looted, a family being driven from their home, a car being stopped by soldiers—a tapestry of the many individual tragedies that made up life in the Lemba district during those days. Mihaljevica, in contrast, takes the countless possible stories of the three-year siege of Sarajevo—a city of half a million at the start of the Bosnian War, reduced by death and displacement to around three hundred thousand by its end—and collapses them all into one, a single narrative evocative of all the city's suffering. There is memory and there is witness within Mihaljevica's film, just as much as in Kibushi's, but it is relayed through the vehicle of its organizing narrative, its father standing for all fathers, its daughter standing for all daughters, and its suffering standing for all suffering, including Mihaljevica's own.

The story of *November 1992 Sarajevo* is perhaps the simplest that could be told of the siege: a father, recognizing there is no more food left at home for his daughter, ventures outside to find supplies and is shot by a Serbian sniper. In that nine-minute tale lies the whole of Sarajevo's experience, of civilians caught in a hell they cannot escape, gunned down unarmed as they try to simply survive. Mihaljevica's unnamed father is as much an archetype of that moment of suffering as an individuated character. But if the father must carry the weight of thousands and thousands of stories, he is never subsumed under that weight. That is to say, Mihaljevica's film always remains intensely personal and detailed, even as it channels all of Sarajevo's experience into the experience of one family. For all the terrible spectacle of the father's assassination on the street, Mihaljevica's main concern in the film seems to be the exploration of the small moments of strangeness made normal by life under siege: the family living at night by candlelight with the city's power grid long gone (plate 22), the constant checking of the cabinets again and again to see if any last piece of food might be found, the fleeting references to the absent mother, seen in pictures but never mentioned or shown and presumably already killed in the siege. Just as Kibushi's work revolves around repeated images drawn by child after child, so too does Mihaljevica's work return obsessively to a few select images: the flickering candle, the empty cupboard, the window that is the family's only connection to the outside world. Such images constitute small tokens of witness to the lived conditions of the civilians in Sarajevo that no newspaper report on casualty figures could ever hope to capture.

Such small, domestic moments are a prelude in Mihaljevica's work to another form of witness, one meant to bring to life an imagery that would be unknowable to anyone not living through the siege. Though his greater focus is on the domestic scenes leading up to the father's departure, Mihaljevica's rendering of the father's journey outside is a remarkable recreation of the heart-stopping experience of walking out of your front door into a once familiar streetscape made unrecognizable and unreal. Glancing nervously from side to side as he steps out of his apartment building, the father seems not to know his own street anymore: the city seems completely vacant, whole buildings have gone missing from artillery fire, snipers might be anywhere. Mihaljevica follows the father's short journey meticulously, taking us through every twist and turn in his attempt to find a way across a few blocks of the city and switching us multiple times into direct point-of-view shots showing us his perspective. When the father is finally shot by a sniper, ignoring the advice of a government soldier that a particular road is not safe to cross, Mihaljevica puts us as close to that moment as a spectator can be: we stay in the father's first-person perspective until the very moment when he is shot, at which point Mihaljevica switches to a third-person perspective next to his body as it falls. In this terrible sequence, Mihaljevica brings his viewers directly into the experience of an imagined civilian casualty of war who signals all the real civilian casualties of war.

Were *November 1992 Sarajevo* a work of propaganda or resistance, an overt statement of protest or a declaration of pacifism, the story of the father's death might be made into a kind of political emblem, a perfect encapsulation of war's devastation or proof perhaps of Croatian nobility and Serbian villainy. But Mihaljevica's minimally sketched, evocative film is more interested in the work of memory and witness than in promoting any single political purpose, and thus Mihaljevica takes pains throughout the film to present his story not as a perfect rendering of the Sarajevo experience but instead as an imperfect one. This limitation is built into the very style of his film. Mihaljevica's drawings, which look like they could have been taken directly from an artist's notebook, foreground their own sketched quality. They appear to us as pictures that have been hastily and imperfectly drawn—urgent and therefore not exact. Around each main image are vast reaches of negative space, each small world of detail surrounded by a total absence of detail: the father and daughter almost floating in space, a candle flickering against a screen that is mostly dark. Within the narrative itself, Mihaljevica acknowledges this story as being just a sketch, a single slice of life that cannot do justice to the whole of Sarajevo's suffering. Trying to explain to the government soldier why he must cross the street even though there is a sniper targeting civilians in the area, the father says, "I have a child to feed." "We all have children to feed," the soldier says in response. "My cousin who just died left five children." There is always a bigger story, uncapturable. No story is all stories, even if they share much in common. Mihaljevica depicts this same idea visually in his film in a remarkable and tragically beautiful sequence showing the nightly shelling of the city. Picturing the city from the perspective of the Serbian gunners positioned in the hills above it, Mihaljevica flickers between images of total darkness over the city and images in which one small part is suddenly illuminated by an exploding artillery shell, small flashes of light and horror, each one indicatory of another terrible narrative and another horrible tragedy for the families afflicted. It is as though Mihaljevica had taken literally Benjamin's mandate to "seize hold of a memory as it flashes up at a moment of danger," recognizing and acknowledging that not all such illuminations can have their stories told.

UNFINISHED STORIES

One sees this awareness of storytelling's inadequacy in the face of war in another narratively driven memory film from a very different time and a very different place, one set not within a city whose suffering drew the attention of the entire world but in the countryside of a nation whose suffering is generally not even known in the West. I am referring here to a short film called *Leaving the Village*, created by the Nepalese animators and brothers Sanyukta and Niyukta Shrestha in

2007, just one year after the conclusion of Nepal's decade-long civil war, which claimed nearly twenty thousand lives. For the Shresthas, memory, war, and animation as a medium of witness are all indelibly connected. *Leaving the Village* was the first animated film the brothers made after founding their studio Yantrakalā and one of only a few such films in the country's entire history. They speak of its origins in terms of their desire to commemorate and communicate Nepal's years of strife, to acknowledge how their nation, "once the messenger of peace for the rest of the world," was tragically "engulfed by its own unfortunate shadow of internal violence."[7] That is, they speak of their work as a way to bear witness. And like Mihaljevica, they endeavor to do so by telling a single story that must stand for the whole, even as they acknowledge the impossibility of that task. Visually, their approach is something of the opposite of Mihaljevica's—whereas *November 1992 Sarajevo* is minimally sketched but richly detailed in parts, *Leaving the Village* is abstract but enveloping. Its human figures little more than tiny outlines seen only from a distance and with no distinguishable features, the film is as much about the total landscape it depicts as any single detail within it. With the whole screen cast in hues of gold and orange, the film looks like a finished painting compared to Mihaljevica's intermittent sketches.

The film is narratively expansive as well, taking on the deliberately repetitive structure of a folktale. Starting with a brief and evocative scene of a mother and child floating down a river on a raft (plate 23), it transitions to a series of scenes of that same mother and child in daily life. Here, the same basic scenario repeats three times: the child sits outside their home in the mountains, staring down at a bridge, waiting for the mother to cross the bridge and return home with their firewood. At the end of the first scene, the mother appears as expected, crosses the river, and the two embrace. The next time the bridge is broken, but the mother crosses the river with a raft and still returns. But in the third scene, the pattern is broken: not by any peril encountered by the mother but rather this time by the child, who watches helplessly as a helicopter appears over the horizon and an unseen figure throws a single bomb overboard, a common practice in the war. The mother returns to a scene of fire and ash, collapsing to her knees. And then, mysteriously, the film returns to its original image: the mother sees her child on a raft, they embrace, and down the river they float, vanishing into the distance.

In the hands of the propagandist, the same story would demand specificity—we would need to know who dropped that bomb, who these victims were, which parties to demonize and which to valorize, whose lives to mourn and whose to curse. For the Shresthas, however, abstraction becomes a tool of witness, casting attention away from questions of *who* and focusing instead on *what*: on the suffering itself, which appears both timeless and tragically connected to the *now* of Nepal's conflict. The deep ambiguity of the film's story is key here. Did the child survive the bombing and wait for the mother on the raft, making this a story both of escape and of displacement? Is the reunion on the raft a fantasy, on the part of the mother or the animators, and an attempt to escape from the actual conditions of war? Has the mother killed herself in that space between the scenes, joining her child in an afterlife in which they float together into the unknown and disappear? War engenders all of these departures: of displacement, of death, of a traumatized detachment from reality. *Leaving the Village* skillfully negotiates all of these variants, leaving them all open possibilities at the end. Tellingly, the entire film unfolds *inside* this ambiguity: the haunting image of the mother and child is the very first image that we see and the last before the film fades away. All of the other action exists between these two mysterious extremities, a narratively untethered image that the main action of the film never in fact manages to secure. How can it? Only a series of overlapping stories—what literary scholars call a *palimpsest*, a rewriting of the same narrative over and over with no version entirely erasing any other—might begin to capture this terrible multiplicity, the different narrative possibilities in the Shresthas' film recalling all the different buildings individually illuminated by the nighttime shelling in that terrible, beautiful scene in *November 1992 Sarajevo*. In the world of the memory film, the narrative is never just one linear arc and never entirely stable.

This sense of narrative instability and purposeful ambiguity also stands at the heart of one of the most enveloping and affecting works in the memory film tradition, a Palestinian computer-animated and mixed-media work called *Fatenah*, from 2009, by the Iraqi-Palestinian animator Ahmad Habash. The film was made with a team of artists and film technicians based entirely in the Palestinian territories, and it is about nothing more and nothing less than the agonizing struggle to survive inside a world defined by a conflict that the characters in the film did not start, in which they do not participate, and which they can do nothing to end. Based on incidents that took place during the Second Intifada of the early 2000s and released just a few years after that period of intense unrest and uprising, the film's focus is neither political nor military. Rather, it is about the doubly difficult trials of confronting the medical tragedies of life in the midst of the geopolitical tragedies of the world. Fatenah, the central character loosely modeled on an unnamed woman from Gaza whose story inspired the film, discovers she has breast cancer and must confront not only the disease itself but the difficulties of trying to treat that disease in the middle of what is effectively an active war zone. Though she detects the signs of cancer early, the Sisyphean delays of checkpoints, paperwork, power outages, and outright wartime conflict mean that by the time she sees the proper specialists in Israel her cancer has metastasized and spread into her spine. In a world where even Palestinian ambulances come under fire from Israeli soldiers when they accidentally turn down the wrong road and interrupt an ongoing military action and where even cancer patients who can barely stand must submit to strip searches in public in front of armed soldiers in order to pass through a checkpoint (plate 24), the search for medical treatment becomes an ongoing battle in itself.

The story of *Fatenah* is powerful enough to make for an effective statement against the militarized conditions of life in Gaza, and on this level the film could have easily been designed as a work of resistance animation. Yet perhaps the most remarkable aspect of the film is the degree to which it refuses to submit to the clear prerogatives of any such politicized genre and instead embodies both the visual and narrative ambiguities of the memory film. To a stunning degree, the macrolevel story of the film, while undoubtedly compelling, serves foremost as a vehicle for reflections on the daily conditions of life inside the Gaza Strip: the family dinner interrupted by an enforced power outage, the teacher's strike to protest unpaid wages, the workday at a tailor's shop broken up by sounds of nearby gunfire that make everyone freeze in place, the exasperation of the doctors and nurses trying to work in a medical facility with the electricity turned off, and most of all, the seemingly endless waiting that makes up one of the primary activities of life within this heavily militarized and supply-deprived zone—waiting for hours upon hours at military checkpoints trying to get to medical facilities in Israel, waiting for whole days in doctor's offices and hospital waiting rooms inside Gaza as the region's limited medical staff travel from clinic to clinic, waiting repeatedly in bureaucratic offices trying to obtain the necessary paperwork and permissions. Such moments are what film theorist Kirsten Thompson would classify as instances of "cinematic *excess*"—elements that are "counter-narrative" and "counter-unity"—and they are everywhere within the film, impeding and subverting the narrative at every point just as Fatenah herself is impeded and subverted in her struggle to find proper treatment.[8] The degree of narrative interruption that the film sustains is nearly avant-garde in its disruptive impact, and this is exactly the point: it is in such fissures that the conditions of life in Gaza come through most clearly, conditions that no proper narrative can possibly contain and that most stories would seek to simply excise and erase. But above *Fatenah*'s commitment to tell a story stands the film's commitment to bear witness to the conflict itself and to the everyday suffering it engenders.

This commitment to witness is reflected even in the visual style of the film, which ingeniously combines computer-animated graphics and photographic images into a vivid and immersive collage. The computer-animated portions of the film are relatively rough by the standards of most commercial animation, limited as Habash and his collaborators were by conditions inside the Palestinian territories. Yet the filmmakers turn this limitation into a virtue, rendering the characters in the film in stylized, figural form with only minimal detail—almost like a series of mannequins come to life. Against computer-rendered figures and equally pared-down computer-generated backgrounds stand interspersed throughout the film other backgrounds and figures that derive from actual photographs of locations and people within Gaza. When Fatenah enters an Israeli checkpoint, she stands inside the photographic image of a checkpoint lined up amidst crowds of lightly rotoscoped Palestinians waiting alongside her. Or when Fatenah and her mother emerge from a store, they must wait to cross the street as footage of an actual street rally with chanting protesters and masked men carrying rifles proceeds to fill the foreground space in front of them. But perhaps the most disarming moments of collage come within those endless scenes of waiting, when the computer-generated background is punctuated only by a single photographic or video image somewhere in the frame: an actual medical poster of the human breast on a doctor's office wall, photographic portraits of Yasser Arafat and Mahmoud Abbas in a bureaucratic waiting room, or, most astounding of all, actual television news footage of Israeli military incursions into Gaza playing on animated televisions in the hospital rooms and institutional cafeterias in which the film unfolds.

The photographic presence of the real world can be found everywhere within the imagined realm of *Fatenah*—a visual decision that serves not to minimize the effect of the film's animation but to magnify it. There is no hierarchy of realities within the film, the photographic portions proving no more important or serious than the animated locations and animated figures. Both are merely an evocation of a time and place that the film means to reference—both are treated as symptoms of memory, in other words. Habash, who has worked in both live-action and animated filmmaking, has in fact stressed the importance of this element of remembrance in all of his works: "cinema is also memory," he has said in interviews.[9] Neither the photographic nor the animated can in fact bring us into Gaza during the period of the Intifada, but both together can take us into that region as an imagined space grounded in the real, pointing us toward the invisible and inaccessible origins of the memories depicted here. Taken in total, what the mixed-media style of the film most evokes is an obvious yearning for witness, for a testimony that does not try to actively make its imagery real but rather tries to use that imagery to convey an unreachable real that can never in fact be seen by anyone not living through it, that can only ever come to us through the filters of memory and artistic interpretation, as here. Trying to use computer-generated imagery, or CGI, to evoke the hard material conditions of occupied life in the manner of so many documentary-minded live-action filmmakers before him, Habash has created in *Fatenah* what might be best understood as a kind of *CG–neorealism*, embodying every aspect of that deep stylistic contradiction. (In fact, in 2009 *Fatenah* was one of the recipients of Italy's Roberto Rossellini Award, named for the legendary film director who helped invent the neorealist style in the immediate aftermath of World War II.) Here Habash is an animator before he is a documentarian, and that distinction is vital to understanding his project in this film: he is urgently trying to render in pixels that which would otherwise be invisible to the world, understanding that the photographic is just another conduit to witness that holds no more special access to a truth that cannot in fact ever be seen.

Fatenah, like so many memory films, actually makes this invisibility and unknowability central to its own story, opening in its final moments into the profound ambiguity that is always a hallmark of the memory film. After following Fatenah's journey so closely over the full length of the film, the final set of scenes refuse to bring any closure to her tale. Our protagonist has nearly collapsed at her last checkpoint stop in the penultimate scene of the film, trying to enter Israel to obtain a medicine that is supposed to be effective in treating her condition. We never learn if she has in fact made it through, for in the film's final scene she is back home, still weak, asking that the window be opened so she can see the Mediterranean. She is bathed in light, and the story portion of the film ends. We return to an image of Fatenah vibrant and healthy and standing before a pure white background, the same image that opened the film when she directly addressed the viewer. But this time there is no address. She merely smiles at the viewer, then walks away. Has Fatenah died from failing to obtain the medicine? Did she receive it but fell victim to her cancer regardless? Or is the imagery of the brilliant white light and the smile of her healthy self at the end of the film a sign of optimism instead, a reassurance that though she is weak now she will get better? Turning back to Fatenah's very first words of the film, as she stands healthy before that white background, gives no further indication of the truth. "I was very busy last year," she says at the opening of the film. "Now I'm free and I can tell you my story." Is she addressing us from a position in the afterlife, free because she has been freed from the bonds of this world? Or is she healthy and recovered, free because she no longer needs to spend her every waking moment trying to treat her disease?

Habash refuses to tell. The woman on whose story the film is based did in fact tragically die from her cancer, but the film itself makes no reference to these facts. Though its title card declares that the picture is "inspired from a true story," the film opens with a disclaimer that "the events and characters depicted in this movie are fictitious. Any similarity to actual persons, living or dead, is purely coincidental." How much the film hews to the true story of Fatenah's real-world counterpart remains entirely unclear. As in *Leaving the Village*, all possible endings are contained within the film's ambiguous framing device: the entirety of the film is set *inside* this ambiguity. Perhaps Fatenah succumbed to the terrible conditions of war itself, unable to reach the medicine she needed. Perhaps she received the medicine but still succumbed to her disease, one of the many tragedies of life that continue regardless of whether a war is ongoing or not. Perhaps she has survived despite all of the obstacles placed in her path and therefore is a point of inspiration. No single story could ever capture the entire experience of life under such hardships as those faced by Fatenah and her family. The most honest possible story is the story that is no story at all, that is all stories all at once, that does not even try to find a way to provide a sense of closure for a situation that in life cannot ever have one, at least not yet.

THE DRAWING THAT CAN NEVER BE DISCARDED

The frustrating, maddening impossibility of fully capturing wartime experience in any cohesive narrative or any singular style, which so animates *Fatenah*, is a central feature of all animated memory films—so much so that in some such works that very impossibility becomes the overt subject of the film itself. *Black Notebook*, a 1996 film by Burundian animator Benjamin Ntabundi, is an especially enthralling instance of a wartime memory film that makes the process of its own generation as much its subject as the wartime events that spurred its creation. Ntabundi was a Burundian artist who worked with animators Michel Castelain and Jacques Faton from Atelier Graphoui to tell the story of his escape from the violence surrounding the outbreak of the Burundian Civil War in 1993, in which ethnic conflict between Hutus and Tutsis, similar to that in neighboring Rwanda, led to an estimated three hundred thousand deaths over more than a decade of fighting. The story of his escape and the ongoing struggle to capture the events around him in artistic form make up the intertwined storylines of the film, which cycles through a variety of animation techniques in the attempt to convey its narrative—from stop-motion to Claymation to live-action "lightning sketch" sequences like the ones that used to be common at the very beginnings of animation's history, when artists would sit before the camera, draw some figure on a sheet of paper, and then marvel as that figure suddenly came alive.

The problem for Ntabundi is that the figures he draws never do come alive or instead come alive in all the wrong ways, his artistry always inadequate to the horrible situation he confronts. The use of live-action drawing embedded within a mix of other animation techniques is a brilliantly recursive means of storytelling as Ntabundi deploys it in the film, with each form of animation corresponding to a different layer of lived and recalled experience. The film opens with a vivid mixed-media cutout animation of Ntabundi himself sitting under a tree listening to a radio announcing the presidential assassination that began the war—a scene whose animated version of reality is shattered by a live-action insert shot of Ntabundi's own hand drawing that radio in his notebook, a live-action copying of an animated representation of whatever actual radio Ntabundi used to listen to the news, if such a radio ever in fact existed. Within the first two minutes of the film, in other words, we are already cast deep into a realm of visual uncertainty where it is nearly impossible to tell the difference between what is origin and what is copy, what real and what artistic reflection. The question of *index* that so vexes scholars of documentary animation is here entirely exploded, with the artist's *real* hand drawing a *real* picture of a *fake* radio issuing a *fake* announcement about a *real* coup, all of which may or may not correspond directly or indirectly to anything from Ntabundi's own actual life. The only two things whose status we know for certain are the hand that we see drawing, happening in the present moment of the film, and the coup itself, from the historical past. Everything else between that present of artistic creation and that past of historical experience is a free-floating mystery: that is to say, a memory.

It is in this context that the main action of the film unfolds, taking on the distorted logic of a dream and the terrifying imagery of a nightmare. Almost as soon as the radio announces the coup, paratroopers fall from the sky, tiny plastic figures who seem no more real than toys. But they are undoubtedly real within the context of the film, and over their image Ntabundi layers disembodied voices asking desperate questions: "Why are they killing us?", "What is our crime?" Ntabundi flees the marauding troops, but as in a dream they cannot be outrun. Boarding a bus filled with other civilians, he tries to draw the soldiers from memory in his little notebook—another live-action insert of his actual hand drawing an actual sketch—and just like that they are conjured: the soldiers stop the bus, tell the passengers to get off and lie down in a field, and then shoot them all where they lay. The content of the imagery is absolutely brutal, but the artistry of Ntabundi's colorful paper cutouts is mesmerizing: his animated alter ego, escaping the massacre, floats off a cliff like a sheet of paper and hides in the jungle. With the film's extremely shallow depth of field, which deliberately compresses the visual layers on screen into a strictly two-dimensional world, the soldiers walking by him in the distance look as though they are marching directly into his head.

Ntabundi finally finds a kind of safety from the violence, though even this seems no more stable than any other image in a dream. Walking through an abandoned, burned-out village, he finds a young boy hiding from the soldiers in a tree, and together they build a new home from sticks that they gather in the jungle, just like that. Their shelter made, Ntabundi immediately returns to his notebook, and for a moment we watch his live-action hand sketch the torched houses that we just saw in their animated forms. The boy, who wants to play despite all that has occurred, confronts his new companion about his obsessive drawing. "What are you scribbling all the time?" the boy asks. "I draw for current and future generations," Ntabundi responds. The boy is unimpressed, and he tears a picture of a soldier out of the notebook and throws it on the ground. "I hate this person. Why are you drawing him?" he demands, thinking that if he can eliminate the drawing, he can eliminate the pain: thinking, that is, that he can forget. Ntabundi does not immediately go to pick up the torn-out page, nor does he begin to sketch again. The idea of simply leaving the drawing discarded there, the idea of *not* remembering, is appealing.

But whether that act of forgetting is ever truly possible is another question. The discarded picture of the soldier that we see on the ground is not actually the same picture that we saw Ntabundi drawing earlier. We witnessed that drawing being sketched in live-action. What is left on the ground within the animated world of the film is not the live-action picture itself but a miniature version of that drawing, now reproduced at a smaller scale and set inside the mixed-media landscape of the animation. It is, in other words, not actually the original drawing that is discarded but a drawing of the drawing. Nor is it truly discarded. It may have been angrily thrown on the ground, but the drawing of the drawing ultimately remains within the world of the animation and does not disappear from or rupture the film like the images of live-action sketching did before. It in fact becomes the film's closing image, the camera lingering on it at length before the screen finally fades to black. In trying to escape his own recollected images of war, Ntabundi has not so much discarded his anguished drawings as he has simply cast them into the endless circulation of disconnected and dreamlike images that make up the substance of the film itself. The act of making art may help to enter images into memory, Ntabundi says, but it cannot necessarily help to take them out. Instead, those images will be endlessly reproduced, like the drawing of the drawing of the soldier, flowing through the processes of memory. Like the soldiers themselves within the film, the memories of wartime trauma become both omnipresent and inescapable, as traumatizing in their way as the original experiences that they depict. The very title of the film conveys as much. The animated notebook that Ntabundi's character carries around throughout *Black Notebook* is not in fact black, and neither is the spiral sketchpad that we glimpse in the live-action sequences. One is tan; the color of the other is never actually revealed. The blackness of the title—*noir* in the original French, which can also mean dark, murky, or obscure, as in *film noir*—has nothing to do with the color of the book and everything to do with its contents: memories that seem like they can never be escaped, incidents that can never be controlled, drawings that can never be discarded no matter how much one may wish to do so.

BIOGRAPHY AFTER WAR

How does one fit the memory of a war into the narrative of a life? What does one do with that drawing that can never be discarded and will always instead be reproduced? That is the question at the heart of

Black Notebook, and it is one that defines the work of so many anima-tors who have survived the experience of war and escaped its envel-oping conditions, as Ntabundi did, artists who now must find a place for those experiences as they move on to a longer life of which war is just one part. Here the work of the memory film begins to encom-pass something different than the immediate memory of the artists still in close proximity to the conflicts they depict, those just ended or just recently escaped. Instead, the memory film becomes shaped by the long-term memories of animators for whom remembering war is not a matter of recollection but a deeper excavation, one that pulls up other memories along the way, other formative experiences, other thoughts of who that artist is or used to be. The questions such artists must confront are far-reaching: what if the disruptive *discon-tinuum* of wartime experience is not a disruption to narratives of his-tory but rather narratives of the self—of the *continuum* that we so of-ten impose on our own notions of a self-consistent and self-evident personality and personhood? What to make of wartime experience then? In other words, where does war fit into one's biography? How does one represent war even to oneself? What biography is even ever possible after war?

These are the questions at the heart of an unusual work of ani-mated biography called *Point of Mouth* by the Bosnian animator Midhat Ajanović. Prior to the outbreak of the Bosnian War in 1992, Ajanović was an established animator in the region. He directed seven animated shorts between 1984 and 1992, with his latest premiering at the prestigious World Festival of Animated Film Zagreb in the same year that the fighting began. With the outbreak of that war, his ani-mation career effectively stopped. He left Bosnia and Herzegovina in the midst of the war in 1994, relocating to Sweden and pursuing work as a teacher and writer. For nearly twenty years, Ajanović did not make another animated film. And then, in 2010, he released *Point of Mouth*, his first work of animation since the war and an attempt to grapple with the place of that war within his life story. The ani-mated portions of the film are set between two very brief live-action sequences showing a man who looks to be in his thirties or forties standing in the parking lot of the Sarajevo airport, staring at the terminal as he prepares to leave the country. The animated scenes that follow the opening shot are quite literally his memories, proceeding from the moment of his birth to the months and days just before his departure—a whole life from childhood through adulthood rendered in witty, comical, and sometimes wrenching cartoonal form.

The conceit of *Point of Mouth*—an unusual one, to be sure—is that the entire memory sequence is filmed from a point somewhere inside the mouth of its main character: each individual scene starting with a set of gums or teeth parting as we gain a brief window into the character's world and surroundings, the scene disappearing whenever the mouth is closed again or something is inserted into it—a baby's pacifier, a piece of food, a tablet of ecstasy at one point. *Point of Mouth* is one of the few animated works in the memory film tradition that takes seriously its status as a cartoon: Ajanović worked in newspaper comics at various points in his career—we see his animated alter ego in the film handing samples of his drawings to a local Sarajevo newspaper editor, his mouth agape from nervousness—and his animated works often had a sardonic edge and a taste for the grotesque. Here those same traits manifest in the bright-colored, clownish design of nearly every character in the film, be they family members, friends, or lovers, and in Ajanović's eagerness to expose his own worst personal traits: he is the kid in school who goes from ignoring his teacher to trying to look up her skirt. To judge from Ajanović's animated mouth at least, he was ultimately far more interested in drinking and drugs than in almost any other activities in his life.

It is of course exactly this irreverence that makes the scenes of the Bosnian War so shocking and unsettling when they appear late in the film. The staccato, episodic nature of the film's progression means that the scenes of war and bloodshed seem to come out of nowhere, which is surely how it must have felt for an artist premiering a film at a prestigious international festival one moment and confronting dead bodies on the street the next. The immediate lead-up to the war within the film is a scene in which the main character is drawing an editorial cartoon of a man with a rear end for a face. In the very next image, we see him staring at five bloodied bodies on a Sarajevo street, the word *Bosnia*—the name of a country that had just come into existence—spray painted in graffiti on the wall behind them. In the next scene, our protagonist is clumsily loading a rifle with bullets and firing into the night across a battlefield (plate 25), ducking for cover when machine-gun fire erupts in return. And then, just like that, the war is over.

The two wartime scenes in *Point of Mouth* comprise no more than thirty seconds in a ten-minute long film. Yet what is remarkable is how completely they commandeer and redirect the narrative. Those two brief scenes effectively eclipse great swaths of the character's life. In the last scene we see before the war, he is a young cartoonist spending his nights at local dance clubs. By the time of the second scene from the Bosnian War, the one on the battlefield, he is staring at a drawing of a child, presumably his own; on the back it says, in a combination of Croatian and Swedish, "In Swedish they say *I love you*." In the film's last brief animated scene after the battle, we see the protagonist returning home to a family greatly aged since the last time we have seen them—his mother and father now elderly, his sister with a child of her own. Ajanović's approach to his life story is pointillist, to be sure, and the film includes several time jumps between childhood, adolescence, and young adulthood. But even within that established narrative system, the war almost entirely takes the place of his adult existence, blocking out all the milestones implied by that postcard and the final microscene with his aged relatives: for anything that exists in the protagonist's life in any kind of proximity to the war itself, the war completely dominates what he remembers and what he can show. And that war also effectively ends his memory and the film itself. The animated portion of the film lasts only a few more seconds after the nighttime battlefield scene. Upon the next mouth opening, it is daytime, and our protagonist is staring at a dopey redheaded teenager in a Red Cross helmet—the return of the cartoonal coinciding with the intervention of the international community and the cessation of hostilities. We see the main character's return home to see his parents and his sister with his passport and his plane tickets in hand, and then the film fades back into the live-action shot of the man at the airport. No extended scenes of homecoming, no celebration of the war's end. Just a few seconds of film culminating in Ajanović's departure, the flight leaving Sarajevo that will define the rest of his life.

The Bosnian War makes the telling of a coherent life story ultimately impossible for Ajanović. He understands memory as always fragmentary and disjointed, the brief vignettes afforded by his inside-the-mouth conceit providing an effective metaphor for the disconnected flashes of our life experiences recalled. Yet even within the established conceit of memory as fragmented, individuated, and comically weird, the disruptions of the wartime scenes are profound. How are we to reconcile the happy scenes of Sarajevo life with the image of a street strewn with bodies and with blood? How to reconcile the kid drawing cartoons with the man firing a rifle into the night? There is a broad coherence to the prewar scenes in their cartoonal irreverence, one that entirely disappears in the artistic style of the wartime casualties and fighting. And though Ajanović tries to return for a few moments to this style with the Red Cross worker and his comically aged family, he almost immediately abandons the effort—literally so. In the live-action scene that ends the film, the man in the airport parking lot begins to cough. Out of his mouth comes a tiny motion picture camera, which he spits into his hand, stares at quizzically, and then puts into his pocket. The man, representative of Ajanović himself and his decision to leave a homeland that had only just formed, will no longer be the same, his life no longer captured by that strange camera in his mouth. There will be no more animation, no more cartoonal irreverence, no more attempts to make coherent that which refuses to cohere. Ajanović does not abandon the camera—as in *Black Notebook*, the picture of war can never actually be discarded— but he puts it away, stores it in his pocket, determines that this

portion of his life is over, the vision of who he once was entirely severed from his future self, with a rupture point defined by the experience of war.

PERSEPOLIS AND REMEMBERING

This vision from a relatively obscure Bosnian-Swedish animated short
showing a male graphic artist approaching middle age staring at the
exterior of an airport contemplating a departing flight from his homeland is almost an exact mirror image of a far more famous sequence
in a much-heralded Iranian-French feature-length animated film
released three years earlier. That is, the framing device of *Point of
Mouth* offers a powerful echo of that used in Marjane Satrapi's 2007
film *Persepolis*, where a female graphic artist approaching middle age
finds herself emotionally frozen inside the Paris Orly Airport as she
contemplates a departing flight back to a homeland that she left long
ago. In both cases, the airport scenes are rendered graphically distinct
from the rest of the film—live-action in *Point of Mouth*, colorized in
the otherwise black-and-white world of *Persepolis*—and in both cases
the life left behind feels different, unreachable, like the life of another
person remembered by someone else. The parallels of these two framing devices are not necessarily an instance of direct artistic influence
so much as a condition of a shared emotional situation, of the same
struggle with biography in the face of utter catastrophe. In both cases
war is minimized—just thirty seconds of film in Ajanović's work,
almost entirely unseen in Satrapi's. And in both it is absolutely central to the struggles with personal narrative and personal coherence
that both animators face, the paralyzing struggle with memory that
leaves them both stranded and frozen at literal points of departure in
their lives, dealing like Ntabundi with drawings that simply cannot
be discarded.

On its face, *Persepolis*, codirected by Satrapi with Vincent Paron-
naud based on her best-selling graphic memoir, is not really a film

about war. Its main concern is a kind of before-and-after picture of Iran in the years leading up to and the years immediately following the 1979 Iranian Revolution. Marjane is a child in the tense years before the revolution, which erupted when she was ten, and her experience of Iran under the shah is deeply colored by the unique circumstances of her upbringing in the loving, middle-class household of two committed Marxists firmly opposed to his rule and unusually connected to the greater history of the nation—her mother in fact descended directly from the last ruling member of the Qajar imperial dynasty that governed Iran, then known as Persia, until 1925. The years after the revolution correspond to those of Marjane's adolescence, her parents' political restiveness now filtered through her own youthful rebellion against Iranian religious conservatism, a rebellion expressed in contraband Michael Jackson pins and secret Iron Maiden air guitar sessions in her room. Though the greater story of *Persepolis* is world-historical, its main settings are persistently domestic: most of the scenes shown directly, as opposed to those involving stories or flashbacks of some kind, unfold in the living rooms, bedrooms, and schoolrooms that defined Marjane's fairly sheltered world.

Yet war is everywhere in *Persepolis*, even if Marjane never steps on a battlefield. Her parents regularly attend violent rallies against the shah in the years of her youth, rallies that will culminate in pitched street battles in the days leading up to the Ayatollah Khomeini's ascension to power. Her beloved uncle Anoosh is made a prisoner of the state after the revolution for his Marxist views and previous subversive activities, and she visits him in his jail cell not long before he is executed. With the outbreak of the Iran-Iraq War in 1980 in the aftermath of the revolution, Marjane hears endless stories of the war, both personal and propagandistic, and is made to participate in rallies at school commemorating the country's fallen in that ongoing conflict. The very streets of Tehran are turned into memorials for the war dead, named after fallen soldiers and decorated with giant murals honoring their sacrifice. "Walking in Tehran now is like walking through a cemetery," Marjane's mother at one point observes. And that war also becomes briefly, fleetingly direct for Marjane when her neighborhood is shelled and her neighbor's home demolished. War is as inescapable for Satrapi as it was for Ajanović. And though their relationships to the conflict forced upon them could not be more different—she a sheltered child and he an adult combatant—its tremendous impact on them and on their sense of themselves is much the same. Satrapi's position in the world of *Persepolis* is roughly akin to that of the unnamed child at the end of *Point of Mouth*, the one to whom stories will be told. Those stories, coupled with whatever bloodshed the child has herself seen in a conflict that does not spare civilians, will prove just as monumental or radically unsettling as any battlefield experience.

Fundamentally, *Persepolis* is about Satrapi's struggles with the discoherence imposed on her by war, those same struggles with a personal *discontinuum* with which Ajanović grappled from his own similar vantage point as a wartime émigré unwilling to return home. Unlike *Point of Mouth* or other wartime memory films like *Black Notebook*, however, *Persepolis* hides its basic discoherence and does so masterfully and beautifully—though the effort is ultimately unsuccessful, as it always must be. Much has been made by critics of the film's distinctive black-and-white color scheme, an adaptation of the pure black-and-white imagery of Satrapi's hand-drawn memoir and a point of her insistence in early preparations for the film, here adapted into a palette that also includes various shades of gray within the backgrounds for emphasis and contrast. The results are stunning, and they give the film an unmistakable and immediately iconographic visual language. But as aesthetically rich as such visuals are, they are unmistakably an attempt to enforce coherence where there is none. The strategy is essentially the same as that used by Kibushi in creating *Kinshasa, Black September*, wherein the standard white chalk and black paper distributed to all the children gave a visual continuity to a film defined by its vastly different drawing styles and personal voices.

That same figural and stylistic discontinuity is everywhere apparent in *Persepolis* and is one of the film's strongest features. For every scene that exists outside of Marjane's immediate experience, a different animated style is used, sometimes radically disrupting the aesthetics of the rest of the film even as it maintains the same black-white-gray palette (plate 26). Hence the sequence where Marjane's father describes to her the story of the shah's rise in Iran, which plays out with a vastly shortened depth of field and figures who, like stick puppets, move only at the joints. Or a scene set during a violent anti-shah rally and cast entirely in shadow and silhouette, recalling the techniques of silhouette animation pioneered by German animator Lotte Reiniger in her 1926 classic *The Adventures of Prince Achmed*. Then there is the Soviet realist mixture of grand heroics and Russian iconography that the film deploys when Anoosh tells his tale of the abortive independence movement in Iranian Azerbaijan, after which he flees to Moscow to continue his studies in Marxism. Elsewhere the beginnings of the Iran-Iraq War are rendered in a highly realistic series of graphic silhouettes, the images of tanks rolling over a mountain immediately recalling the rotoscoped war sequences of *Peace on Earth*. Still elsewhere the film departs entirely from realism and engages in a stunning abstract play of symbols, as when the thousands of political prisoners executed in the darkest days of the Iran-Iraq War are represented by a few dozen stylized prisoner figures, falling and disappearing one by one as Marjane's father speaks of their refusal to declare loyalty to the state. The total scope of references and influences embedded in the visuals of *Persepolis* is staggering—everything from puppet animation to silhouette animation to the propaganda films of the Soviet Soyuzmultfilm to American work in rotoscopy to the iconographic approach of protest and avant-garde animation. Absent the all-defining black-and-white approach, the film would look like a collage.

Of course, none of this encroaches on the visuals of the film's central storyline concerning Marjane and her immediate family, and that visual displacement is exactly the point. *Persepolis* is the story of a life, and a story that is quite literally told to us by its own subject. The adult Marjane's first words in the film are "I remember," and the rest of the film's narrative unfolds from there. Against the openly pointillist approach of a work like *Point of Mouth* or the hallucinatory, dreamlike remembrances of a film like *Black Notebook*, the main storyline of *Persepolis* comprises a determined attempt to assert a unity of person and a coherence of experience. "I loved fries," "I wore Adidas sneakers," "I saw the mountains," "I went to the Caspian Sea," "I went to the prison where Uncle Anoosh lay"—at its beginning, at its middle, and at its end, Satrapi's narration returns to and reiterates the continuity of its central subject. Its whole purpose is coherence, an insistent telling the story of the self to the self—a kind of personal *continuum* a la Benjamin's descriptions of official state history. The refusal of the main storyline of the film to engage with any of the stylistics of its many embedded stories, remembrances, descriptions, or historical summations is part and parcel of this highly protected and highly valued sense of coherence. It is one that is even more closely guarded in Marjane's case than in most subjects, as the society around her seems determined to strip that inner coherence from her and impose instead a version of its own—a scripted coherence based on strict religious adherence. Every challenge that Marjane issues to this new scripted coherence that she refuses is also a defense of a different coherence that she wants to maintain, one that remains true to the conditions of her childhood and the general worldview of her family. "You criticize us yet our brothers here have different hair and clothes," she says in a cumulative moment of outspokenness, challenging the gender segregation and religious clothing requirements at her university in an act of verbal protest that also registers as a defense of the basic egalitarianism under which she was raised, a protection of a private life and private history that is under assault from a new public discourse in her nation that wants to erase that history—*her* history—and make it scandalous.

Marjane can protest such cultural assaults to her personal identity and can ultimately escape them. And the film devotes much time to chronicling these micro- and macrolevel moments of rebellion, from the Michael Jackson pin to her outspokenness at university. But what Marjane cannot challenge and cannot escape is war itself. As with

Ajanović, the appearance of war in Marjane's life immediately and irrevocably changes the trajectory of her biographical narrative. And even though these intrusions are minimized in terms of the time and attention devoted to them in the film—as in Ajanović's work, again—the impact of such moments is immense. In fact, the single greatest rupture in Marjane's story turns on the moment when the conditions of the Iran-Iraq War most directly intrude into her life. Prior to the incident of the shelling in her neighborhood, Marjane has endured much—but always from a distance. Her parents' participation in the anti-shah protests, her uncle's imprisonment and execution, a visit from a family friend tortured by the shah's secret police, reports from the Iran-Iraq War, ritual mourning for the fallen soldiers at her school—all of these were known to Marjane before her neighbor's building was exploded, but always filtered through stories and tales of something that seemed far away. It is the direct experience of war that utterly changes her life—epitomized in the moment where she approaches the building that has been shelled and sees a single human hand sticking out from the rubble, still wearing a pearl bracelet, possibly that of her neighbor and friend. It is this transformative encounter that leads to Marjane's parents' decision to send her away from the country, enrolling her in a school in Austria and forever severing her connection to the childhood version of herself.

The change in Marjane's life when she is sent abroad for schooling is monumental. From being primarily an audience for stories throughout the early portions of the film—a position that she relishes as a child—Marjane becomes the unwilling teller of stories. But the struggle to form a narrative around what she has seen is almost insuperable. "You saw a revolution and a war?" asks one of the kids she tries to befriend in Vienna. "You saw a lot of dead people?" Marjane, suffering from inarticulateness almost nowhere else in the film, here finds nothing to say. "Well, yeah," she says to the first question. "A few," to the other. Always an outsider, Marjane quickly grows disillusioned with Europe, a place she once romanticized. Part of it is cultural, part of it is romantic. Bad friends, bad boyfriends, and the changes of puberty make it a terrible time to be alone. And that is just the point: she is utterly alone in Europe, long before she finds herself actually homeless. She has been alone since the beginning of her stay there. Her status as someone who "saw a revolution and a war" renders her position in a country where war seems far away untenable in and of itself. Her entry point to acceptance may initially come by way of stories of the war that the other teenagers find so fascinating, yet the stories themselves are never forthcoming, never able to be formed. Any story to be put around the violence of war is a false or at least imperfect story. Satrapi emphasizes this fact in the scene in which Marjane is kicked out of the religious dormitory where she first stays in the country—the expulsion that in her own words "marked the start of a series of moves," her long period of rootlessness in Europe. Ostensibly the incident involves a prejudicial comment over dinner about how ill mannered Iranians are, prompting an expulsion-level response from Marjane in turn. The conflict had been long simmering, but it is not incidental to the scene that the nuns in the dining hall are all watching a vapid murder mystery on television. The scene of the expulsion in fact opens with the animated figure of a body on the ground stabbed by a knife, and only after a few moments does the camera pull back to reveal that the image is on television. Marjane looks on incredulously from behind the other nuns as they watch this show of perfectly packaged and entirely explicable violence broadcast as entertainment. "It's murder," says the wise detective, as if every act of violence could be explained.

In many ways, Marjane never recovers from that initial period of exile, limited though it may be. She ultimately returns to Iran and attempts to resume some semblance of a normal life, but she never feels at home again. "Nothing had changed," she says, "but deep down, I knew, nothing would be like before." She has known life in the West and the freedoms enjoyed there—entirely overlooked and unappreciated by the other teenagers around her—and she cannot countenance the repressions at home: the private acts of rebellion once enacted in her own bedroom by way of a contraband cassette tape become dangerous public statements at university against the hypocrisies of the Iranian regime. But neither does Marjane feel entirely at home in the West. "In the West nobody cares if you die in the street," she tells a boyfriend who wants to emigrate. In the West, in other words, you are alone; in Iran, you are repressed. What Marjane does not realize then but what she will come to recognize by the very end of the film is that the dynamic of isolation and repression is not just born of her position between two worlds. It is also a product of the war experience itself: the dynamics of isolation and repression are within her, and both feelings will follow her wherever she goes. She will always feel as alone as she did on that day she was alone in the street, staring at that rubble, watching a world torn apart. She will also always feel as unable to express herself, as repressed and shut inside. When she and her family decide that she should return to Europe and make a life for herself in France, it is a deeply mournful moment. It is not just the people left behind: it is the loss of that sense of coherence itself that came from a time before war's disruptions.

Like Ajanović's, Satrapi's story essentially ends when she gets on that plane leaving Iran, and the visual style of the film entirely changes. The colorization of the scenes set years later in the Orly Airport not only marks the fact that these moments occur in the present; it also marks the fact that they occur in a world, and a *self*, apart and different. As Satrapi prepares for the trip in the first scenes of the film, she tries to reenter a version of her old self, putting on a hijab that she presumably has not worn in many years. As she sits in the airport, unable to bring herself to take that flight back home, she takes it off again. The passport photo that she shows the customs agent upon her reentry has no headscarf in it. She is a different person now, irrevocably. There is much to this difference, as there is for any émigré as well as for anyone approaching middle age and looking back upon their youth. But for Satrapi the experience of war stands at the fissure point of that transition, as it did for Ajanović. The film in fact reemphasizes this point through its insistence on identifying the protagonist figure in the film with Satrapi herself: it is not just that the main character's first name is the same; it is not just that the fictional Marjane's family circumstances are similar. The passport that the animated Marjane shows to the customs agent in fact spells out her name in full on the screen. She is Marjane Satrapi, the world-famous graphic novelist, artist, and animator. She is the same woman who has spent her life drawing and redrawing the images from her youth, putting her memories into visual form. Meaning that, within the world of the film, she will make a graphic novel and then an animated film of this experience. And within that animated film, another Marjane will appear who will make another graphic novel and then animated film of this experience. The drawings will exist within drawings, over and over again—like the recursive drawing of the solider at the end of Ntabundi's *Black Notebook*. Satrapi's situation is much the same as Ntabundi and his notebook trying to outrun the Burundian Civil War. She has been drawing the same images over and over, trying to sort through her memories. She will continue drawing them again and again. As in *Black Notebook*, the drawings of war can never be discarded.

WALTZ WITH BASHIR AND FORGETTING

Although they can, in fact, become lost. This idea of a wartime memory lost and then recovered stands at the center of the 2008 Israeli film *Waltz with Bashir*, directed by Ari Folman. Released within a year of one another, *Persepolis* and *Waltz with Bashir* form an unlikely pair in the general Western consciousness of animation from and about the Middle East. Apart from being two of the most internationally successful animated films with roots in the region (*Persepolis* in fact being a French production), they also stand as negative-image versions of one another in their thematic and narrative concerns: the one about a girl, a civilian, largely on the outskirts of war but deeply affected by it nonetheless; the other about a man and a soldier who, as he explains at the start of the film, seems curiously untroubled by

PLATE 21. *Kinshasa, Black September* (Zaire/Belgium, 1992)

PLATE 22. *November 1992 Sarajevo* (Croatia/Bosnia and Herzegovina/Belgium, 1995)

PLATE 23. *Leaving the Village* (Nepal, 2007)

PLATE 24. *Fatenah* (Palestinian territories, 2009)

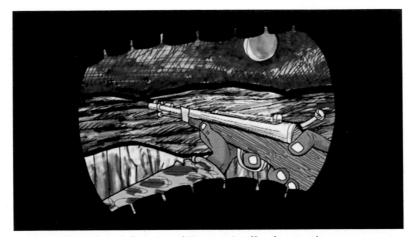

PLATE 25. *Point of Mouth* (Bosnia and Herzegovina/Sweden, 2010)

PLATE 26. *Persepolis* (Iran/France, 2007)

PLATE 27. *Waltz with Bashir* (Israel, 2008)

PLATE 28. *Tale of Tales* (USSR, 1979)

PLATE 29. *The Sinking of the Lusitania* (USA, 1918)

PLATE 30. *Children of War* (Kenya, 2013)

PLATE 31. *Men in Black/Operation Homecoming* (USA, 2007)

PLATE 32. *Birthday Boy* (South Korea/Australia, 2004)

PLATE 33. *White Tape* (Israel/Denmark, 2010)

PLATE 34. *Bear Story* (Chile, 2014)

PLATE 35. *We Shall Never Die* (Israel, 1959)

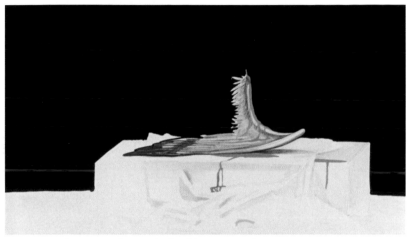

PLATE 36. *The Games of Angels* (Poland/France, 1964)

PLATE 37. *Silence* (UK, 1998)

PLATE 38. *Nyosha* (Israel, 2012)

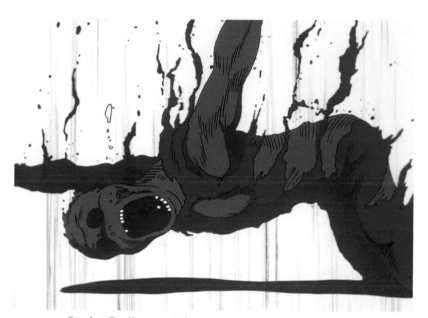

PLATE 39. *Barefoot Gen* (Japan, 1983)

PLATE 40. *Grave of the Fireflies* (Japan, 1988)

his time in war. The former focused on the attempt to build a coherent sense of self out of memories that cannot be forgotten or erased; the latter centered on the gaping hole in the protagonist's sense of identity caused by his unexplained inability to remember his time at war. *Persepolis* and *Waltz with Bashir* stand on opposite sides of the memory film tradition in many ways, even in terms of their graphical styles—the one highly stylized and abstract, the other at times disorientingly real. Yet they thematically coincide in at least one important respect, as do all works in the memory film tradition: they both understand the experience of war as an indelible aspect of identity formation for those who have lived through it in any way, the violence of war constituting a rupture to the self that must always be faced, even if it can never be fixed. For those who have lived through war in some capacity, these films argue, it is impossible to even begin to understand oneself without doing so in relationship to the war experience.

This is, of course, exactly the problem that Folman, who is himself the central figure in *Waltz with Bashir*, faces at the start of the film. Nearing forty-five when the film opens, Folman finds himself haunted not by any specific memory of war but by a strange absence of such memories in his life. He knows, as a matter of pure fact, that at age nineteen he was a soldier in the Israeli Defense Forces, or IDF, who participated in the country's invasion of southern Lebanon during the ongoing Lebanese Civil War in an operation that would come to be known in Israel as the 1982 Lebanon War. He can remember clearly all of his furloughs from the war, and he has scattered memories of the wartime experience itself. But he suspects that some of them are false, and he has absolutely no recollection of where he was or what he was doing at the greatest crisis point of that conflict: the horrific Sabra and Shatila massacre in which a Lebanese Christian militia allied with the Israelis murdered upward of 3,500 Palestinians living as refugees in Beirut. It may seem an unusual psychological condition to be haunted by an *absence* of traumatic memories. "The truth is, that's not stored in my system," Folman says in the very first scene of the film. But one quickly recognizes a kind of displacement in his unpeaceful equilibrium: he has substituted melancholy for trauma, as he seems generally beset by a depression whose origins he cannot pinpoint. Clearly, he has made no peace with those lost memories; he has merely shut them out. But as Ntabundi shows us in *Black Notebook*, such memories can never actually be discarded; they are still in circulation within Folman's psyche. In fact, those misplaced memories seem to be holding up his entire life. Whereas the assemblage of friends and former wartime colleagues that Folman visits in trying to discover the mystery of his missing memories seem for the most part to be hitting all the expected milestones for middle-class, middle-aged success—one is a therapist, another an accountant, most of them with spouses and families—Folman stands noticeably apart from these peers. He identifies himself as a filmmaker within the first scene of the film, but we see little professional context for that work and no scenes of any home life. Isolated and lonely, Folman seems detached not just from his own past but from his present as well. He seems not all that different from the nineteen-year-old that we see in flashbacks throughout the film. Of course, he has not moved on with his life, as the others have: he does not know who he is.

In this way, *Waltz with Bashir* establishes another parallel with *Persepolis*. Whereas *Persepolis* concerns itself with a protagonist trying desperately to maintain a coherent sense of selfhood against the encroachments of war and violence—a drive toward a personal sense of *continuum* represented in the strict segregation of animated styles within the film between its core narrative and moments of outside remembrance as well as its overarching black-and-white aesthetic—*Waltz with Bashir* concerns a protagonist with no coherent sense of selfhood to enshrine and no special memories to protect. Folman's experience is pure *discontinuum*, and the film reflects this fragmented sense of memory and self in every frame. Although the film looks rotoscoped, built on the traditions of filmmaking where animators draw directly over live-action footage, it in fact is not. Rather, the technique used by its animators involves cutout animation from illustrations that are not directly drawn over film but modeled on real actors, arranged and moved by computer programs meant to simulate the movement of those same actors. Quite literally, the film is cobbled together from parts and strung together by algorithms, which accounts for the floating quality of much of the imagery, the way in which the characters—and Folman most especially—seem to glide across the background in a mildly uncanny trance. (The effect is roughly equivalent to the double dolly shot in live-action filmmaking, a means of altering the perception of movement in the frame that has the effect of detaching the actor from the surrounding world.) Unlike in *Persepolis*, there is no careful sequestration of animation styles nor one single overarching aesthetic to the film. Though largely in the realist vein, the film's scenes adopt a variety of stylistic approaches: from the broad expressionism of the Beirut swimming dream that recurs throughout the film to the delicate, almost impressionistic imagery of the orange grove memory with the child and the rocket-propelled grenade to the hyperrealism of the final scenes in Beirut on the night of the massacre. Whereas *Persepolis* endeavored to maintain a system of center and periphery in its deployment of animation styles—one for Marjane's memories, one for remembrances and stories told to her—the very nature of *Waltz with Bashir*'s engagement with the *discontinuum* of war renders such a rubric impossible to enforce. How can Folman possibly keep his own memories separate from those around him? He does not even know which ones are his.

This is in fact one of the most arresting aspects of *Waltz with Bashir*, and it is unlike almost anything else in the memory film tradition. Folman's sense of traumatic disassociation and disequilibrium runs so deep in the film that he does not even fully distinguish between his own memories and those of the others all around him. At least in a film like *Black Notebook*, as surreal as its imagery is, one understands it to be representative of the memories of its animator Ntabundi himself, centered on his fleeing of the war. The approach in *Waltz with Bashir* is something more like the multimemory work of an animator like Kibushi in *Kinshasa, Black September*, except there the multivocality of the project is foregrounded throughout. Here, the overlap and distinction between different wartime memories is purposefully left vague, with memories from multiple different campaigns within the Lebanon War being invoked at different points (plate 27). There is, at the start of the film, one friend's memories of serving on targeted missions to apprehend wanted adversaries, which were quite different from Folman's own assignments. Another speaks of serving in a tank company. Another reports on visiting the headquarters of the Christian militia allied with the Israelis, where he believed that they tortured and mutilated prisoners. None of these memories and none of these traumas belong to Folman; he knows none of these experiences himself. Yet all these scenes are presented in styles that resemble, overlap, and bleed into the scenes from his own memory, scattered and fragmentary as they are. Without keeping very careful track of the narration, it is easy to overlook when Folman is in fact present in a wartime memory and when he is not, which are his and which are not—especially as he is not always the protagonist even in his own memories, often casting himself in a background role within his own stories. As an epitome of this psychic confusion, the film even opens with images from a dream that are not Folman's own: a vision of barking dogs that comes from the nightmares of a friend assigned to shoot the village dogs who might wake up the enemy before a raid. So lost is Folman in searching for his own place in the Lebanon War that he will even appropriate the posttraumatic nightmares of his friends as a kind of substitute for his own absent dreams.

Of course, if *Waltz with Bashir* presents a fragmented disarray of other people's memories and other people's dreams that take the place of Folman's own—a veritable posttraumatic quilt made in compensation for his own absent recollections—that is at least in part a product of the degree to which Folman's few known memories themselves conform to no set rules and no appreciable logic. So deep is his sense of fragmentation—much like Ntabundi's in *Black Notebook*—that his own memories overlap and spill into one another and even at times intrude into his present reality. Waiting at a Lebanese villa for his next set of orders at one point during his recollections of the war, Folman sees a young Israeli woman walking toward him wearing only a shirt but lets the image exist within the scene without any comment whatsoever. Only later do we learn that she is his ex-girlfriend, and that he is struggling with their breakup while he is deployed at war. In another memory scene shortly thereafter, he imagines being killed in war and envisions her walking toward his casket as he watches from the transport plane in which he is then flying, overjoyed at the prospect of her terrible guilt for having left him before his death. These images point to a high level of narrative breakdown in Folman's story of himself: time, place, and people all seem to collide in his head, unmoored as he is from any firm sense of place or purpose within the war.

The most troubling manifestations of such overlaps come not in the collage of Folman's memories, however, but in those scenes where such dissociative elements intrude even into his present day. The markers of such intrusions in the film are subtle but unmistakable. In one scene where Folman is talking to his therapist friend, the friend's young son rides back and forth repeatedly on a small bicycle in the background—displaying an obsessive repetition that most likely belongs more to Folman and his current thought patterns than to the son himself. In an even more brash example from earlier in the film, the background outside his friend's house literally transforms in the midst of their conversation. As the friend describes a psychological experiment wherein participants were tricked into believing they had visited a carnival as a child by looking at manipulated photographs, a fairground suddenly appears outside his window in the background. In another moment later in the film, a military cargo plane can be seen landing outside a window as Folman talks to another friend in a trendy bar—only to disappear from view entirely in the reverse shot of the same conversation, the window now suddenly empty. A few scenes later, Folman will board exactly that kind of transport aircraft in a memory in which he returns to the front from furlough and begins to contemplate his death. The boundaries in the film between past and present, real and imaginary, self and other eventually become entirely collapsed, the whole of Folman's earnest expedition to find the truth turning into a surreal, absurd experience—one that leaves him with an even thinner grasp on any sense of objective reality than the one he had before.

This is another way to say that Folman remains entirely haunted by war, even though—especially though—he cannot remember the specifics of his involvement. Rather than help to resolve his dissociative and surreal relationship to the world around him, his reclaimed memories of war only serve to highlight where that disjointed sense of self and world originates. For, real as they may be, the actual scenes of war that Folman is able to reconstruct through his memories and investigations are as unhinged as any overlapping memory sequence and as much of an affront to any sense of normalcy or logic. Hence the absolutely bizarre wartime scene that constitutes one of his most complete reclaimed memories from the conflict: a scene that he pieces together from several accounts and then replays in full as his own, revealing a battle that is not just terrifying but also absurd. Caught in a deadly street-corner ambush, Folman and his fellow soldiers huddle for cover and try to fire back at an unseen enemy high in the apartment buildings above. Behind them, Lebanese civilians gather on the balconies of their apartments and calmly watch the battle as though it were a play. Meanwhile, a war-weary television reporter walks calmly and slowly down the street in the middle of the crossfire, too unfazed to duck for cover, while his absolutely terrified cameraman crawls along the ground in front of him. At the same time, one of the trapped Israeli soldiers makes a desperate bid to end the stalemate by running into the middle of the open street and opening fire on the apartment buildings while doing a bizarre waltz-like dance with his feet, a giant poster of Lebanese commander and president-elect Bashir Gemayel glaring down at him the entire time. It is this pivotal scene that gives the film its title, and it is unlike any scene of war in almost any other animated film—or any wartime film at all. The total impact of the war tableau is pure Samuel Beckett—the huddled soldiers, the calm strides of the television reporter, the cameraman crawling for safety, the distressed soldier doing a machine-gun waltz with no one, the silent audience of civilians staring down upon it all. It is a near-perfect surrealist image of battle—and *this* is the actual reconstruction of an actual experience that Folman has heretofore forgotten. In the face of such utter discoherence, it must have seemed as though forgetting was the surest route to some semblance of a *continuum* of self and personal story that might still remain.

This is ultimately the great paradox of *Waltz with Bashir*: that the further Folman goes in his quest to reclaim lost parts of himself, the further he gets from any sense of completion or coherence. He is not in any way made whole by this process of recovery. How can he be? The nature of war's *unmaking* involves a fraying of set narratives and a destruction of normal boundaries: a making real of the unthinkable, including the unthinkable about one's self. The experience of war as described by Folman's friends who remember it distinctly is unreal—"like being on an LSD trip," as one friend recalls; in other words, it is nothing that will ever serve to sooth his anxieties or ease his persistent discomfort. This is the explosive, unsettling condition that Folman must face at the film's emotional climax, as he finally comes to understand where he was and what he was doing during the massacres—the idea that recovering the memory of war will not serve to help him settle his identity but rather to unravel it even further, that the illumination that he seeks will not bring any insight. The terrible irony of what Folman learns about himself and his role is that his position was literally one of illumination: he was part of the ring of soldiers whose job it was to send flares over the camps that night so that the Lebanese militia could see what they were doing as they supposedly looked for enemy combatants in the camp but in fact perpetrated mass killings.

Folman's question upon realizing his role in the massacres is, inevitably, what does this make him? Part of the reason this particular memory remained repressed for so long—for all of Folman's adult life, in fact—is because this question proves so hard to answer and because the possible responses are so devastating. The child of Holocaust survivors, Folman seems to have been party to another gruesome act of genocide. As his therapist friend says, summarizing what he thinks is Folman's own opinion, "Unwillingly, you took on the role of the Nazi." He insists that this interpretation is not correct and that Folman should think of his involvement in different terms. "You were there firing flares, but you didn't carry out the massacre," he says. But Folman is never clear as to whether the film wants us to accept his friend's exculpatory assessment. At two other points within the film, former Israeli soldiers speak of how their actions during war came to define their sense of self in persistent and destructive ways. The film opens with Folman's friend describing his assignment to shoot the dogs in the villages they were approaching. He presents the job as important—"Someone had to liquidate them. Otherwise our men would have died"—but when Folman pushes him on this assessment, he admits it was a sign of his failure as a soldier. "They knew I couldn't shoot a person," he says. "They told me: 'Okay Boaz, go ahead and shoot the dogs.'" Ultimately, he recalls the role as humiliating, acknowledging even twenty years later a strange inverted moral universe where the refusal to kill is seen as a moral failing. Later in the film, another friend remembers his first excursion into Lebanon and speaks of how he ran terrified from his tank as soon as it came under fire, forgetting all his training immediately and fleeing as far from the battle as he could. He says he is still haunted by the supposed cowardice of this moment. "I felt like it was me who had abandoned my comrades. . . . I wasn't the hero type who carries weapons and saves everyone's life. That's not me. I'm not the type."

Such statements beg the question: if one's actions in wartime, whether honorable or dishonorable, are part of what define one's *type* as these soldiers claim, what does that make of Folman and his role as accessory to genocide? Just a lowly soldier following orders, as another soldier present during the massacres insists in the film? The moral equivalent of a Nazi, as Folman's therapist friend suggests that he actually fears? Something in between? Folman does not definitively answer the question in the film, in large part because it cannot be definitively answered. The nature of war and its action of total *unmaking* is that it undoes all set standards and disallows all easy definitions. The true horror that Folman has confronted is less the horror of how to define himself than it is the horror of how to comprehend the total victimization of all involved in war. The work of the soldier, as Scarry observes, is always self-injuring. "The form of world alteration to which he devotes himself does not simply entail the possibility of injuring but is itself injuring," she writes.[10] Simone Weil knew this well from her own time serving in the Spanish Civil War. "Violence obliterates anybody who feels its touch," she writes, forming "a destiny before which executioner and victim stand equally innocent, before which conquered and conqueror are brothers in the same distress."[11] Folman, like all who are subject to war's violence either as victims or as perpetrators, found himself turned into a *thing*—not a casualty or a victim but a person stripped of agency nonetheless. He was an accessory to the worst forms of wartime violence—this the film establishes beyond any doubt. But he was also extremely compromised in his agency in those moments, unsure of what was proceeding and unable to stop what was happening, pulled through the motions of soldiering just as he is pulled through the film itself via the double dolly effect that defines all the movement in the frame. Folman must deal with both of these conditions, both his ultimate culpability and what he sees as his fundamental lack of agency.

In the end, Folman argues, there may be no reconciliation to be had. It is in this context that we must understand the final moments of the film, moments that have proven controversial among scholars of documentary and animation. After presenting nearly an hour and twenty minutes of enveloping, often stunning animation, *Waltz with Bashir* reaches a moment where it seems that animation can take the film no further. Several times throughout the story, Folman confronts a false memory that places him outside the military action the night of the Sabra and Shatila massacre: he imagines himself swimming in the Mediterranean while the killing occurs, then walking through the streets of Beirut, then coming upon a side street teeming with mourners and survivors from the massacre. Having finally confronted his actual role in the events that night, Folman returns to this image of the mourners, realizing its proper place within his experience. It comes not from a dreamlike wandering through the city but from his repressed memories of entering the devastated camp with the rest of his unit the next morning. In the final moments of the film, we see that scene of horrified mourners one final time, only now not through animation but in live-action footage that appears to have been taken that very morning, as Folman himself came face to face with what had happened at the camps.

The images are devastating, pure pain captured on film. Watching feels both unbearably intrusive and also necessary. For two agonizing minutes Folman shows us these video images of human misery, never returning to animation again: the film ends with the wailing of the mourners and then fades to black. It is a tremendously powerful ending, but also troubling in terms of its relationship to the film that comes before it. Is it a critique? A statement of animation's fundamental inadequacy to capture the face of atrocity? An insistence on photography as the only standard of the real? For scholars who study the intersection of animation and documentary, many have read the scene in this way and found its implications unsettling, as it seems to perpetuate an argument against the idea of animated documentary from one of the most famous instances of the form itself. As the film critic Jonathan Murray argues, the shift to live-action at the end seems to indicate that one would need "quite literally—another kind of film" to do proper justice to the events of the massacre, perhaps rendering the whole animated project questionable.[12] Folman himself has seemed to confirm this view, if not necessarily acknowledging its wider implications, explaining his decision to include the live-action film as part of a forced encounter with the real for his viewers. The move, he says, was a way to ensure that no one could "leave the theater thinking 'This is a very cool animated movie with great drawings and music.' I wanted people to understand this really happened."[13]

Yet viewed through the tradition of the memory film, the final scene takes on a different resonance entirely. Ntabundi's drawings in *Black Notebook* are the most apropos example. Those drawings do not document or represent or serve in any way as material evidence of the atrocities endured: in the case of *Black Notebook*, they are not even drawings taken from actual events but drawings of things already drawn, literally drawings of drawings and then eventually drawings of drawings of drawings. And this repetition is exactly the point: the drawings do not represent life in its unrepeatable instances but instead evoke memory in its inevitable and endless process of return. As such, they do not help artists to document events but rather are part of the means by which they process and preserve them in memory. They are not witness to atrocity so much as they are witness to the artist as the victim of atrocity, a person trying to reconstitute a self and trying to give meaning to the memory of events that defy such efforts. The imagery in Kibushi's *Kinshasa, Black September* does not need documentary footage to supplement its children's drawing because it is not about documenting specific incidents of violence; it is about documenting the children who were witness to such violence, witnessing their witness, witnessing their selves.

In this regard, the turn to live-action imagery at the end of *Waltz with Bashir* is evidence not primarily of the massacre itself but of just how far Folman's character in the film still has to go in understanding and accepting his place within that incident and all its horrors. As the film scholar Garrett Stewart notes in his evaluation of the film, the degree to which Folman presents the live-action images at the end without any sense of context or explanation is almost unconscionable from a strictly documentary perspective: "We don't know for sure who took these documentary images, if or when they were ever broadcast, whether or not they correspond to what Folman was positioned to see on the scene," he writes.[14] But as evidence of Folman's failure to complete his project of self-understanding, it is masterful. Folman the character only ever exists within the world of the film as an animated figure within an animated universe beset by animated memories. As a rupture with that all-encompassing animated aesthetic, the live-action footage is in a sense totally inaccessible to him, to Folman the character. Though it presents as real to the viewer, within the world of the film's own protagonist it is not so much real as *unreal*—unknown, unprocessed, entirely different from anything he has ever known, even in his worst memories. Still, even after all this searching, the events of that night remain out of Folman's reach and beyond his understanding. Folman has come to an acknowledgment of the actual facts of his involvement in the massacre and has glimpsed the enormous scope of his culpability. But the actual human pain involved remains as yet entirely inaccessible to him. Only once it has become animated will it actually become real to him, as with Ntabundi's drawings in *Black Notebook*. That process may yet be a long time coming. There is tremendous work that still remains for Folman beyond the film, work that will likely take the rest of his life. The ending of *Waltz with Bashir* is in this sense just the beginning of his journey to reclaim some sense of his self and to understand his past.

SURVIVING MEMORY

The question at the heart of so many memory films that stand at a long remove from the experience of war is essentially a question of survival: How does one survive a war that one has in fact already survived? How does one handle the continued discontinuum of a life lived after war? Must the only relationship to the past be one of sorrow and suffering? These questions of transformation and transcendence stand at the heart of one of the most profound and beloved animated works ever put to film: the 1979 animated short *Tale of Tales* by the legendary Russian animator Yuri Norstein. A surreal and hallucinatory journey through the archives of Norstein's childhood recollections, *Tale of Tales* is among the most celebrated films in the history of world animation, consistently ranked as one of the most accomplished works in the form. It also shares all the basic properties of the animated memory film, from its fractured and recursive structure to its absence of cohesive narrative to its varied and unreconciled animation styles to its focus on constituting Norstein himself by way of some of his most troubled memories. Yet in contrast to almost every other film in the tradition, *Tale of Tales* evinces a sense of peacefulness, warmth, and balance even as it confronts the traumatic experiences of war. Like much of Norstein's work, the whole film is bathed in a soft and gentle glow, a product of soft-focus effects. Animated primarily by using cutout techniques that keep a shallow depth of field, moving images forward and backward over and past one another, the film has the look of a storybook folktale come to life. Yet it is a tale that leads to no clear morals or obvious resolutions, a tale whose very story is not even obvious. Concerned more with feeling and impression than logic and sequence, the film's sense of transcendence is achieved not by way of surety or conclusiveness but by a profound acceptance of incoherence as an inevitable aspect of memory and an indelible condition of selfhood in the aftermath of trauma.

That the film is in fact any of these things—grounded in memory, personal to Norstein's own experience, or even touched by war—is not immediately obvious to viewers, such are the enveloping and overlapping layers of surreal and sometimes inexplicable action. The film cycles through a series of repeated locales, images, and events, arranging them in no obvious order with only limited apparent connection: there is an infant nursing as a folk song is sung, a wolf figure derived from that song, a townhome covered in snow, a light shining through a door as it is opened, repeated scenes of a minotaur at a picnic, a dance set sometime in the 1940s, a mother and a child walking through the snow, a recurring image of a shining, golden apple. These scenes, unarranged and disarrayed, are actually the scenes of a life, derived from Norstein's own disjointed memories of childhood. The home pictured at points throughout the film is based on the one in which Norstein grew up outside of Moscow, the light from the door is an image he recalled as a child, and the folk song is one that his mother used to sing.[15] *Tale of Tales* is thus a deeply personal collage, a fractured recounting of formative experiences whose wider context is always left out.

Or rather, whose wider context is consistently eclipsed and replaced by the one historical instance to which the film returns over and again: the experience of World War II. Born in 1941, Norstein was just old enough to have a few impressionistic memories of the lean and fearful war years. The privations of that moment are everywhere apparent in the film, indicated by a table set for a feast but left entirely empty, a wind blowing through its tablecloth, and emblematized in the recurring image of the apple that takes on the luster of a religious totem, an object of reverence as much as a childhood treat. But what is most apparent in the film in relation to the Second World War is the tremendous loss of life that the Soviet Union endured in those years. Over ten million soldiers and perhaps twice as many civilians perished on the Soviet side during the war, a staggering level of losses felt everywhere throughout Russian society. Representatives of those millions are glimpsed in Norstein's film in the longest single sequence featured in the story, one to which the film returns twice more. Here a popular 1940s tango, "Weary Sun," plays on a gramophone as several couples dance under a streetlight. Elegant and happy, these delicate cutout figures eventually leave the earth and float into the sky, dancing gracefully above the street where Norstein grew up like the airborne figures in a painting by Marc Chagall. Yet suddenly the gramophone begins to skip, and each time it does another man disappears from the dance—a few at first, then more and more until all of them are gone, the women left dancing alone as the music continues to play.

It is here that the soldiers of that war enter the film: faceless, ghostlike, they begin to float across the dance, their backs turned to the camera as they bisect the frame and disrupt the entire system of Norstein's visual arrangement. Eventually, they eclipse the dance completely on their long march into the distance. The dancers gone, we see the troops march in rain, then reappear in snow, then reappear again in the empty night. From a world that was once so carefree that dancers filled the sky, Norstein's childhood realm has become a universe of marching soldiers, always leaving, always disappearing, absolutely relentless in their evaporation from this realm. And most of them never come back. Instead, the screen is filled with tiny paper triangles and the sound of angry knocking on a door: the iconography of death notices being returned accompanied by the exhausted, endless knocking of the postman. "Faithful," "military," "honor," "courage," "valor": these pro forma words fill the screen in Russian, the last remembrances of the men who filled the dance.

In the total scheme of Norstein's twenty-seven-minute memory reel, the sequence of the soldiers leaving from the dance and the casualty letters returning home comprises only three minutes toward the beginning of the film. But it also completely dominates the tone and the aesthetics of the remainder of the work, commandeering the story much like the Bosnian War sequences do in *Point of Mouth* or the encounter with the destruction of the neighbor's home in *Persepolis*. Near the exact center of the film, the sequence returns in a heartbreaking repetition. As fireworks celebrate the end of the war, the music and the dancing resumes, but only three men out of ten have returned from the war, one of them missing a leg. Two dance gracefully with their partners, the third sits with an accordion and his sweetheart, and the other seven women perform the dance steps alone, arms reaching up for their absent partners (plate 28). An image of a platter containing vodka and bread—the traditional Russian meal of mourning—is interspersed with the dance, which doubles for victory celebration and funeral at once. And then, at the very end of the film, the echo of these losses appears again, with the music from the dance sequence playing subtly over the final moments of the film as the screen fades to nothing other than the lamppost under which the soldiers once danced.

The tremendous Soviet casualty figures of World War II are everywhere in *Tale of Tales*. Norstein never saw the war itself, but he saw its afterimage, the negative space left by all those men taken away

and never returned, leaving him with a childhood defined by departure, absence, and mourning. In a sense, these very elements take
on a leading role in the film, embodied in the mysterious figure of
the wide-eyed, childlike wolf who seems to be the main recurring
character within the dreamlike story. That wolf is a manifestation
of a figure from the folk song that a mother sings to her infant in the
opening moments of the film, a song that warns,

> Baby, baby . . .
> On the edge you musn't lie
> Or the little grey wolf will come
> And will nip you on the tum
> Tug you off into the wood.[16]

Suckling at his mother's breast, the infant glances up and sees the
wolf staring back at him—not menacing, just present. We will follow
this wolf throughout the remainder of the film. And no wonder. Norstein's entire childhood was defined by people being snatched away,
most of them never to return. He would have to make a kind of peace
with the idea of these departures if he was ever to surmount their
trauma.

In its way, *Tale of Tales* is defined as much by war as any memory
film. Like *Point of Mouth*, the fact of war once it appears eclipses all
other historical concerns and all other markers of time. It is only in
these scenes of the soldiers leaving, the letters returning, and the wid-
ows dancing alone that the film shows any identifiable connection to
a time and place that exists outside of Norstein's sheltered childhood
remembrances and imaginative spaces—the lighted hallways and
mythological picnics of the film's other scenes. And as in *Persepolis*,
the encroachment of a war that lies far beyond the child protagonist's
ability to understand or in any way affect marks a kind of crisis that
envelops the entire narrative of childhood, turning the trauma of the
adult figures that surround the protagonist into a unique burden for
the child, who must experience and remember that which he or she
cannot yet begin to explain. The result is a deeply fractured process

of recollection, every bit as unsettling, in its way, as the discohesion that defines a film like *Waltz with Bashir*.

Yet as much as Norstein's tale is defined by trauma, it is ultimately not consumed by it. The war scenes inevitably recur, appearing or being referenced at the film's beginning, middle, and end. Yet they cannot take away the delicateness of the film's other imagery: the mother and child, the picnic, the apple. Norstein ultimately takes his film's disorder as a point of aesthetic departure, crafting an associative work that never tries to establish any hierarchies amidst its imagery. There is no one story that can capture the wartime experience, and the film never tries to build one. Its tale is the *tale of tales*—the greatest of all tales, in one sense, but also a collage of tales in another sense: a story made up of other stories, all nested inside one another. Like so many wartime memory films, it never tries to build a perfect narrative. But neither does it try to build a perfect self or lament the impossibility thereof. Norstein need not force his stories or styles to cohere, because he does not seek to force himself to cohere. There is instead a free circulation of images, an interplay of the mournful and the magical, signs of a life lived in the shadow of grief but also marked by joy and peace and comfort, by turns. There would be no way to avoid or overcome the traumatic imagery of war: such drawings, as Norstein knew, could never be discarded. But that would not mean that other drawings could not be made over time, that the images of a life could not accumulate regardless. Sometimes in the memory film, the highest form of witness is not to the events of war themselves, though those remain ever present. The highest form of witness is to acknowledge the witnesses themselves as being more than the sum of the violences they all have known—showing not just the mournful dance but also the joyful feast, with neither one eclipsing the other.

CHAPTER 4: MEMORIAL

The McCay family lives at 1901 Voorhies Avenue in Brooklyn, New York, in a home that smells of acetate and India ink. It is an elegant three-story mansion with a wide front porch and charming awnings over every window, set on a quaint suburban corner in an affluent part of town. It is March 1918, and the house looks perfectly respectable from the outside. Inside is another story. Winsor McCay, the world-famous editorial cartoonist, animator, and sometime vaudevillian—father of two, grandfather of one, and husband of twenty-seven years to his wife Maude—has been caught up for nearly two years in another one of his obsessions. For the past twenty months, he has spent nearly every waking moment outside of his employment at the *New York American* drawing picture after picture after picture of a sinking ship: nearly twenty-five thousand of them, hole-punched and tightly stacked on binding posts all around his home.

Across the East River in Manhattan, other animators of the day have developed professional production systems involving teams of draftsmen and technicians working in tandem. John Randolph Bray, with whom McCay once got into a spiraling series of lawsuits over Bray's attempts to steal and patent his techniques (McCay ultimately won these legal challenges), has a staff of thirty over at his studio on Twenty-Sixth Street. Uptown in the Bronx, the Barré-Bowers Studios has another twenty animators set up in a similar system. But not McCay. He is not some sort of industrial manager who can barely draw a picture on his own—he considers himself an artist, and he prefers to work alone, out of his home. He has just two assistants on this current undertaking: his friend and fellow cartoonist William Apthorp "Ap" Adams from Cincinnati, whom he has convinced to come and help him on this work, and a local artist from the neighborhood named John Fitzsimmons. Both are tasked with filling in the drawings between key points in a character or object's movement in a process known as inbetweening, while Ap has the additional, laborious task of lining up all of McCay's thousands of drawings in the proper order for photographing. In just a few more weeks McCay will be finished, at which point he will cart these thousands of drawings a few miles down the road to the Vitagraph Studios, where he will pay out of his own pocket to have them shot on film and processed. The premier he has arranged will take place in May at the National Press Club in Washington, DC: an institution more accustomed to hosting speeches by politicians and dignitaries than screening animated films. But this is not just any cartoon. It is, according to the wording on one of the intertitles that McCay will have them insert in the film at Vitagraph, "the first record of the sinking of the *Lusitania*."

For McCay, *The Sinking of the Lusitania* was more than just a film. It was a mission. According to all accounts, McCay was horrified at the 1915 sinking of the luxury passenger liner by a German submarine off the coast of Ireland during the First World War. Perhaps it was the fact that the United States remained a neutral nation in the war at that time and the ocean liner, though British, had departed from an American port and was carrying hundreds of Americans. Perhaps it was the fact that McCay's employer, William Randolph Hearst, maintained a strict antiwar (and largely pro-German) stance even after the incident and forbade his editorialists, McCay included, from openly advocating for the United States to join the fight. Perhaps it was simply the tremendous loss of civilian life, 1,198 innocent passengers and crew drowned in total. Perhaps it was the fact that so many of those passengers moved in the same social circles as McCay himself—financiers and famous authors and Broadway producers from the upper echelons of New York society. Whatever the cause,

McCay determined almost as soon as the news hit that he would make an animated film depicting its events, and he committed to producing and paying for the entire enterprise himself outside the scope of his employment with Hearst. Were it just a work of propaganda—a rallying cry to urge America to enter the European conflict at last— then perhaps he might have stopped somewhere around the halfway point of this self-enforced ordeal, as President Woodrow Wilson asked Congress to declare war on Germany some nine months after McCay began his drawings. Yet McCay persisted, filling his stately home with more and more drawings of women and children drowning at sea. His own son Robert went off to war during that time and participated in the excruciatingly bloody attempts by the American forces to break the Hindenburg Line, the main German defensive position on the western front; he would return with terrible shell shock. Still McCay persisted, trying in picture after picture to capture an event now two years in the past that he himself had never seen. Just what was McCay trying to achieve with all those drawings arranged in binders and filling up the rooms and hallways of his home?

If you believe the press at the time, it was nothing short of the conjuration of the past. "Loss of *Lusitania* Shown on Films" read the headline in the *Washington Post* the morning after McCay's premier at the National Press Club.[1] The film was immediately picked up for distribution by Jewel Productions, which marketed the picture with outlandish claims about its impact. The film "will burn in your brain forever" declared one ad. The film itself claimed in an introductory intertitle to be "a historical record of the crime that shocked Humanity." In a world where hand-drawn newspaper illustrations were still more common than photographs, the film purported to be something like a documentary account of an event that had caught the attention of the nation, an event for which no actual footage existed or ever could exist. Both the film itself and its promoters made sure to play up the factual aspect of the work. One news report stressed how McCay and a commander from the navy "worked out the mathematical problems necessary to make the picture absolutely accurate."[2] In an

opening live-action sequence before the start of the animated portion of the film, McCay likewise shows himself sitting down with
reporter August F. Beach, the Hearst Corporation's correspondent in
Berlin and the first to report on the tragedy, who is described as "giving Winsor McCay the details of the sinking—necessary for the work
to follow." McCay even included photographs of several of the more
famous victims as well as facts and figures about the sinking and
the carnage interspersed throughout the film. Yet the claims to total
historical and scientific accuracy seem more than a bit far-fetched
coming from a figure like McCay. Though he was an exquisite and
uncompromising draftsman capable of rendering the world in ex-
traordinary detail, he was an editorialist first and foremost and an
early master of the comic strip. As an animator, he was a downright
fabulist, a figure whose very first animated film concerned a boy who
wakes up at night and enters the world of his dreams and whose last
animated film before *Lusitania* involved a giant pet dinosaur with
whom McCay interacted live on stage in a vaudeville routine. McCay
also stressed his scientific accuracy in that film, *Gertie the Dinosaur*,
from 1914, supposedly consulting with paleontologists at the American Museum of Natural History to learn about the proper dynamics
of dinosaur movement. But that did not mean he did not then go and
ask his dinosaur creation to bow, dance, and play catch once he got
her up on screen. The very title of McCay's most popular comic strip,
Little Nemo in Slumberland, which subsequently became the subject
of his first animated film, gives a name to the entire body of McCay's
animated work that followed—all of which, according to Scott Bukatman, operates under the "poetics of slumberland."[3] As much as
he was a draftsman of record, McCay was also a dispenser of dreams.

Both aspects of McCay's artistry are at work within *The Sinking
of the Lusitania*. The technical precision of the film is unmistakable.
Using overlapping cell sheets that convey different visual layers and
planes of space—a process that was becoming standard practice in the
animation industry at the time but that was entirely new for McCay—
he creates a world of billowing smoke curls and rolling waves that

give depth and texture to the carefully rendered ocean liner. An opening shot where the ship is viewed through the frame of a window, a curtain blowing in the foreground as the Statue of Liberty stands in the back and the ship glides out of New York harbor, is a miniature masterpiece of dimension and movement, one that can seem as though it is shot in live-action if you look quickly enough. Later, as the ship suffers the torpedo attack, damage and debris are sent high into the air by the impact and the blast, only to rain down in the foreground of the frame a few moments later, as though we were actually viewing the destruction from a vantage point some several hundred yards away. The actual sinking of the ship, both lugubrious and enthralling, displays in every moment McCay's supposed consultation with those naval and mathematical experts. This is no work of scurrilous excitement or exaggerated scandal-mongering; it is a carefully plotted study in the actual mechanics of how a great ocean liner sinks (plate 29). (Fans of the 1997 James Cameron film *Titanic*—another cinematic study of disaster that loudly tries to foreground its technical precision—may notice more than a few visual allusions to McCay's depictions.) Here McCay earns every bit of his reputation for "keenly draftsmanlike emphasis on weight, mass, and sophisticated movement," per the descriptions of illustrator and animation historian D. B. Dowd.[4]

And yet, for a film about an event that is objectively so horrible—a "blood stirring pen picture of the blackest crime of all history" in the words of one promotional ad—*The Sinking of the Lusitania* is also strangely beautiful. McCay's drawings, both in his editorial and illustrative work and in his animation, always tend to have a curvaceous art nouveau elegance. But the cinematic arrangement of sea, smoke, and ship here goes beyond good design and takes on the contours of artwork. The first shots of the ship at sea, tiny in the far left of the frame as a swirl of clouds dominates the upper-right reaches and the undulating sea defines the bottom, are, on the level of pure composition, simply stunning. Likewise, the elongated final moments where McCay lingers on the spray bursting from the ocean surface as the disappeared liner sinks deeper and deeper below, its ghostly geyser-effects being its only remaining record. The push and pull of beauty and technical precision is perhaps embodied best in the introduction of the German submarine that deals the fatal blow. In the first shot, we see only its periscope cutting through the rolling waves and then disappearing below, a technically proficient case study in the dynamics of propulsion and the details of modern ship construction. In the next, the U-boat has surfaced, and we see it only in silhouette, a series of featureless figures moving back and forth across its bow like actors on a faraway stage, the waves below rendered in all white against the black of the hull, undulating like the moving shapes of an abstract painting. Taken only as a work of art, *The Sinking of the Lusitania*, for all its bellowing about blackest crimes and historical records, is simply gorgeous.

What is the point of rendering in such captivating form an event that one means to decry? On one level, the film seems like an especially meticulous instance of animated propaganda, one that ultimately traffics in the same vitriol as other instances of the form. "And yet they tell us not to hate the Hun," a title card declares indignantly near the end of the film, chastising all those who supposedly refused to condemn Germany's aggression. Yet the obvious obsolescence of this message profoundly undercuts the film's propagandistic purpose. McCay spent two painstaking years getting his film exactly right, in which time the United States went from a neutral nation to an active combatant in the war. Though Germany had its defenders in America circa 1916 (including Hearst, McCay's boss at the *New York American*), by the time of the picture's premier there were precious few figures in American public life still actively defending the Germans. Yet McCay declined to either update the title card or pull it all together, tying the film to the moment of its inception and creation rather than its premier, actively removing it from the actual discourse around the war as it existed in 1918.

It seems, then, that McCay was not so much trying to move public opinion in the present as he was trying to document a very specific moment in the recent past. For many scholars today, this is part of what makes *The Sinking of the Lusitania* a prime example of the genre of documentary animation—the very origin point of that genre according to some.[5] As a matter of historical fact, the idea that McCay's work might serve as the beginning of that form misses the mark. McCay's competitor and nemesis John Randolph Bray had an entire division within his studio dedicated to animating technical and educational films under the direction of J. F. Leventhal, and they started producing works like *The Gasoline Engine* and *The Rudiments of Flying* as early as 1916. Yet none of Leventhal's films looked anything like *The Sinking of the Lusitania*, and if McCay is given undue precedence within the field of animated documentary, that is in part because the marketing tag line of that newspaper ad actually in some way came true: McCay's film truly is a work that "will burn in your brain forever." It has been remembered far longer than *The Gasoline Engine*, surely. And that is exactly the point. It is designed not so much to actively inform as to be remembered.

McCay's own designation for the film, which he uses twice in the intertitles, is *record*: "a historical record of the crime that shocked humanity," "the first record of the sinking of the *Lusitania*." The purpose of a record, of course, is its longevity: a record not only documents but preserves, it marks something in place for the future. It is not just the ship itself that McCay wants us to remember, that which he so desperately wants to record. Nor even the attack and the international incident in and of themselves. Vitally, it is also the *people* most affected that he wants to capture and preserve in some way: the elite and celebrity passengers whose photos and descriptions he includes; the distant, barely decipherable figures seen falling from the ship as it sinks; the lost souls frozen in the water and bobbing lifelessly near the rescue boats, an image repeated twice within the film; or the drowning woman framed in an iris as she falls below the waves and tries desperately to push her infant child up to the surface. Apart from those shown in the photographs, these are not of course the actual victims of the attack: they are representative of them. There is another word for a record of wartime death or destruction involving representative figures primarily. It is *memorial*. *The Sinking of the Lusitania* is a memorial to the dead.

How does one remember something that one never in fact experienced? That is the question behind all memorials, which exist not just for the veterans and survivors but for the uncomprehending public and for unknowing future generations beyond. "The memorial . . . is not complete without those who visit it, in whom memory is invoked," as the literary theorist Richard Crownshaw writes.[6] Next to and beyond the memory film in the traditions of wartime animation stands what I call the *memorial film*: a work that comes into being at the intersection of remembrance and fantasy, whether a shared imagining between survivor and artist or else an interpolative reconstruction of an event never recorded, a collaborative construction or a communing with the dead. In the *memory film*, the experient of war, whether soldier or civilian, speaks from his or her own knowledge, whether through story or in direct recollection. Disordered and disruptive, the memory film is the testimony of Walter Benjamin's *discontinuum* itself, an attempt to "seize hold of a memory as it flashes up at a moment of danger."[7] The *memorial film* stands in the calm after that dangerous storm—it is the story of the storm and not the storm itself. Though its subject matter and point of inspiration is that same voice of *discontinuum*, its purpose is less to unsettle than to cement; the memorial film in fact seeks entry into history's *continuum*—into official narrative and recognized discourse, into the *public transcript* of history itself. In the memorial, the cultural theorist Andreas Huyssen writes, memory "has its chance to inscribe itself into history, to be codified into national consciousness."[8] McCay's decision to premier his *Lusitania* at the National Press Club is no anomaly within the tradition. The memorial film almost always solicits official recognition, seeking to become part of the apparatus of sanctioned remembering. From major film studios to recognized nonprofit organizations to the state apparatuses of television broadcasting and film production, the backers of the memorial film are often synonymous with officialdom.

Its artists are established figures by and large—the legendary Winsor McCay, not his shell-shocked son Robert. From their acknowledged powers of imagination, they offer to the survivors of atrocity a voice and to future generations a vision. McCay called his film a *record*, as a noun, but we might also just as easily say that it is an attempt to *re-cord*, as a verb: to transcribe in pictures that which was not witnessed to begin with but is now being retold nonetheless. It is not an unproblematic process. In the very best works of wartime memorialization, the tension and the problems of remembering that which was not and cannot be seen give these works a special and lasting power, making them truly what Julia Kristeva might call an *art for the invisible*.

ANIMATION AND TESTIMONIAL

For some, remedying war's too frequent condition of invisibility is exactly the point of such work. The drive against invisibility was arguably part of the all-consuming motivation that McCay felt in creating *Lusitania*—he the great inventor of imagined, unseen worlds called to use that imagination toward the recreation of an unseen but all too real event. A similar impulse seems to stand behind the work of the Kenyan animator Allan Mwaniki in his collaborative film *Children of War*, from 2013, a kind of twenty-first-century update to the tropes of McCay's faux newsreel footage and the idea of an animated reporting on an event that could never be seen. For Mwaniki, his invisible crisis is the ongoing plight of the child soldier in Africa and around the world, and his immediate point of documentary reference is not the newsreel but the television news broadcast. Like *The Sinking of the Lusitania* long before it, *Children of War* positions itself as an animated answer to an absent news narrative. The entirety of the film unfolds inside the drawn image of a television screen, with the opening moments given over first to television snow and static and then to the striped *stand-by* screens of old, with a message "Do Not Adjust Your TV." Interspersed throughout the film are statistics and facts about the situation of child soldiers, akin to those that punctuate

McCay's story of the *Lusitania*. And underneath the images of child soldiers that Mwaniki and his student collaborators draw are the program identification bars of television news broadcasts: the French TF1 News, the British Sky News.

Of course, the condition of the child soldier is not unknown either in Africa or beyond. Neither is it entirely unseen, with images of war and interviews with former child soldiers appearing regularly in television news broadcasts and documentaries on the topic. But Mwaniki's motivation, similar to McCay's, is that this knowledge and this record are simply not enough. Though we know of this barbarity and though we can see its after-effects clearly enough or even hear from its survivors, we cannot *see* the barbarity itself. Thus the animator steps in to document the unseen and the unseeable. Mwaniki's images of life as a child soldier, though they are positioned as faux news broadcasts, are nothing like what one would actually ever see on any news show. They are images from *within* the unseen world of the child solider, the events conducted far away from the eyes of local news cameras and Western interventions. Mwaniki shows in brutal detail the village massacres from which child soldiers are recruited, their closest relatives murdered before their eyes. He shows the brutal camp life of the child soldier: the regular and vicious beatings used to instill fear and discipline, the forced ingestion of drugs that are used to numb the children and sever their ties to reality and their own memories. And finally the combat itself, the children holding weapons that are far too large for their tiny hands, firing into the distance or scanning the rubble for enemies (plate 30). When we finally get to the kinds of images that might be more familiar from typical documentary work or television reporting—the dead-eyed children holding weapons and staring at the camera but not actively engaged in conflict, the aftermath of battle, the interviews with those who have escaped—we know, because we have seen, the terrible conditions that lead to these states: the invisible crisis behind the visible one, the secret world of the child soldier finally unveiled in all its horror.

Like McCay's work, Mwaniki's animations walk a delicate line between exactitude and artistry. This is not entirely Mwaniki's story to tell, and he is careful. His work is figural and graphic, bounded by reality with no trace of the cartoonal. But neither is it perfectly detailed or entirely immersive. Mwaniki's figures are often faceless or so lacking in character detail that we cannot even tell if they are facing us or not, their eyes and features appearing as a surprise as they adjust their heads and turn to us, sometimes staring directly at the viewer in a flash of frontality. They are both specific child soldiers and all child soldiers, both an unveiling of the invisible and an acknowledgment of the actual impossibility of that task. They are an attempt to bear witness to that which cannot in fact be witnessed by anyone who is not already immersed in this world: there is simply no way to see what happens inside those hellish rebel camps if one is not a monster who kidnaps children or a victim of such monsters. Mwaniki, a prominent animator in Kenya and a beloved mentor to other local artists, bears no direct connection to the world of the child soldier, nor has his native Kenya ever been party to such atrocities. Rather, his film draws on the experiences of children at Kenya's Kakuma and Dadaab camps, which together house nearly half a million refugees fleeing wars and famine in Sudan, Ethiopia, and Somalia, and was created in collaboration with Kenyan youth via the United Nations–backed Global e-Schools and Communities Initiative (GESCI).[9] What Mwaniki lends to the struggle to bring recognition and intervention to the plight of child soldiers is not any power of witness himself but a power of visualization and imagination based on the testimonials and accounts of others. The very structure of Mwaniki's film seeks to enter the *discontinuum* of those testimonials into the overt public transcript of the age: to place their experiences directly on television as part of an official state broadcast, albeit in imagined form. *Children of War* is a work of activism, to be sure. But it is not only a work of activism or even primarily one. It is an attempt to create a *record*, as McCay might say, of atrocities unseen, to give not just a voice but a *picture* to those who have long had neither. It is an attempt to make their suffering—their invisible suffering—officially legible at last.

In this way, *Children of War* stands alongside a much wider tradition in the wartime memorial film that seeks to animate actual, specific testimonials from individual veterans and survivors, substituting for the amalgam of testimonial accounts that lie behind a work like Mwaniki's a single recorded interview animated directly on screen. This is documentary animation in its purest state, and it is a widespread technique. The BBC ran a number of such animated testimonials in conjunction with Aardman Animations, of later *Wallace and Gromit* fame, during the late 1980s and early 1990s under the *Lip Synch* series; the American folk history nonprofit StoryCorps has turned many of their recorded interviews into animated films posted online, with animation from various independent studios; and the nongovernmental organization Vital Voices Global Partnership has used the technique to promote stories from women leaders around the world, to take only a few examples. In the case of veterans and other survivors of war, such films represent perhaps the most direct possible manifestation of the memorial tradition. Yet the gap between the two disjointed strands of filmmaking—the audio interview track on the one hand and the animated accompaniment on the other—can oftentimes be so great as to be actively disconcerting, drawing our attention not to a work of co-imagination but to the deep inaccessibility of the story being told for the animators who do not know it as their own. There is a difficult double bind for the animators involved in such projects, many of whom may not have been to the places of these conflicts and may not even have met the speakers of these stories: either render their tale in a series of delicate abstractions, taking what is a very specific life experience and translating it into the realm of the broad universal, or else overillustrate a story that is not their own and imbue it with imagined detail that may seem unmoored from the actual experiences described.

In some of the most effective of such works, this tension and struggle is acknowledged directly within the film and becomes an active part of its construction, with the film asking viewers to recognize and consider the limits of third-person witness even when it is tied to a first-person account—that is, asking viewers to consider the limits of the animated memorial itself. Such is the case in the short film known as *Men in Black*, a seven-minute animated portion of the 2007 Oscar-nominated documentary *Operation Homecoming: Writing the Wartime Experience*, which grew out of a National Endowment for the Arts project to collect testimonials and writings from veterans returning from America's wars in Iraq and in Afghanistan. *Men in Black* animates a story written and read by army infantryman Colby Buzzell about a particularly affecting combat situation during his most recent tour of duty. On its surface, it is an action-packed, graphic novel–style illustration of a straightforward, reportorial account of a Stryker armored vehicle coming under fire in an unnamed Iraqi city. Buzzell sticks largely to the facts in his account, narrating as though he were a witness in the most literal sense, one providing testimony to establish the basic details of a case. His battalion has been ordered to hunt down enemy soldiers firing mortars at their base, they come under fire from individuals clad entirely in black, they return fire, escape, and then return to the scene of the ambush to continue the operation and try to eliminate the attackers. *Men in Black* is a soldier's story, filled with recollections of Buzzell and his fellow soldiers "hootin' and hollerin', yelling their war cries" and marked throughout by the pumping adrenaline of battle. "I put the cross-hairs on him and engaged him with a couple good ten-round bursts of some 50-cal. right at him," he says in a typical description. Like any soldier in the midst of combat, Buzzell has little time to humanize the enemy. We never learn who these attackers were or on what side they stood in the multiparty violence that Iraq had descended into at that time. In Buzzell's descriptions, they are only "a man dressed in all black with a terrorist beard" or "two guys with those red and white jihad towels wrapped around their heads."

The film, animated by Evan Parsons based on drawings by artist Christopher Koelle, follows Buzzell's lead in crafting a visual story grounded in the accumulation of detail. Koelle's illustrations have the look of a hyperrealist graphic novel (plate 31): the vehicles and weapons rendered with the precision of a technical readout, the sol-

diers often envisioned with looks of grim determination or mounting
fury in the heat of battle. Parsons uses cutout animation alongside a
highly active camera that pans over and zooms into the drawings to
create the illusion of action, all of which adds to the sensation of reading a graphic novel account of the battle, the reader's eyes moving
across the page as the action unfolds. Undoubtedly exciting, the animation also seems troublingly unnuanced—on the verge of turning
an actual combat experience involving real risk and casualties into an
imagined adventure modeled most on video-game shooting action.
(In fact, Parsons's very next animation credit after *Men in Black* is a
video game called *Metal Gear Solid 4: Guns of the Patriots*.) The effect is
so unreal that the entire enterprise of pairing veteran narratives with
civilian animation seems to come into question. Just what exactly is
being reproduced here, an actual story or a broad cultural imaginary?

And then, in a stunning coda, the entire previous story and animation style both fold in on themselves, urging us to question everything we saw before. The first hint that something is purposefully
amiss comes after the battle, when Buzzell dismounts from his tank
and sits alongside it, smoking and thinking about the day's events.
His sergeant senses something might be wrong and asks if he can sit
next to him, taking out a cigarette and talking. It seems like a standard moment of decompression after the rush of battle, but something
in the visuals appears immediately questionable: the character design of Buzzell and his sergeant seem so alike that they could practically be doubles of one another, iterations of the same figure stuck in
conversation with themselves. The proximity and centrality of the
two characters makes the doubling especially apparent, but in fact
such iterative use of character types is a visual motif of the film if
one looks closely enough: from the enemy fighters encountered on
the street to the officers issuing the orders for the soldiers to return
to the combat zone, the figures in the film again and again double and
triple one another in a *Matrix*-like maze of looped identities. *Men in
Black* in no way appears haphazardly made: funded by the National
Endowment for the Arts and nominated for an Academy Award, it is

a work of extremely deliberate construction. That is to say, the doubling motif of Parsons's design is no shortcut born of circumstance
but a choice derived from the thematics of the tale. The advice that
Buzzell's sergeant ultimately gives to him says much about the experience of war and the attempt to convey it accurately during its long
aftermath. Buzzell confides to his sergeant in their scene together
outside the tank that he thinks he may have hit civilians while they
were battling in the streets. "Not everybody that I engaged today
had a weapon in their hands," he says. His sergeant does not deny
the profundity of such a realization, but he urges Buzzell to defer
any examination of its emotional reality or consequences until some
other time, the battlefield being no place for moral quandaries. "Put
all the things that bother you and keep you awake at night and clog
your head up, put all those things in a shoe box, put the lid on it,
and deal with it later," he says, reiterating advice given to him by his
father, a Vietnam vet. Buzzell accepts the recycled advice from this
recycled character. "I've put the events of that day in a shoe box, put
the lid on it," he says. "I haven't opened it since."

The final phraseology is revelatory: "I haven't opened it since"—
a declaration that he makes in the midst of telling the story of those
events. In a remarkable act of bravery, Buzzell admits in a nationally
distributed and widely publicized documentary that he still has not
confronted the reality of that firefight and that this story he is telling
in no way constitutes that reckoning. He admits to it being for him
a series of unassimilated microevents: a situation in which he knows
all of the facts but none of the meaning. Though he has lived through
these experiences, he is in no way ready yet to bear witness to them
according to the double mandate that Julia Kristeva lays out for the
witness: "the act of looking truth in the face and, simultaneously, the
translation of this vision into meaning."[10] If Buzzell himself does not
yet understand those events and is as yet unable to ascribe meaning to them, how can we? How can the witness that Parsons offers
through his animation be anything other than a play of preexisting
tropes from the world of video games and graphic novels and war
flicks and the broader American imaginary? How can characters like

Buzzell and the sergeant not be redoubled versions of each other—
insofar as they are all just iterations of the idea of the soldier? Inside the actual contents of Buzzell's shoe box lie the components of
a wartime *memory film*: disjointed, confusing, contradictory, possibly unsolvable. Perhaps, Parsons's *Men in Black* seems to suggest, the
memorial film can only ever be premised on the erasure or at least
indefinite deferral of actual wartime memory, in all its messy and
troubling uncertainty.

ANIMATING ABSENCE

This is a possibility explored directly in another animated testimonial film from a very different time and a very different place than
Men in Black. Titled *1947: Haunting Dreams*, the Indian animator Pari-
tosh Singh's 2012 illustration of a recorded testimonial from a Sikh
man who lived through the bloody aftereffects of the partition of
India and Pakistan in 1947 by the departing British colonial forces
is a harrowing example of the limits of the memorial film, or any
animated documentary, to capture the most disturbing elements of
war's great *unmaking*. Of course, the partition itself was not an act
of war but part of the unraveling of a centuries-old colonial occupation that included a violent military component, from the Uprising
of 1857, or "Sepoy Mutiny," to the Amritsar massacre in 1919. The partition in turn led to further decades of conflict, to four different wars
between India and Pakistan, the first starting just months after the
partition, and to ongoing violence in the region of Kashmir. The story
told in *1947: Haunting Dreams* is just one small part of that decades-
and centuries-old legacy of violence and in some ways not at all representative of the broader contours of those struggles. Though arguably that exceptionalism is exactly the point; all wartime violence is
exceptional and unique to anyone who must live through it.

At its outset, *1947: Haunting Dreams* seems to be a story of the partition writ large. Singh opens with a recorded speech by Jawaharlal
Nehru, the first prime minister of India, delivered on the eve of the

partition and heard over the image of a radio: the voice of officialdom establishing the public record of a new nation. "At the stroke of the midnight hour, when the world sleeps, India will awake to life and freedom," Nehru intones. Yet the voices of history's *discontinuum* will always complicate the narratives of its *continuum*, and Singh quickly switches to animating a story told in a 2008 interview with Bir Bahadur Singh, who relates the events that unfolded one night during the lead-up to the partition, in March 1947 in the village of Thoha Khalsa in what was to become Pakistan. The story is almost too horrible to tell, and Bir Bahadur audibly breaks down into tears as he reaches its most challenging moments. In the midst of three days of violent struggle between the region's impoverished Muslim laborers and its Sikh landowners, Bir Bahadur, then just a teenager, learns of a demand that one of the Muslims has made for a Sikh woman to be given to him as a bride. Bir Bahadur's father, as a show of defiance, decides to behead his own daughter by sword rather than submit to this ignominy. Trapped in the other room, Bir Bahadur remembers listening helplessly as his father executed his sister in the violent madness of that terrible night. According to accounts recorded elsewhere, his father and his uncle would go on to execute twenty-five other women in his extended family that evening, many of them submitting willingly to the execution. Another ninety Sikh women in the village would commit mass suicide in the following days by jumping into a well, while Bir Bahadur's father would be among the hundreds of villagers killed in the continuing struggle until the army arrived to quell the local violence nearly a week later.[11]

What can animation do with such a story? What can history? *1947: Haunting Dreams* exists on the very margins of relatable experience, illustrating a story that its own teller, speaking sixty-one years after the fact, has trouble even finishing. Animating the early moments of the tale in a mix of silhouetted images with occasional flashes of detail and color, Singh all but abandons illustration in the moment that Bir Bahadur's father first raises his sword, seen through a crack in the door leading to the other room. Instead, Singh puts us in the perspective of Bir Bahadur himself, lying on the floor and breathing heavily, staring at the twirling ceiling fan above, its simple turning blades almost unwatchable in this context. There is no easy explanation in which to fit Bir Bahadur's horrific recollections. They were born of the partition experience and the rush of civil violence that surrounded that event, yet they were also specific to the power structures of that particular town and personal to the patriarchal dynamics of Bir Bahadur's own family. Bir Bahadur refers to the figure who made the demand for a bride as "an evil man," yet the violence that we are closest to in the story is perpetrated by a father against his own daughter, while the British officials who made the partition arrangements that helped give rise to such ethnic violence were half a world away from these events. How can one possibly classify this violence? How does one divide its characters into heroes and villains? Where does it fit in the story of India and Pakistan's bloody twentieth century? Recognizing these impossible questions, Singh ends not with any acknowledgment of the deep specificity of this testimonial but rather an engagement with the problems of any attempt to tell the stories of war's violence in an official, documentary capacity. Images of Indian newspapers displaying stories about interethnic and interreligious violence flash across the screen over an audio montage of disconnected fragments taken from different testimonials: "We thought that night is the last night of our life," "We were tired of keeping on running," "Even today when we remember it, we wake up and cry in the night." Eventually, the newspapers are replaced by a montage of different animated faces, Hindu, Muslim, and Sikh as indicated by their diverse clothing and head wear, all staring at the camera as the testimonial fragments continue to play underneath the images and start to bleed into one another, indecipherable. How can animation possibly capture all such stories? How can history?

For some animators working in the memorial film tradition, the only conscionable answer is absence. Faced with the impossible task of visualizing and bringing to life experiences that they have not directly known and whose singularity they can never fully appreciate, their response becomes one of profound refusal, and their films center on an absence of wartime depiction rather than any engagement with the impossible task of picturing such conflict. Among the most famous of these efforts is the 2004 film *Birthday Boy* by the Korean animator Sejong Park, who was then a student at the Australian Film Television and Radio School and who had previously served in the South Korean military.[12] Nominated for an Academy Award and honored at festivals worldwide, *Birthday Boy* has taken on a surprising life in secondary school classrooms the world over, where it is regularly taught as an antiwar film. If that is the case, however, it is true only in the most absolutely literal sense: *Birthday Boy* is an *antiwar* film only insofar as it deliberately refuses to depict the war that stands at its absent center, focusing instead on the conditions of war's periphery where most of its audience dwells as well. The entire film is arguably about the deep inaccessibility of war, no matter how much we may think we understand it. Set in an unnamed Korean village in 1951, during the second year of the Korean War, the film centers on a young boy, Manuk (plate 32), playing soldier alone throughout the village: jumping up from behind rocks and pretending to fire an imaginary rifle, taking aim at the fighter jets he can see far away in the sky. Witnessing Manuk alone in the wreckage of a fighter jet that has crashed in his town, we know that this is not just empty boyhood play: Manuk is approximating his vision of the actual events unfolding in those exact moments just outside his sphere of experience, perhaps only miles away, though it might as well be another world. We can see the transit of war interrupting his spaces of play: a train carrying tanks to the front rushes past at one point, a brief blur of wartime imagery that yields no greater understanding of wartime experience.

And then, as if in a kind of economic exchange, the war also sends something back from the front: another set of wartime objects, this time with tragic resonances and still no greater shred of understanding. Arriving at home, Manuk discovers a box that has been delivered to his house containing a set of soldier's dog tags and a pair of soldier's boots. We in the audience know exactly what this means, but

Manuk is entirely uncomprehending. He takes it as a present to assist him in his play, putting the dog tags around his neck and wearing the boots on his feet as he marches around the house as if standing guard. Eventually, he falls asleep exhausted on the empty floor of his home, splayed out in the late afternoon sunlight in a pose that unconsciously evokes his father's passing on the battlefield. His mother returns home at last, and the film ends as she calls to her son on his birthday. His father's artifacts now incorporated into his toys and the box discarded, it is unclear if his mother will ever even realize the message she has missed.

At bottom, *Birthday Boy* is a film about misunderstanding—or rather the false presumption of understanding. Manuk has a certain naive understanding of war centered on danger and heroics, one that he enacts and repeats obsessively throughout the film. Not even the confrontation with war's starkest material realities—the last remaining possessions of his now perished father, delivered directly into his home—can shatter that false understanding; they are merely incorporated into his continued misapprehension. Can there be a starker statement of war's deep inaccessibility, even its total invisibility—an experience wholly unrecognized by son and mother alike, though in vastly different ways? Surely, Manuk's misunderstanding is contingent upon his young age; the deep dramatic irony of the film's title and of the sequence where he receives the package are dependent upon the idea that the adult audience knows more than him. But do they? In fact, that supposed act of understanding is itself premised on a deliberate instance of cultural misunderstanding that Park programs into the film from the start. Working and living in Australia after having grown up in Korea just a generation removed from the war, Park stands at the threshold of two cultures, and the central irony of *Birthday Boy* depends on a cross-cultural perspective. As Park recounts, the tradition of birthday presents is not a significant part of birthday celebrations in Korea: "In Korea when I was growing up, even still now these days, the present really is not that important for birthday [*sic*]."[13] The very idea that Manuk would think the package on his doorstep is a present because it is his birthday is it-self a form of misunderstanding premised on a certain Western ig-norance of the limits of its own cultural practices and traditions. In other words, Park lulls his Western viewers into the same assumptive trap that his central character unwittingly makes, of thinking that they *do* understand when in fact they do not.

Whether through age (as the boy), culture (as the viewer), or sheer invisibility (as the mother), every figure connected to *Birthday Boy* is forced to confront a limit to their understanding, even if they do not recognize it as such. In fact, the film purposefully makes the pro-cess of recognizing this limit extremely difficult. Part of its appeal and success lies in the film's extraordinarily polished visual appeal, an extremely clean 3-D graphic rendering that seems like a contem-porary update to a classical Disney realism. Manuk is adorable, the world is vivid, the detail exquisite: it seems as though we can make out every tile on every village roof, every rock in the road, every grain in the wood floor of Manuk's home. Everything seems explicable. And yet absolutely nothing is. Within the space of the film itself, Manuk never comes to understand his tragic mistake in treating the items in the box as toys. The audience never comes to recognize or be informed of their own oversight in making assumptions about the universality of Western birthday traditions—the boy's happy re-sponse to the items in the box being a symptom not of his birthday enthusiasm but his general inability to think of war in anything other than the terms of play he has already established for himself. And the mother, as far as we know, never comes to recognize or dis-cover the objects that have been hidden from her, even though they are already in her home. Perhaps she will at some point see that her son seems to have some new objects in his playtime armory, but who knows how long that might take? In the meantime, war remains a distant phenomenon even for those closest to it, whose incomprehen-sion proves insurmountable even when the records of war are deliv-ered to their doorstep.

This idea of the fundamental inaccessibility of the wartime expe-rience also stands behind a very different film from *Birthday Boy*, one drawn from conflicts in a very different part of the world. The experimental film *White Tape*, a brief two-minute animation from 2010 by Denmark-based Israeli animators Michelle and Uri Kranot, is a study in inaccessibility even as it seeks to memorialize as well, or at least to mimic the process of memorialization. The origins of *White Tape* lie in the B'Tselem Camera Project run by the Israeli Information Center for Human Rights in the Occupied Territories, or B'Tselem, which in 2007 began distributing handheld digital cameras to Palestinians living in the West Bank, allowing them to film their encounters with Israeli soldiers and other aspects of their daily life. *White Tape*, made as part of a still unfinished trilogy of animated films drawn from those digital recordings, uses a brief ten-second clip that records a group of Palestinian men being made to stand behind a line of white tape by an armed Israeli soldier. We have no context for the event depicted—no sense of who these men are or why they are being made to line up, whether this is at a checkpoint or in a city street or even inside someone's home. In fact, we cannot even recognize what we are looking at for nearly the first full minute of the film—or approximately half of its entire running time. The screen is just a blur of white paint and dynamic brushstrokes, and only slowly do a few identifiable figures emerge. Even then we cannot entirely tell who they are or what they are doing, the film clip being shown only in parts and irregularly repeated—we catch a glimpse of a soldier's helmet here, then a shot of boots walking that is repeated several times, then several shots of just the tape itself. Only in the last ten seconds of the film does the clip play entirely from start to finish, its whole expanse visible at once: a soldier lays out a piece of white tape on the ground, makes the men back up to stand behind it (plate 33), and the film is over.

Nearly incomprehensible and seemingly trivial in the greater context of the ongoing Israeli-Palestinian conflict, *White Tape* is a profound commentary on what it means to use film and animation as vehicles of witness and tools of memorialization. In the abstract, the film replicates the conditions of basic documentary animation with amazing precision: take the testimony of a witness and animate it. Such is literally the mandate of countless animated documentary projects, only here the testimony is visual rather than aural, and the results are entirely impenetrable. What possible context could make us actually understand the situation in that video footage, of the men being made to stand behind the tape? Short of actually being in that moment and living through that context, anything else will just be a poor approximation of an explanation, one that might lead to a sense of understanding that only ever covers over a deeper, total lack of comprehension, as in *Birthday Boy*. *White Tape* asks us to question whether any attempt to document conflict can ever be anything more than a series of brushstrokes and time skips that obscure what they are meant to show. In this sense, the film enacts a kind of *anti-rotoscope* process: taking the basic conditions of rotoscopy, wherein live-action film is carefully painted over by animators, and using it to obscure rather than to clarify. The final few seconds of the film more or less approximate a basic rotoscoped animation, yet by this point we are primed to recognize that even such moments of seeming visual clarity will yield no new understanding at all.

White Tape does not entirely discount the role of the artist as witness. In fact, it mimics the process of memorialization quite perfectly: taking a work of testimony by an actual participant within a zone of conflict, animating that testimony, and submitting it to the public record, where it will be remembered and recorded far longer than had the testimony never been so used. That ten-second and seemingly inconsequential clip shot by the unnamed Palestinian using the B'Tselem camera most likely would never have the extended afterlife it has been afforded by being entered into the Kranots' extensive and well-regarded catalog of work. In that sense, the Kranots have created every bit as much of a *record* as McCay himself, one that lives on in a way that scattered testimony alone could never do. What the Kranots do not subscribe to, however, is the supposition that such a process will ever lead to a greater sense of understanding or a new-found comprehension for those who are not subject to the conditions of conflict and occupation here shown. Any attempt to submit such experiences into the *public transcript* can only be a distortion. They are pure *discontinuum*, the uncontainable counternarrative to the smooth storytelling and careful arguments of the *continuum*. The animation in *White Tape* must obscure its subject, lest in making it too clear the film erases it entirely.

BEAR STORY

Perhaps the process of memorializing war and atrocity through art of any type is an impossible project. Perhaps the act of witness must belong only to the witnesses themselves, as any other attempt to tell their stories will be a failure. And yet perhaps even in the face of failure and incomprehension that effort to memorialize remains necessary, even urgent. This is the position put forward by the 2016 Academy Award–winning animated short *Bear Story* (2014), by the Chilean animator Gabriel Osorio Vargas, credited here as Gabriel Osorio. There may be no animated film that deals more directly with the question of memorial than Osorio's does: the entire film, in fact, is about an animated memorial to the dead and much of the film in fact takes place *inside* that memorial. Of course, we do not realize until the very last moments of the film what we have been watching or how it serves as such a memorial, and the power of that realization accounts for much of the film's impact. Wondrously animated throughout, the film tells the story of a sad old bear who spends his days making mechanical models of a father, mother, and boy bear (plate 34). Waking alone one morning in a home that seems to have other inhabitants but is at the moment strangely empty, the bear takes his models and other mechanical contraptions out to the street where he solicits coins from passersby to play his mechanical show. There is a cub who begs a coin from his father and goes to watch the performance, whereupon a magical tale unfolds of animals captured by carnival goons and forced to perform in a traveling circus until one day the star show-bear escapes and returns home to his wife and son. The mechanical play ends with the tiny mechanical bear family happily reunited, but as the actual bear takes out a photo that he keeps in his pocket watch showing his own happy bear family—the same photo featured in miniature within the mechanical show—we realize that in reality there was no happy ending. The story of the circus bear is his own, and the part about the reunion is pure fantasy. The mechanical play he has created is his living memorial to the tragedy of his life.

To a degree that is extremely unusual for any animated film, *Bear Story* is actually about the role of animation in dealing with atrocity: not just in a metaphorical sense but in the most literal way possible. The mechanical play that the bear creates is essentially a work of animation, a vivification achieved through a vast technological trickery—an instance of object animation par excellence. Surely, part of the film's great success is due to the exhilarating ingenuity with which Osorio animates this clockwork dumb show. The crisp realism of the film's computer graphics gives weight and texture to each little tin object and mechanical gear, making it all the more fascinating to watch as Osorio conceives elaborate uses of forced perspective, rotating scenery, and flyaway objects to make it seem like the bear's expansive story is all being told within the fixed dimensions of his wooden theater-box. Watching the story unfold, we are as mesmerized as the little bear cub on the street holding the coin from his father. And yet, all the ingenuity in the world cannot convey the weight of what has actually happened to the bear and to his lost family. The bear cub with the coin just blinks uncomprehendingly as the bear's story concludes. He hands the bear showman his coin, gets a toy pinwheel in return, and then skips off to join his father, who hasn't been paying attention. What exactly was the point of this elaborate edifice, and is it objectively a failure?

We might ask the same question of the film itself. For anyone who knows the history of Latin America or has some familiarity with the region's animation, the references within the bear's story are immediately apparent: the metaphor of the animal catchers and the captured creatures is almost exactly the one used in Walter Tournier's *In the Jungle There Is Much to Do*. Set within the film's Chilean context, the story is evocative of the nearly thirty thousand citizens secretly detained and tortured during the military dictatorship of Augusto Pinochet. (Given the prominence of Tournier's *In the Jungle* among communities of leftists and dissidents in Chile and Argentina during the dictatorships of the 1970s and 1980s, the references in *Bear Story* seem likely to be a direct homage.) Osorio, who was born in 1984 during the waning years of Pinochet's rule, has little direct connection to that world, which vanished during his early childhood. But he has a deep family connection. His grandfather, Leopoldo Osorio, was a Socialist Party official imprisoned when Pinochet overthrew the democratically elected socialist government of Salvador Allende; detained and tortured for two years during the beginning of Pinochet's rule, he eventually fled to England and was unable to return to Chile until after his own son, Gabriel's father, had already died. *Bear Story* is an act of witness to the experiences of Leopoldo Osorio, an act of animated memorial, just as the mechanical bear story within the film is the bear's own attempt to give witness to and to memorialize his suffering and that of his family. (The Spanish title of the film, *Historia de un oso*, makes the connection even more apparent, as the word for story and history is here one and the same and the Spanish word for bear, *oso*, is a partial homonym of Osorio's own surname.) In the end, though, are we the audience any more comprehending than the overwhelmed bear cub on the street who just wants a toy for his coin? *Bear Story* is an elaborate, beautiful film: a visual wonder. But does that element of spectacle not simply put us in the same position as the cub, gawking at the elaborate show? From start to finish, the film is marked by a lilting music box melody, one that punctuates the mechanical performance just as much as the nonmechanical sections of the film: the extensive use of that melody seems to indicate that the whole of the film itself is no different from and no more successfully communicative than the mechanical theater story, the animation within the animation.

And yet maybe it is not the cub who matters so much as the bear showman himself. He does not grow angry when the cub misunderstands. He smiles, happy to give him his toy. This elaborate system of mechanical memorialization is truly more for him than for anyone else. The bear lives in a world apart, frozen in the past. He spends his days refining his models of loved ones who have passed, wakes up in the morning in a bed that still bears the impression of his lost wife, checks in on the untouched, empty room of his lost son. The clock on the wall when the bear is leaving home in the morning says 3:10 even though the early light of day is streaming into the house. When the bear checks his pocket watch just a little while later out on the street corner, it is a few minutes before ten. The bear lives in the world of his tragedy, his home frozen in time and set in another universe; that misery is his permanent residence, and he cannot escape it. The only thing that brings him out on the street into the world of the public and the time of the present is the possibility of having his story told—even if no one understands. He merely wants them to see. That is the purpose of his elaborate memorial, and if it takes elaborate tricks to hold his audience's attention, so be it. What matters most is that someone at least look inside that box. What matters is that they *see*, even if they can never truly comprehend.

WITNESS TO ATROCITY: THE HOLOCAUST

It is in this context that we might begin to understand two of the most difficult and gravely important projects in the realm of animated memorial: the work of Holocaust remembrance and the commemoration of the victims of the atomic bomb blasts at Hiroshima and Nagasaki. While vastly different from one another, these two projects, each of which has been ongoing throughout the second half of the twentieth century and into the twenty-first, share an important core component centered on the absolute and literal invisibility of the atrocities they mean to remember. In the case of the Holocaust, that invisibility was the deliberate product of a meticulous process of erasure on the part of its Nazi perpetrators, who imagined that the complete destruction of Europe's Jewish population and other undesirables could be accomplished totally in secret. As Shoshana Felman writes, the Holocaust represents "the unprecedented, inconceivable historical advent of an event without a witness, an event which historically consists in the scheme of the literal erasure of its witnesses."[14] The call to witness in the aftermath of that unprecedented atrocity would be a moral imperative like no other, part of what Felman calls the sudden and urgent need for "articulating . . . history's presence to itself."[15] In contrast, the atomic bomb detonations at Hiroshima and Nagasaki were acts of public spectacle whose effects were meant to be immediately observed by the Japanese high command so as to prompt a swift and unconditional surrender. Yet as a product of their immense destructive power, the explosions would leave no trace of witness in the most immediate sense: no up-close recording of their destructive power in the moments of detonation, no survivors from the immediate blast zones. In both cases, nearly everything and everyone within a one-mile radius of the detonations was entirely destroyed. What was left in these cities was just a gaping emptiness—the instantaneous ending of over one hundred thousand lives combined and the decimation of miles of homes and infrastructure, to say nothing of the victims of and damage from the ongoing fallout. Here the question of invisibility is no metaphor: the genocide of the Holocaust and the near-apocalyptic impact of the atomic bombs were atrocities that, in different ways and for different reasons, were designed for the world not to see.

Thus the imperative to *show* would be especially pressing in these cases—though the question of how to show such terrors would prove extremely difficult to answer, so difficult that it would take decades before animators even began to approach these subjects. For the Holocaust, what seems to be the first work of animation dealing with the subject does not appear until 1959, when Yoram Gross releases *We Shall Never Die*. Born in Kraków, Poland, in 1926, Gross survived the Holocaust by passing as a gentile in Kraków and later Warsaw, where he worked with the Polish underground; his mother, who also spent many years in hiding, was eventually discovered and sent to Auschwitz, though she ultimately survived. Leaving Poland for Israel in the aftermath of the war, he made *We Shall Never Die* in tribute to the recent passing of his mother and to the millions lost in the Holocaust. Technically, one might consider Gross's work that of a memory film, given the centrality of the war to his own life. Yet his approach in *We Shall Never Die* is that of the living paying tribute to the dead rather than an exploration of his own personal experience of that time. Indeed, the very composition of the film invokes the traditions of memorialization within the Jewish faith. Made using stop-motion animation techniques with candles, the film is an abstract study in the interplay of light and movement: isolated flames scattered across the screen, the appearance and disappearance of candles, melting wax and its reformation. That such images are meant in reference to the Holocaust is declared in the opening moment of the film, which features barbed wire alongside the title. Such Holocaust imagery returns around the midpoint of the film, when the candles suddenly display the striping of the concentration camp prisoners' uniforms and the numbers of the prisoners' tattoos, with three such candles positioned behind barbed wire (plate 35) followed by a superimposition of objects that evoke the destruction of normal life—an abandoned child's toy, a smashed pair of glasses. Tellingly, the imagery does not derail the film or change its trajectory in any way. As those scenes complete, Gross returns to his abstract study of candlelight, the candles melting or the flames flickering but never entirely disappearing or going out. The history of the Jewish people, stretching thousands of years before the Holocaust, will continue unabated into the future: the title card, reoccurring here at the end of the film just as it appeared at the beginning, declares "we shall never die."

Gross does not yet dare to depict in any direct way the imagery of the Holocaust itself, leaving unseen such experiences for now—though he will change his position on this substantially much later in his career. Yet if the specific historical circumstances of the Holocaust are purposefully left unseen, they are nevertheless far from invisible. All of Gross's film is premised around acknowledging, mourning, and memorializing those lost in the Holocaust, a memorialization rendered most powerful in the film's moments of looking forward. The central physical metaphor of the candle is an apt one: integral to Jewish tradition, it is a beacon of both illumination and impermanence, a light that is constantly consumed. So much of Jewish belief and Jewish lore is centered on the idea of this fragile source of light being preserved in the face of loss and adversity: on the one-year anniversary of a loved one's death within Judaism, a *yahrzeit* candle is burned for twenty-four hours, as is also done on the high holy day of Yom Kippur and, beginning in 1949, on Holocaust Remembrance Day. Powerfully, Gross does not allow a single flame to go out within his film, even those bearing the striping and the numbers of the Holocaust victim. The lives being here preserved are not those of Jewish individuals alone but those of the Jewish people writ large, and in this sense the flame is rendered eternal. But of course those lit candles are also always a memorial for the millions departed. Candles must be lit by the living, but in burning they help us to remember the dead.

We Shall Never Die is, by design, an inspirational and forward-looking work, one that finds its act of memorial in a testament to Jewish perseverance. Its careful avoidance of any Holocaust imagery beyond the iconographic is strategic. But if it did choose to depict that nightmare, what imagery could it possibly show? This is the question that motivates the deeply abstract and deeply disturbing 1964 film *The Games of Angels* by the Polish animator Walerian Borowczyk. Borowczyk was a teenager during the years of his country's invasion and occupation by the Nazis; though he was not Jewish and his family is not known to have suffered directly in the Holocaust, the necessity of bearing witness to such suffering profoundly influenced his early animated works. An avant-gardist, he was prone to take in a more literal way than most Kristeva's questions as to "What art is possible for the invisible? For the unthinkable?"[16] Thus in *The Games of Angels*, he deploys an assemblage of visual and audio tropes that cohere into no comprehensible story, message, or pattern but that powerfully evoke the industrial horror and unfathomable terror of the camps. The film begins with a direct invocation of the Holocaust, indicating in an intertitle that "the music in this film is based on an original chant from the Polish concentration camps."[17] Yet after that, any identifiable connection is at best only implied. Borowczyk's images, deployed seemingly at random but also in a progression of greater and greater intensity, always evoke but never quite represent the known imagery of the Holocaust: walls that seem to be of concrete but are also only just shapes; a room that might be a shower but the equipment is absent; a rapidly passing blue-black pattern that might be the inside of a train car; liquid that pools and moves like blood but the color is wrong; an object that seems like a disembodied torso but the structure is off—it seems perhaps like it might have room for wings, which have since been detached; and image after image after image of cylinders or tubes—pipes perhaps, or smokestacks. Borowczyk's imagery swirls around the iconography of the Holocaust without ever landing on an identifiable scene. When his camera does pause, it is usually on an image both disconcerting and unplaceable: in perhaps the film's most memorable tableau, a giant blue wing lies on a white sheet and starts to drip blue blood, as though it had just been severed from some being (plate 36). Yet if Borowczyk's imagery is abstract and evocative, his sound track is disarmingly concrete: the sounds of a train rushing over tracks, water dripping, the chanting referenced at the very start of the film, all placing us clearly within the vicinity of Holocaust stories.

For anyone who encounters *The Games of Angels* entirely without context, it will surely seem like an exercise in pure surrealism. But there is something more at work in Borowczyk's avoidance of definitive imagery than abstract artistry alone. He acknowledges that the experiences of the Holocaust's victims demand an imagery, but he also regards that project as impossible: any straightforward attempt at witness will be unconscionably incomplete. Instead, he attempts to render the fissure between image and meaning, that gap between the two sides of the witnesses' mandate according to Kristeva, "the act of looking truth in the face and, simultaneously, the translation of this vision into meaning."[18] Borowczyk's imagery points at the literal truth of the camps but always falls short of the identifiable image. Meanwhile, that same open and associative imagery allows for a superabundance of meaning and interpretation, an uncontainable excess of possible readings, none of them definitive, all of them in contrast with one another. Juxtaposing the angelic and the concrete, the organic and the mechanical, the heavenly and the hellish, Borowczyk engages in an ongoing play of signs that admits no stable or definitive locus of meaning. In this way the film both approaches and steers clear of overt Holocaust remembrance, never assuming a final totality or set interpretation yet always pointing back to the event as the origin point of its depictions. It is a special kind of witness, one that recognizes the absence of imagery as being a necessary component of Holocaust commemoration but that also demands an imagery in acknowledgment of the victims' suffering and experience. *The Games of Angels* attempts to provide both without ever fully committing to the stability of either.

THE IMAGE OF ATROCITY

The reticence to engage directly in the imagery of the Holocaust that Gross and Borowczyk share is understandable and admirable, fully attendant to the perhaps insurmountable limitations of the memorial film. Yet there is also a sense in which such avoidances can seem like another form of silence, even if reverent. Though the abstraction and absence that define these early works of Holocaust animation would remain the standard for decades, such approaches would begin to shift toward the end of the twentieth century. One important impetus toward such change was undoubtedly the landmark publication of Art Spiegelman's graphic novel *Maus*, first serialized in the magazine *Raw* between 1980 and 1991. A pioneer in the use of comics for purposes of testimonial, his work being grounded in the personal account of his struggles to understand his father's Holocaust experiences, Spiegelman broke ground in his sheer willingness to engage with the unfathomable imagery of that atrocity: to actually show, via a cartoonal world of cats and mice, pictures that evoked his father's profound suffering.

In the realm of animation, a similar reevaluation of the medium's relationship to the imagery of the camps and the suffering experienced there would come about a decade after *Maus* in the 1998 film *Silence* by the Israeli producer-director Orly Yadin and the French animator Sylvie Bringas, who met and made their careers in England. Based on the oral accounts of a Holocaust survivor named Tana Ross, who was born in Berlin in 1940 and spent most of the war at the Theresienstadt transit camp in Czechoslovakia, *Silence* falls into the tradition of the animated testimonial film. It is one of the most powerful of that form. Ross's story is one that she had held within her for nearly her entire life—"it took me fifty years to tell this story," she says toward the end of the film—and Yadin and Bringas approach the responsibility of animating her long-held experience with reverence and imagination. Their imagery moves in and out of direct representation and abstract metaphor continuously, never settling on one approach. When Ross mentions Berlin, the city is conjured before our eyes in documentary footage with traces of coloration and other animation-on-film techniques. Yet just as quickly those conjurations vanish again: when Ross explains that her mother left her unaccountably one day, the photograph of mother and child transforms into an animated image of Ross spinning helplessly through space. Describing her time in Theresienstadt, Ross recounts how her grandmother kept her carefully hidden to avoid transportation to Auschwitz. Yadin and Bringas show her stepping into a suitcase where she is entirely hidden: an imagery that seems literal in the moment but eventually becomes figurative as well. When Ross later speaks of her isolation in Sweden after the war, the imagery of her in the suitcase reappears, the concrete made abstract and the past made present.

Part of what makes *Silence* so powerful as a work of Holocaust remembrance is the degree to which it pursues Ross's story long after the end of the war. Ross was only a child during the years of the Holocaust, five years old when Theresienstadt was liberated. Her mother mysteriously lost, she and her grandmother went to live with relatives in Sweden, and much of the film centers on Ross's childhood and adolescence there: concerts with her orchestra-conductor great-uncle, parties, parades and Swedish festivals. Yet Ross always feels cast apart from this world, floating through space as she did after the loss of her mother. "I was still invisible, still the best at hiding," she says as we watch her animated representation tuck itself again into a suitcase. When Ross turns twenty, she decides to leave, and upon her departure her great-uncle and aunt give her a package of papers they have never shared before (plate 37). It is here that the Holocaust reenters the film directly, and here that its imagery is most powerful. In these letters, Ross learns the full truth of her mother's experience, including her death at Auschwitz. When Ross mentions this site of horrors, we see it: film footage of the actual entryway to Auschwitz, approached by train, rendered in a grainy black-and-white negative and then subtly recolored in several different hues—of a piece with the rest of the animation in the film, but not. It is this image as much as Ross's story itself that has been repressed for so long, always present in the deep background of other animated engagements with the Holocaust but rarely so directly evoked.

Much of Ross's story is about not just the Holocaust experience itself but about the process of learning to bear witness. It is a task she comes to only reluctantly. "Don't tell, don't tell," her great-aunt tells her as a child. "We don't ever want to know." Yet even as Ross tries to keep silent, the work of witness is one she cannot entirely avoid. Her very name carries forward the memories and effects of those terrible early years. Tana is not the name that her mother chose for her; it is the name given to her by the Nazi state when she was born. "They had special names for us, for Jewish babies," she explains. Ross carries the story of her tragedy wherever she goes; it is integral to her identity, to her very name. What she discovers is the power of bearing witness to what she has known, of building what she calls a "bridge to the past." Yadin and Bringas replicate this act of discovery in the turn to Auschwitz imagery when the camp becomes part of Ross's story. The image of the camps is the great lacuna of Gross's work and of Borowczyk's. Yet it is always there, inescapable. To evoke it directly is not necessarily to give it a totemic power nor to do a disservice to its victims or its survivors. It is part of Ross's story, and Yadin and Bringas assert that it belongs in the film simply by making the decision to include it. It does not dominate or change or control Ross's witness: in fact it helps to resolve it, the image of the camp fading into an image of tracks fading into a butterfly image that has been evoked each time Ross thinks of her lost mother and that now enters the present of the film, following alongside the train leaving Sweden on which Ross is riding. To exclude such direct imagery of the Holocaust from the animated realm runs the risk of coloring not just the past but also the present. *Silence* ends with the image of a train, Ross's train, the one that will take her into her future. Yet we also cannot forget the vision just seen of entering the Auschwitz gate by train and everything the image of the train connotes in the context of the Holocaust. Yadin and Bringas's final image is one of freedom and futurity, but one that is also resonant with everything lost: both past and future united together in the testimony of the witness.

In the years since *Silence*, there has been a sea change in depictions of the Holocaust and the way in which that unspeakable event becomes memorialized in animation. One sees this change in a film like *Nyosha*, made in 2012 by the Israeli animators Yael Dekel and Liran Kapel using interview material from Kapel's grandmother recorded by Steven Spielberg's Shoah Foundation, which archives testimony from survivors of the Holocaust and other genocides. What is remarkable about *Nyosha* in the context of the animated films about the Holocaust that came before it is the degree to which it openly and directly depicts the story being told by Nomi Kapel and the manner in which it does so. Kapel's tale, like Ross's, is one of hiding: as a child in Poland, she is the sole survivor when the Jews of her village are discovered in an attic. Yet whereas Yadin and Bringas are meticulous in blending the representative and the metaphorical, the concrete and the abstract, in their rendering of Ross's words, Dekel and Kapel illustrate Nyosha's story as a straightforward narrative film. Making exquisite use of puppet animation reminiscent of Jiří Trnka's famous work in Czechoslovakia, Dekel and Kapel turn Nyosha's story into what seems like a vivid folktale. Their puppet figures are expertly exaggerated types, stylized and unreal without ever seeming like caricature: Nyosha's figure featuring huge, wondrous eyes that take up most of her tiny head, her worried mother defined by her constantly creased eyebrows. Nyosha's story is remarkable for its material details—she grew up extremely poor and could only afford a single good shoe from the local cobbler, and she remembers being covetous of the other shoe that she could not possess. In Dekel and Kapel's depictions, these objects take on a talismanic quality, the unpossessed shoe gleaming with a luster reminiscent of Snow White's apple.

What are the ethics of turning someone else's tragedy into a marvelously good story? In one sense, Dekel and Kapel's approach seems to be exactly what animators like Gross and Borowczyk were trying to avoid, and Yadin and Bringas are likewise circumspect about ever veering too far into the purely representational. Absent all historical context, *Nyosha* could seem like a beautifully animated folktale, the violence and danger involved being entirely part of the tradition of that form. But of course, Nyosha's story is in fact no folktale, and that seems to be precisely the point. Whatever intersection her story seems to have with the realm of imagination, it is all too tragically real: we hear Nomi Kapel's voice come in and out throughout the film and can never forget her act of witness or misunderstand this story, as fantastical as it is, as being anything other than an illustration of that act. Dekel and Kapel do not shrink from the tremendous violence in Nyosha's tale. When the Nazis discover the villagers with whom she has been hiding, we stay with Nyosha in her hiding spot and hear everything proceeding around her: commands, threats, gunshots, her own mother being taken away and shot just outside the house (plate 38). The imagery switches to hand-drawn animation for most of this sequence, and we witness Nyosha spinning through space, like Ross in *Silence*, yet when Nyosha opens her eyes and emerges from hiding, there is nothing abstract about her world: she is surrounded by blood and glass and bodies. Nyosha survives and like some character in a Brothers Grimm fairy tale goes wandering alone into the woods, where she is taken in by a family of farmers. Dekel and Kapel end their animation at the point where Nyosha enters the dark forest. They end her story exactly where another fairy tale might begin: the point being that Nyosha's story is no such tale. Violent, bloody, and terrifying, it is the story of an actual life lived in the midst of an actual historical nightmare. Dekel and Kapel's animation, buffeted by Nyosha's actual words, does not eclipse the reality of her tale but instead always gestures toward it. The very unreality of their folkloric retelling speaks to the unrepresentable reality of the story itself. What imagery could ever capture Nyosha's remembrances or any of the thousands of others recorded by the Shoah Foundation? How can that reality ever be known? Though Dekel and Kapel's approach is quite different, the sense of the Holocaust experience as being fundamentally unrepresentable as it is for Gross and Borowczyk in some way still remains.

ANIMATION IN MEMORIAM

By definition, testimonial projects like *Nyosha* and *Silence* focus on the stories of Holocaust survivors, who may or may not be party to the process of co-imagination in these works. Yet who is there who can speak for the dead? How might that memorial be constructed? These are the questions that animate the late work of Yoram Gross, who returned to questions of Holocaust remembrance in the last years of his career after many successful decades animating children's feature films and television series in his new adopted home of

Australia, where he moved after leaving Israel in 1968. Though Gross had his own survival story, what most captured his imagination as an artist was the question of how to speak for those who were lost in the Holocaust. *We Shall Never Die* is dedicated to the memory of those lost, and in two of his last films, *Sentenced to Death* and *Don't Forget*, from 2011 and 2010, respectively, he returns to the camps again: to Theresienstadt in *Sentenced to Death* and Auschwitz in *Don't Forget*. Though meant to stand alone, the two films are powerful compliments to one another, each taking a different approach to the question of witness and memorial. *Sentenced to Death* is powerful for what it does not show. The film is dedicated "in memory of my childhood friends who perished in the concentration camps" as indicated in an introductory intertitle, and the imagery with which it opens is evocative of the terrible realities of the Holocaust without directly showing any of them. Zooming in and out of piles of cloth fabric, Gross evokes the specter of bodies and mass graves, the piles of clothes stolen from the victims of the camps or piled outside the showers, yet he does not directly show any such images. Like Borowczyk in *The Games of Angels*, Gross approaches the imagery of the Holocaust but always also pulls back.

Yet this pulling back becomes complicated throughout the film, as Gross layers in additional forms of imagery that bring us closer and closer to the explicit subject of the film, the millions of children lost in the Holocaust. Amidst the piles of fabric, we eventually find stone sculptures of children's heads: disembodied like the detached heads of dolls and staring at the camera with vacant stone eyes, they are chillingly uncanny. Animation is always a study in the interplay of subjects and objects, the one being always transformed into the other, and these terrible statutes force us to think of the lost children to whom the film is dedicated as both the living beings they were and the murdered bodies they became. It is a deeply unsettling series of images, made all the more troubling by yet another layer of images that Gross soon incorporates, the close-ups of the sculptural heads fading into rotoscoped images of children drawing interspersed with flashes of the drawings themselves—the first signs of life in the film, but separated from us by a layer of animation. The drawings are innocent but also tragically resonant within the context of the film: a girl's simple drawing of a train immediately brings to mind all the connotations of that image within the context of the Holocaust. These inserts are ultimately just a prelude to the final two layers of imagery that Gross includes: actual drawings of life in a concentration camp by Helga Weissová, who was sent to Theresienstadt at age twelve and then to Auschwitz at age fifteen, as well as actual photographs from the Holocaust.

The cumulative effect of *Sentenced to Death* is overwhelming, making the brief photographic images that appear toward the end of the film far more affecting than they might otherwise be. The photographs that are the last layer to be added to the increasingly complex sequence of images are not so much the pinnacle of representation as the origin point of the film's iconography, that which the other images are trying to make real. What can a photograph of the Holocaust tell us? Perhaps nothing if we do not know how to approach that image. Gross's explication is not about history or context but about thinking through the human lives and material experience behind those images. There are the flashes of witness from Weissová, which bring us deeply into the experience of the camps as seen and recorded by a child, much as the children's drawings in *Kinshasa, Black September* do—embodying the act of witness not in the perfection of their imagery but the immediacy of the act of recording itself, the child's presence and emotional life tragically placed in front of us on the page. There are the flashes of the present and the future in the rotoscoped images of modern children and the snippets of their drawings that we see, a reminder of what is actually lost when we say that a child has died. There are those uncanny sculptures of the children's heads, like corpses but not quite: objects that remind us of life through its obvious absence and that bring us face to face with the material quality of the body once life is lost. And then the fabric, seen up close at an almost microscopic level such that the weave of the cloth envelops the screen. Such images are a reminder of the tactile, material reality of lived experience that a simple photograph can rarely capture. There is more to Holocaust remembrance than the picture of those scenes. *Sentenced to Death* is an attempt to use the multiple tools at animation's disposal to help prepare and to contextualize the lived reality that stands behind any photograph.

In this sense, it can be viewed as a companion piece to the film that came one year before it in Gross's body of work, *Don't Forget*. Using film footage from the Auschwitz-Birkenau Memorial and Museum in Poland, it consists of a montage of actual Holocaust imagery turned into lightly animated images through the process of rotoscoping. Gross never for a moment lets the photographic imprint of these images be forgotten: the black-and-white newsreel footage bleeds through the animation at multiple points such that you can see the film directly through the drawings, the photographic and the animated existing on top of one another or side by side. Yet he also makes a point of evacuating these photographic images of most of their detail and content. The entire film is cast against a stark white background, and much of the rotoscoped work consists in outlining the images only and leaving the details blank. On one level, such erasure makes the gruesomeness of the worst images somewhat easier to watch. The emaciated bodies, the piles of corpses, the near-skeletal people placed in wheelbarrows to be moved from place to place—these images of historical nightmare will try any viewer's capacity for passively watching the worst forms of human suffering and human cruelty. But Gross's purpose is not amelioration: *Don't Forget* does not exist to make the Holocaust more watchable. It exists as a demand that we cast these images in memory and make them our own, that we accept the process of memorial as being as much about the future as the past.

Like Michelle and Uri Kranot in *White Tape* or like Pierre Hébert in his Living Cinema protest animation, Gross does not just outline in his rotoscopy but also adds, exaggerates, and inserts his own drawings that are not built on a photographic basis: one of the concentration camp victims pictured is Gross's own original drawing, for example, and there are various Nazi figures who transform into evil ravens. Such artistic license, which seems to appear without rhyme or reason throughout the film, is a powerful statement of ownership, the living present meeting and engaging with the living past. Gross's stated purpose in making Don't Forget is to make the story of the Holocaust humanity's story, to take the specific conditions of that historical nightmare and make it part of the common moral inheritance of the global community. Gross's audience is as wide as the world. Though the film begins with a dedication to "the memory of my mother who suffered in Auschwitz and Ravensbrück," it also opens into an even more expansive dedication at the end. There Gross includes a summation that puts the history of the Jewish Holocaust in dialogue with other elements of that genocide, dedicating the film in memory of not only the six million Jews who perished in the Holocaust but also the "20 million Russians, 10 million Christians and 1900 Catholic priests" who died at the Nazi's hands. And then, as a final gesture, a single message repeated in forty-four languages and thirteen scripts: "Don't Forget." The profound point of all those photographic images vacated of their detail and rendered in outline form is not to erase the history underneath but to allow space for viewers to understand those images as also being their own—the true work of memorial being not only a communion with the past but also an ongoing process of co-imagination and co-identification that extends into the future.

WITNESS TO ATROCITY: HIROSHIMA AND NAGASAKI

This meeting of past and future likewise stands at the center of animated depictions of the atomic bomb blasts at Hiroshima and Nagasaki, where the process of memorializing one of the foundational horrors of modern Japanese history meets one of the most highly developed and forward-looking animation traditions in the world. The history of modern Japanese anime owes much to the years of the

Second World War itself: wartime propaganda films like Mitsuyo Seo's *Momotarō, Sacred Sailors* are often regarded as early forerunners of the stylized realism and dramatic themes that will distinguish postwar Japanese anime from more cartoonal and comedic traditions elsewhere in the world. Yet even as anime came into its own in the 1960s and 1970s, direct depictions of the atomic bomb would be virtually nonexistent, though reflections on the bomb blasts would be refracted indirectly through any number of science-fiction and horror tropes. This was not necessarily the case across Japan's varied graphic arts traditions. Appearing in 1972 as a stand-alone *manga* work, Keiji Nakazawa's graphic memoir *I Saw It* would openly recount the author's childhood experience of the Hiroshima bombing, laying out its nightmarish effects in panel after devastating panel of charred bodies and ruined streetscapes. Yet even after the publication of Nakazawa's work, which he would continue to develop and refine over the course of his career, depictions of the bomb attacks in the world of anime would remain rare. One of the earliest overt illustrations within Japanese animation would come in 1979 with a short film called *Pica-don* (more than two decades after American animators protesting the Cold War nuclear arms race had issued their own depictions of nuclear destruction in *Good Will to Men*, from 1955), but other attempts to return to the subject would be scarce. It is not that the years of the Second World War themselves were unexplored. Anime artists frequently adapted memoirs of civilian wartime experience more generally, as in *Kayoko's Diary*, from 1991, based on the autobiography of a woman who lost her family to the firebombing of Tokyo as a child, or *Raining Fire*, from 1988, which illustrates several eye-witness accounts of the firebombing of Fukuoka in 1945. Even those films that more directly addressed the historical context of the bombings often shied away from any deep visual engagement with the specificity of those events. *Summer with Kuro*, a children's feature released in 1990, tries to achieve the difficult feat of creating a heartwarming tale of a beloved pet who lives through the Hiroshima attack, here rendered primarily as a matter of physical destruction with the injuries that the human characters sustain seeming no different than typical burns and bruises. In the 2005 film *Nagasaki 1945: The Angelus Bells*—one of the only anime films to deal specifically with the attack on Nagasaki—the action is set literally on the outskirts of the city and focused primarily on the struggle to care for the injured and the sick, who again show no unusual visual signs of trauma. For these films and for many others, the attacks remain primarily an idea, far less so a visual reality.

The absolute brutality of *Pica-don*, the 1979 short that directly depicts the effects of the Hiroshima bombing, makes it immediately clear why so many anime artists chose to focus their depictions on other aspects of the wartime experience. Only seven minutes long, *Pica-don* is staggeringly hard to watch. Its creators, Renzo and Sayoko Kinoshita, were television animators primarily who often pursued historical and topical subjects in their independent animated shorts, and they conducted extensive research into the accounts of Hiroshima survivors in an effort to convey the events of the attack as accurately as possible. Their goal, as they described it, was nothing less than to "tell the story of the children whose lives were obliterated and buried beneath the ruins that summer morning."[19] The film's very name embodies this documentary purpose, *pica-don* being the Japanese term used to refer to the two parts of the atomic bomb blast, both its initial flash (*pica*), one hundred times brighter than the sun, as well as the subsequent explosion (*don*). *Pica-don* is nothing other than a study in that destruction, telling no story and following no narrative arc. It is nearly documentarian in its objective interest in depicting the effects of the blast, coding its experience in no political perspective and offering no moments of historical reflection. In fact the film provides no context whatsoever other than the before-and-after imagery of the people and structures of Hiroshima itself. The film is, in almost a perfect sense, exactly what McCay would call a *record*: an animated vision of that for which no other visual recording exists or ever could exist. It takes that which cannot be seen, and it insists that it be imagined.

The results are numbing, horrible in a way that only animation could ever capture. Animation is the art of visual transformation par excellence, but here the Kinoshitas render hellish the mutability intrinsic to the form. The film begins with a succession of tableaus of everyday life in Hiroshima the morning of August 6, 1945: a family getting ready for the day, people riding the city's trolley system, children at school, a boy flying a paper airplane. Then, at just about the halfway point of the short, the atomic bomb drops, and the entire world is completely unmade. Each of those previous tableaux is carefully disassembled in turn. Flowers are reduced to ash, buildings are immediately turned into rubble, and the various figures seen in the first half of the film are turned suddenly white then ghoulishly red. At first these color shifts seem inexplicable, but we quickly realize what they mean: the people are actually beginning to melt. In a terrifying scene straight from a horror film, we see in a long shot the trolley encountered earlier in the film. In an instant, the buildings around it are evaporated or reduced to rubble, and out of the trolley stream the confused city-dwellers. As they come closer to the foreground of the frame, we see their skin peeling and melting off of their bodies, their eyes coming out of their sockets, their teeth falling out of their mouths. The Kinoshitas meticulously researched the physical transformations wrought by the bomb's atomic blast and studied the drawings made by survivors. But nothing in the way of background or explanation is offered in any overt form within the film, just the ghastly visual record of such effects, presented entirely without context or account—an expository silence that makes the scenes all the more difficult to view. Again and again, we watch the residents of Hiroshima atomically disassembled: an infant grasping for a mother whose flesh is puddling on the floor, a schoolgirl whose fingers become elongated and loose, piles and piles of bodies charred beyond recognition.

The minutes devoted to illustrating the effects of the initial blast are excruciating; the scenes of attempted recovery immediately afterward even more so. Here, the initial disintegrations being complete, the focus is on the encounters between those who have survived and not survived to various degrees, which raises the question of what survival even means in such a case. The scenes are pure postapocalypse, as half-disintegrated people wander stupefied through the streets. A mother carries a charred lump of a child on her back, bodies lie everywhere without eyes or teeth. A hand sticks out of the rubble, reaching for help, but when someone clasps it and pulls, the skin just comes off like a glove, leaving only blood and bone. *Pica-don* is ultimately closer to a horror film than a war film, and the Kinoshitas acknowledge this inheritance in a final pan across the bodies of the survivors, lined up like monsters against a plain white background, staring out at the viewers as if asking for help yet totally unrecognizable as humans. They fade into an image of black rain, long streaks of radioactive precipitation streaming down the screen like paint dripping down a window, and then resolve into a final montage. We see the remains of a small child whose head is only a skull and who has a gaping hole in his chest leaving his ribs exposed, lying in a pile of debris outside the famous domed building that would later be designated the Hiroshima Peace Memorial, rendered not in a drawing but in a photograph, the only such image used in the film to this point. The image fades, and we return to the boy with the paper airplane who we first saw just before the bomb blast, leading us to assume that it is this boy that we see dismembered in the rubble. He is alive again and happy. When he casts his airplane, it flies clear across the world until it lands back in Hiroshima in the time of the film's present, in the bustling 1970s, again pictured not in a drawing but a photograph. Past connected to present, the film ends.

The bombing of Hiroshima is not a politically neutral event: no historical matter ever is. In Japan, in the United States, and around the world, debates have been ongoing since the days of the initial blast as to the strategic and moral justifications for the attacks, the degrees of moral culpability across various parties involved, and the lessons we are meant to draw. The Kinoshitas are not themselves neutral on these questions. Instrumental in founding the Hiroshima International Animation Festival in 1985, which aims to promote peace

through international cultural exchange, they have also been criti-
cized for the commentary portions of a commemorative book published in conjunction with their film, which focuses on Japan's suffering at the end of the Second World War with little context as to
Japan's role in the war's beginnings.[20] (The topic is inevitably fraught:
commemorative efforts in the United States, such as a Smithsonian
exhibit planned for the fiftieth anniversary of the bombing in 1995,
have received their own criticisms for downplaying the moral questions and moral consequences surrounding the bombs.) What makes
Pica-don the film, as opposed to its later commemorative book, so
remarkable is the degree to which it carefully and self-consciously
sequesters itself from such questions, focusing instead only on the
destruction and the dead. The montage at the end of the film that
runs from the ruined peace memorial to the scene of modern-day
Hiroshima, both presented in photographs and both connected by an
interposed animation of the boy and of his paper airplane, provides a
kind of thesis statement for the film. *Pica-don* is here figured as a set
of images sent across the world and across time, as impossible as a
paper airplane defying time and space to reach its present-day desti-
nation It is a work of imagination, in other words. And it is also a memorial. The focus here is not on politics or history, morality or culpability. The dead play no role in those questions. The film is identified
as a testament to their unimaginably horrendous suffering, an effort
to imagine in order to remember.

THE MORAL IMPERATIVE OF WITNESS

In some ways, *Pica-don* manages to stand as so neutral a memorial
because it is so scant in offering explanation. The film includes no
dialogue, no intertitles, no narration, and therefore no context or
accounting whatsoever. Like any brick-and-mortar memorial, it is
mute. In this way, it contrasts substantially with the other anime
film that is arguably its closest relation, the 1983 film *Barefoot Gen*

from director Mori Masaki. Like *Pica-don*, *Barefoot Gen* is relatively rare among anime films in centering on the attack upon Hiroshima, and in many ways, it seems like a feature-length update of that earlier film. Certainly, the visual elements of the blast and its effects are closely mirrored in both films, so much so that the nuclear detonation sequences in *Barefoot Gen* can read as a direct homage to those in *Pica-don*, cast in the same tones and utilizing the same visual techniques. Here again we see the horrendous change in skin from its normal cast to a bright white, a deep red, and then a charred black; we watch the sudden loss of eyes and teeth, the skin melting off of bones (plate 39). The tableaux are just as terrible: a mother reaching for her nursing infant, both turned to charred husks; a dog trying to outrun the blast and disintegrating before our eyes; a whole world that literally bends and shakes before entirely flying apart, debris being pulled straight up into the air as in a tornado. Yet in a film that is an hour and forty minutes long, the attack on Hiroshima comes in its first thirty-five minutes and lasts in total only five. The remaining hour of film, while set within the world of the bomb's aftermath and ostensibly about the struggles of its main character to survive, are arguably less about survival and more about understanding: about trying to piece through what exactly happened in those five minutes of terror and how we should make sense of it moving forward.

That *Barefoot Gen* should take up both sides of this mandate with equal fervor is explicable at least in part by the nature of its origins. *Pica-don* was a meticulously researched act of imagination on the part of animators who did not live through the blast itself, though Renzo Kinoshita would have known the firebombing of Osaka as a boy. *Barefoot Gen*, though directed by Mori Masaki, is based on the *manga* work of Keiji Nakazawa, the author of *I Saw It*, who lived through the Hiroshima blast as a six-year-old and spent much of the rest of his life reflecting on the experiences of his youth and trying to communicate them to others. Nakazawa's *Barefoot Gen manga* series, published between 1973 and 1975, was an outgrowth and extension of *I Saw It* and is divided into two parts, only the first of which deals with the immediate situation of the attack; in the second, Nakazawa's alter ego Gen must confront his mother's death from cancer later in the 1960s, caused by the radiation to which she was exposed in the blast. (It would also be made into an anime film, *Barefoot Gen 2*, in 1986.) Thus the act of witness at work in *Barefoot Gen* is of a substantially different kind than the direct memorialization in *Pica-don*. *Barefoot Gen* is ultimately far closer to the animated testimonial accounts of a work like *Silence* or *Nyosha* than the pure memorialization of a film like *We Shall Never Die* or *The Games of Angels*. Everywhere, you can hear Nakazawa's voice, refracted through the character of Barefoot Gen.

This background perhaps helps to explain one of the most utterly puzzling aspects of the film: the strange degree to which Gen seems personally exempted from the terrible events happening around him. It is not that he does not suffer: he loses his father, brother, and sister, and later another baby sister all as a result of the bomb; later, in *Barefoot Gen 2*, he will lose his mother as well. But Gen himself is remarkably unafflicted in any bodily form by the blast. Ostensibly, this is because he knelt down to pick up a pebble at the exact moment of the blast and was shielded by a stone wall: but for a blast that can evaporate whole buildings and that lays waste to almost every structure around Gen, the degree of his protection seems extreme. All around him during the scenes of the explosion and its aftermath, we see the same terrible imagery as in *Pica-don*. Even after the blast, most of the characters take on a red or yellow tinge in their skin to indicate their continued damage and injury. But the character design for Gen remains almost exactly the same before the blast and afterward. Bright and vibrant from the first frames of the film, he remains so through the last. Even the sudden loss of his hair about an hour into the film—literally the only physical affliction that we see him suffer—comes with little other lasting damage. Now bald, he still seems much the same. In fact, the character design for Gen has stood out from the rest of the characters even from the very beginning of the film. The overall design of the feature is largely in keeping with the somber traditions of adult-oriented anime, that which deals with complicated dramatic themes or sometimes violent future worlds: highly stylized, it offers an artistic vision clearly drawn from the tenets of live-action filmmaking. Gen himself, though, appears transplanted from another tradition in anime, one geared more toward children and comic treatments of the world. Highly geometrical in his design rather than carefully realist, Gen seems like the adorable comic protagonist of a children's movie caught inside a dark anime realm.

Masaki, while not one of the foremost directors in the anime tradition, was no novice, and the mixing of styles within *Barefoot Gen* cannot be regarded as an accident. Rather, it seems like an acknowledgment of Gen's special role as witness within the film, specifically his role representing Nakazawa as witness. Within the *manga* books that Nakazawa wrote and illustrated himself, Gen does not seem obviously different in his design from any of the other characters, and he suffers directly as much as any other figure: covered in flies that swarm around the city on the bodies of the dead, burned by debris in the aftermath of the explosion, his own skin visibly charred by the initial blast, he is far more of an active participant in and victim of the situation of the bombing and its aftermath in Nakazawa's books than in Masaki's film. For Masaki, Gen quite literally acts as witness again and again, even to the point of describing out loud the events that he sees before his eyes—an effect that, for the viewer, is not unlike the audio track of a survivor's testimonial running underneath a film, as in *Silence, Nyosha, 1947: Haunting Dreams*, or *Men in Black*. Seeing a street full of bodies, he remarks on how many bodies there are. Encountering black rain for the first time, he comments on its color and its properties. Later, when Gen encounters a soldier suffering from the radiation, he will literally narrate his sickness to him, commenting on the same disintegrations that we see before us on the screen: his shivering, his profuse bleeding, his sudden loss of hair. The soldier grows furious at the narration but proves too weak to do anything about it, and Gen watches him utterly collapse.

As much as *Barefoot Gen* is about the actual experience of the atomic blast at Hiroshima, it is also about the moral imperative of witness. That is, as much as it is about the terrible disintegrative effects experienced by that soldier, it is about Gen observing and narrating that experience, relaying it back to the soldier and to himself and to us. In a way, the film is beset by a superabundance of narration. There is Gen's narration of nearly every major event in the film, his constant articulation of that which he sees immediately before him. There is also an omniscient narrator who exists outside the story and describes to the audience certain effects of the bomb blast or certain elements of the historical or political situation—narrating the arrival of American bombers over Hiroshima, for instance, or explaining the ultimatum that the United States issues between the attack on Hiroshima and the one on Nagasaki. And then there are elements of visual narration that exceed the possible scope of Gen's direct experience, as when the film takes a detour to display the suffering at Nagasaki despite no character in the film being present at that site. Narration is not just an element in *Barefoot Gen*; it is an imperative. It must be. In the face of atrocity, the only moral response is that of witness.

In this sense, the true villains in the film are those who prevent or shun the act of witness. The Americans in fact go largely unmentioned in the film's accounts of moral culpability. Instead, it is the Japanese government making certain "that the full extent of the damage to Hiroshima was little reported," in the words of the narrator, which receives the most direct moral critique—a refusal of witness that the film argues led to the repeat of the Hiroshima experience at Nagasaki. Likewise, the most villainous figure that Gen confronts is not an enemy of any direct sort but a wealthy Hiroshima resident who pays him to look after the terribly injured and grotesquely deformed brother that he cannot stand to look at or listen to, a figure whose suffering he cannot bear to witness. Gen is a caretaker of a sort—his first assignment is to wipe the thousands of maggots off the man's terribly destroyed flesh—but he is also more than that: he is a designated witness to the man's suffering, just as he was to the soldier's. His physical tasks completed for the day, Gen shows his greatest act of generosity in offering to simply stay and sit with the man after his work is done. In response, the man is inspired to finally get up from the bed where he has been trapped since the bombing. His first act is to paint, which he must accomplish by gripping the brush between his teeth. His first act, in other words, is to bear witness in turn, to find expression for what he has seen and all he has experienced.

In the postapocalyptic world that Hiroshima became in the days and weeks after the attack, survival and death as it is depicted in *Barefoot Gen* came to depend on interpersonal economies of generosity or selfishness: who will share food and who will horde it, who will give shelter and who deny it. Gen's greatest frustration is the refusal of help when it is needed most: "Everything's gone crazy, there's nobody to help me," he reflects as he surveys the damage after the blast and realizes he and his mother are on their own. Likewise, his greatest source of pride is the help that he gives to others, as when he and his mother take in an orphan boy who reminds them of Gen's lost little brother and treat him as a member of the family. Attention and witness are figured in the film as resources like any other: deadly when withheld, transformative when shared. For Gen, it is the government's silence that compounded the country's suffering in the space between Hiroshima and Nagasaki. Likewise, it is his attention that transforms the life of the invalid man who becomes his ward. Even for the soldier whose life he cannot save, Gen's reporting on his condition to the doctor at the local field clinic helps him to understand the scope and extent of the radiation damage that has befallen the city and its people. The act of witness is not just an emotional necessity in the world of the film. It is actively salvific. For all the unmitigated suffering it depicts, the film ends on a remarkably positive and forward-looking note. In a dream, Gen communes with his lost father, who speaks of the need to put down roots and grow strong like the wheat sprouts that push through the soil even after the blast. Gen accepts the challenge to regenerate himself and his nation, but his first act in accepting this mission has nothing to do with personal health or physical reconstruction. With his mother and his adopted brother, he stands before the Ōta River that runs through Hiroshima and releases a paper lantern on a boat. It is a ceremony known as *tōrō nagashi*, a means of commemorating the dead. His first step toward the work of growing strong and regenerating both himself and his country, in other words, is an act of memorial.

GRAVE OF THE FIREFLIES

Yet what if there is no one left to tell your story? What if war's destruction and erasure is rendered complete and all its suffering is completely forgotten? That is the fearsome scenario considered in one of the greatest wartime anime films, and by some accounts simply one of the greatest war films of all time, Isao Takahata's 1988 film *Grave of the Fireflies* (plate 40). Based on the classic autobiographical novel by Akiyuki Nosaka, who was a teenage boy of fourteen when the Second World War ended, and produced by Japan's legendary Studio Ghibli, *Grave of the Fireflies* is one of the most profound works of memorial animation ever put on film. It is not a story of Hiroshima or Nagasaki, nor of Tokyo or Osaka or any of the other more well-known sites that suffered grievously in the last months of the Second World War. And that is exactly the point. It is set in the city of Kobe, a mid-sized city on the island of Honshu that was firebombed by the Americans in March of 1945 in a mission that is rarely recounted on either side as being particularly transformative to the war. It concerns two children of no particular status who witness no especially world-historical events and whose parents hold no special place in the nation: she, a wife who perishes largely unnoticed in the bombing; and he, a sailor on an unnamed naval ship who drowns in the war without so much as a notification sent to his family. Everything about *Grave of the Fireflies* speaks to the unremarkableness of its central story and its central characters, who ultimately are central to nothing but themselves. They are no one who would ever normally be memorialized. They are the true *discontinuum* of history, its utterly forgotten afterthoughts. Which is what makes the act of memorialization that *Grave of the Fireflies* enacts all the more transformative and profound, a true testament to the power of animation as a vehicle of remembrance.

The total isolation and utter insignificance of the main characters in *Grave of the Fireflies* is established from its opening moments. "September 21, 1945. That was the night I died," says the character of Seita as we are shown the image of an emaciated boy slumped against a column in a busy train station. He is abandoned and homeless, almost entirely unnoticed by the busy travelers walking in every direction; even the woman who quickly stops to leave him food does not look him in the eye or say a word. It is too late, and in the first minutes of the film we watch him die of starvation and malnutrition. The rest of the movie will center on understanding how Seita came to this place, bearing impeccable witness to a life that in its own time was not deemed worthy of any consideration at all. Part of what makes *Grave of the Fireflies* so extraordinarily powerful is the careful attention that it lavishes on the most seemingly inconsequential things. The details of daily life that are normally the excess of other more traditional narrative films are here the substance of the story itself. Dressing, bathing, finding food, eating, even urinating and defecating— Takahata offers a veritable master class in constructing a story out of what would be the narrative refuse of other works, focusing in where others would choose to look away or move on. As a war film, *Grave of the Fireflies* is relatively unique. It contains hardly any scenes of war as we typically understand it other than the firebombing in its opening minutes. Its two main characters, Seita and his sister, Setsuko, both die of malnutrition and starvation, a product of the war but not one typically considered in straightforward casualty figures. (Their mother is grievously injured in the raid, bandaged to the point of unrecognizability, and taken away early in the film, never to be seen again.) Seita and his family are the unseen, unheralded victims of war, all but invisible to everyone but the animators themselves.

It is arguably this sense of profound isolation that gives the film its sweeping emotional resonance—and its status as an infamous tearjerker, "a three handkerchief movie on a scale of one to three," according to its American distributor.[21] There are any number of stories in the world about family members dealing with tragedy and trying to do right by one another through their suffering. But each step in the growing isolation of Seita and Setsuko serves to further amplify the stakes of their ordeal: they lose their home, they lose their mother, they lose their mementos of her when they are sold by the heartless aunt who has taken them in, they lose their second home when that aunt compels them to leave, they lose any source of food as wartime rations become harder and harder to obtain. By the later portions of the film, Seita and Setsuko have come to live inside the very metaphor of their own isolation. With nowhere else in the world to turn, they take up residence inside an abandoned bomb shelter, little more than a cave deep in the countryside. They have lost everything: home, family, memories, food, shelter, even civilization itself. All they have is each other, and the pain of that scenario is overwhelming.

Why is it so emotionally affecting? For the simple reason that we are *witnessing* it: the film demands that we focus our attention where no one else will, and our forced recognition of that which everyone else ignores is transformative. The legendary artistry of Takahata and his collaborators at Studio Ghibli makes even the most mundane actions beautiful and arresting, each animated character's performance rendered as vivid and detailed in its physicality as that of any flesh-and-blood actor. It is simply astounding what the film is able to make dramatically interesting: the eating of gumdrops, the observation of fireflies, the gathering of firewood. For Nosaka, author of the autobiographical novel on which the film is based, this hypersensorium is precisely that which he tried to convey in his writing: a profound awareness of the world and of life afforded by the wartime experience. "We could all see so well back then," Nosaka remembers. "After all, we were about to die, so it was the terminal vision of people about to die. Everything looked so fresh. . . . Death was nearby, so the feeling of life was overwhelming."[22] Seita and Setsuko have literally been made to live in a world apart, and in the film's superabundance of detail and beauty we as viewers are subsumed by that heady experience. We are forced not only to see them but to see *with* them, one of the most empathic of all actions. We might say that for Takahata, as for Emmanuel Levinas, ethics is an optics.

In this way, *Grave of the Fireflies* is not just a film that tries to bear witness to the particular experiences of Nosaka, who lived through a scenario much like the one described and who lost his sister to malnutrition and starvation. It is a film that is actually about the process of bearing witness and the importance of that act. For Nosaka, the experience of war is a profoundly isolating one, one that begets a sense of alienation that can last an entire lifetime even as the rest of the world seems to move on. No matter the skill of the artist, he insists, it is "hard to depict a time when dying was taken for granted. It must be beyond imagination. That you might wake up next to a corpse one morning. That after an air raid like a passing storm, there'd be corpses lying everywhere. The townscape is changed overnight."[23] *Grave of the Fireflies* makes literal that feeling of separation, enforcing it socially and geographically on Seita and Setsuko, who eventually become severed from every part of the world they once knew and must exist inside a darkened cave constructed of the war itself—a bomb shelter, an isolation chamber of war. Though Nosaka wrote about his own experiences in the depths of such isolation and became famous for those efforts in Japan, his novel being widely taught in secondary schools for its picture of the Second World War experience, he himself admitted to wondering if it was ever really possible to communicate his experiences to someone else: if the possibility of bearing witness was even real. This is in part why he refused so many offers to make a film version of his book. "There were many offers to make that novel into a movie, but they never materialized," he remembers. "It was impossible to recreate the barren, scorched earth that's to be the backdrop of the story, and I thought today's children could never play the main characters in live-action."[24] It was specifically the idea of recreating his story through animation that convinced him to allow an adaptation. "I realized this could only have been done with animation," he said before the film's release. "It's just the way it was. . . . That wouldn't be possible filming at some location in live-action. I've looked for a photo of that place from that time period, but I've yet to find it."[25] For Nosaka, *Grave of the Fireflies*, lovingly made in a work of co-imagination with Takahata, is the elaborate mechanical show of the haunted bear father from *Bear Story*. We are the gawkers on the street who stop and watch, transfixed, even if we can never truly understand. Whether or not we fully understand in the end is immaterial. The story must be told. And to be told it must be conjured, for it is a story of invisibility. And for it to be conjured, it must be animated. It must be brought to life.

In the end, the act of witness is not just for Nosaka or his generation or the memory of his sister or any survivor, veteran, or victim of any war. It is also for us, all of us who may never fully understand but must watch anyway: we who must give our attention like the precious resource that it is, as Gen knows. *Grave of the Fireflies* ends in a haunting and transformative image on this theme. Perished in the train station, Seita's soul emerges from his body and joins the soul of his sister. There are other emaciated bodies in the train station all around him, we realize as he leaves, others who are dying or may soon be dead. Seita's story is not the only story; it is all those stories as well, all those souls. Seita and Setsuko ride the train back to the shelter where they once lived in total isolation from the world. But that shelter does not remain a place of isolation forever. Time goes forward, and as it does, they watch it. The film ends with them sitting on a bench overlooking the modern city of Kobe, lights and skyscrapers all aglow. Their story is part of that modern world too. It must be. The past is always there, ghostly, watching us, asking if we see it. Through the art of animation, through the powers of witness, we can. As Sergei Eisenstein once remarked, the *anima* that gives us the word *animation* actually means *soul*.

ACKNOWLEDGMENTS

It is a pleasure to acknowledge the many people who have made this book possible. Above all, I want to thank the animators featured in these pages, those living and those passed, whose work has so inspired and moved me. Many have risked their lives in creating these films, and all of them have engaged in acts of remembrance and witness at great personal and psychic cost. I am grateful for their art, their grace, and their humanity and for all the ways in which they have enriched our understandings of history and the human condition.

At the University of Chicago Press, I want to give my deep thanks to my editor Timothy Mennel, whose guidance shaped this book from the outset and whose support for this project has been immutable. I am also thankful to Mark Reschke for his keen eye and contributions, to Jim Farned for his detailed work, and to Susannah Engstrom for her assistance throughout. At the Kneerim and Williams Agency, I am grateful to Ike Williams and Lucy Cleland for supporting and shepherding this project from its earliest days.

I want to thank Jerome Morrissey, chief executive officer of the Global E-Schools and Communities Initiative, or GESCI, a United Nations–founded initiative in Nairobi, Kenya, for permission to use an image from *Children of War* on the cover of this book. GESCI's work training students and young adults in animation and other arts is an inspiration, and *Children of War* is just one testament to their achievements. My thanks to Angela Arnott and Rachel Wambua at GESCI for their assistance as well. I also want to extend my thanks to Johns Hopkins University Press for permission to reprint portions of my article "Animating the War: The First World War and Children's Cartoons in America" (*The Lion and the Unicorn* 31, no. 2), where some of the material in this book first appeared.

This book would not be the same without the input of friends and colleagues. In particular, I would like to thank Scott Bukatman for his always trenchant comments. Likewise, Peter Knox and his colleagues at the Baker-Nord Center for the Humanities at Case Western Reserve University, who responded to an early version of this work. In my home department at the University of Texas at Austin, Elizabeth Cullingford and Douglas Bruster both read pieces of this project, and I am grateful for their attention. I am doubly grateful to Liz in her capacity as department chair for the years of guidance and assistance she provided throughout, and to Doug for his unfailing wisdom and mentorship. My thanks also go to Janine Barchas, James Loehlin, and Elizabeth Scala for their help and sage advice throughout. Within the College of Liberal Arts, I am honored to thank Dean Randy Diehl for his steadfast support and encouragement, and I am obliged to Deans Richard Flores and Esther Raizen for the subvention grant that they generously made available.

I am especially thankful to my research assistant on this project, Dylan Davidson, who played an essential role in helping this work come into being. I have every confidence that Dylan will soon be writing his own books on film and animation, and I greatly look forward to reading them. I would be remiss if I did not also thank the many students who have enrolled in my courses on animation history and theory over the years. Those students, some of whom have gone on to become animators themselves and all of whom have inspired me, were deeply influential in shaping the ideas contained here, and I am grateful for their probing thoughts and questions. I am equally grateful for the influence of one of my own teachers from when I was an undergraduate first studying animation. John Culhane's class on the history of animation at New York University's Tisch School of the Arts will always be a touchstone of my intellectual life, and this book would not exist without him.

On a personal note, I want to thank the friends and family who were with me throughout this process. To Diane and Tom Dickinson, the Popolizio family and the Trotto family, and to my uncle John Andriulli, I offer my continued gratitude and appreciation. To my mother, Donna, who has been by my side since my earliest days watching cartoons in the living room, thank you. To my husband, David, who has been watching animation with me for close to two decades now, thank you. To my children, Cyrus, Sophia, and Gabriel, who all now have their own favorite cartoons that I can watch alongside them, thank you too: this book is dedicated to you, with love.

NOTES

PREFACE

1. Tom Shales, "A Duck for All Seasons," *Washington Post*, June 24, 1984.

2. See, for instance, Tracey Mollet, *Cartoons in Hard Times: The Animated Shorts of Disney and Warner Brothers in Depression and War, 1932–1945* (London: Bloomsbury, 2017); and Michael S. Shull and David E. Wilt, eds., *Doing Their Bit: Wartime American Animated Short Films, 1939–1945*, 2nd ed. (Jefferson, NC: McFarland, 2004). For a world history of propaganda animation during the Second World War, see Sébastien Roffat, *Animation et propagande: Les dessins animés pendant la Seconde Guerre mondiale* (Paris: Editions L'Harmattan, 2005).

3. See, for instance, Hikari Hori, *Promiscuous Media: Film and Visual Culture in Imperial Japan, 1926–1945* (Ithaca, NY: Cornell University Press, 2018); and Peter B. High, *The Imperial Screen: Japanese Film Culture in the Fifteen Years' War, 1931–1945* (Madison: University of Wisconsin Press, 2003).

4. See, for instance, Rolf Giesen and J. P. Storm, *Animation under the Swastika: A History of Trickfilm in Nazi Germany, 1933–1945* (Jefferson, NC: McFarland, 2012).

5. See, for instance, the chapter "The First World War: British Animated Cartoons and Their International Contexts" in Malcolm Cook, *Early British Animation: From Page and Stage to Cinema Screen* (London: Palgrave Macmillan, 2018); Ülo Pikkov, "On the Topics and Style of Soviet Animated Films," *Baltic Screen Media Review* 4 (2016): 17–37; and Maya Balakirsky Katz, *Drawing the Iron Curtain: Jews and the Golden Age of Soviet Animation* (New Brunswick, NJ: Rutgers University Press, 2016).

6. See Annabelle Honess Roe, *Animated Documentary* (London: Palgrave Macmillan, 2013).

7. See Hillary L. Chute, *Disaster Drawn: Visual Witness, Comics, and Documentary Form* (Cambridge, MA: Harvard University Press, 2016).

INTRODUCTION

1. For the most comprehensive source on Arthur Melbourne-Cooper, from which his connection to the 1899 Empire Theatre screening comes, see Tjitte de Vries and Ati Mul, *"They Thought It Was a Marvel": Arthur Melbourne-Cooper (1874–1961), Pioneer of Puppet Animation* (Amsterdam: Amsterdam University Press, 2009). For alternate views of Melbourne-Cooper's early career, see Frank Gray, "Smith versus Melbourne-Cooper:

History and Counter-History," *Film History* 11, no. 3 (1999): 246–61; and Stephen Bottomore, "Smith versus Melbourne-Cooper: An End to the Dispute," *Film History* 14, no. 1 (2002): 57–73. On the controversy around the dating of *Matches Appeal*, see note 6 below.

2. Tom Gunning, "The Cinema of Attractions: Early Cinema, Its Spectator and the Avant Garde," in *Early Cinema: Space, Frame, Narrative*, ed. Thomas Elsaesser, 56–62 (London: BFI, 1990), 57. Cf. André Gaudreault and Tom Gunning, "Le Cinéma des premier temps: Un défi a histoire du film?," in *Histories du cinema: Nouvelles approaches*, ed. J. Aumont, A. Gaudreault, and M. Marie (Paris: Publications de la Sorbonne, 1989), 49–63.

3. De Vries and Mul, 54. De Vries and Mul's description is specifically of Melbourne-Cooper's later film *A Dream of Toyland* (1907), though they connect all six of the director's surviving animated films to his ability to create "miracles which still satisfy our stubborn and ineradicable want of sanctuaries." See De Vries and Mul, 36.

4. Stanley Cavell, "Words of Welcome," in *Cavell on Film*, ed. William Rothman, 205–20 (Albany: State University of New York Press, 2005), 212.

5. Dan Torre, *Animation: Process, Cognition, and Actuality* (London: Bloomsbury, 2017), 233. Torre's use of irreality derives from the work of philosopher Nicholas Rescher. For a different discussion of animation and irreality, drawn from philosopher Gaston Bachelard's idea of the "irreality function" in human psychology, see Scott Bukatman, *The Poetics of Slumberland: Animated Spirits and the Animating Spirit* (Berkeley: University of California Press, 2012), 7. Cf. Nicholas Rescher, *Imagining Irreality: A Study of Unreal Possibilities* (Chicago: Open Court Publishing, 2003); and Gaston Bachelard, *The Poetics of Reverie: Childhood, Language, and the Cosmos*, trans. Daniel Russell (Boston: Beacon Press, 1971).

6. For a useful overview of the controversy surrounding the date for *Matches Appeal*, see Donald Crafton, "Arthur Melbourne-Cooper's Shadow of Doubt," preface to Tjitte de Vries and Ati Mul, *"They Thought It Was a Marvel": Arthur Melbourne-Cooper (1874–1961), Pioneer of Puppet Animation* (Amsterdam: Amsterdam University Press, 2009), 11–18. De Vries and Mul present their case for the 1899 date at length in the chapters that follow.

7. Gilles Deleuze, *Cinema 2: The Time-Image*, trans. Hugh Tomlinson and Robert Galeta (Minneapolis: University of Minnesota Press, 1989), 57.

8. Annette Wieviorka, *The Era of the Witness*, trans. Jared Stark (Ithaca, NY: Cornell University Press, 2006), 96.

9. See Walter Benjamin, *Gesammelte Schriften*, vol. 1, ed. Rolf Tiedemann and Hermann Schweppenhäuser (Frankfurt: Suhrkamp, 1972), 1236; quoted and translated in Matthias Fritsch, *The Promise of Memory: History and Politics in Marx, Benjamin, and Derrida* (Albany: State University of New York Press, 2012), 121; and Deleuze, *Cinema 2*, xi.

10. Julia Kristeva, "For Shoshana Felman: Truth and Art," in *The Claims of Literature: A Shoshana Felman Reader*, ed. Emily Sun, Eyal Peretz, and Ulrich Baer, 315–21 (New York: Fordham University Press, 2007), 316.

11. Kristeva, 316.

12. Bukatman, *The Poetics of Slumberland*, 2. Bukatman's use of the term *illogics* is taken from Bachelard.

13. Walter Benjamin, "Theses on the Philosophy of History," in *Illuminations*, ed. Hannah Arendt, trans. Harry Zohn, 253–64 (New York: Schocken Books, 1969), 255.

14. Elaine Scarry, *The Body in Pain: The Making and Unmaking of the World* (Oxford: Oxford University Press, 1985), 61.

15. Scarry, 63–64.

16. Scarry, 58.

17. Scarry, 25.

18. Virginia Woolf, *Three Guineas*, in *"A Room of One's Own" and "Three Guineas,"* ed. Anna Snaith, 87–216 (Oxford: Oxford University Press, 1992), 95. Quoted in Susan Sontag, *Regarding the Pain of Others* (New York: Farrar, Straus and Giroux, 2003), 4.

19. Simone Weil, "The *Iliad*, or the Poem of Force," trans. Mary McCarthy, *Chicago Review* 18, no. 2 (1965): 5–30, 6.

20. Weil, 6.

21. Weil, 7.

22. Weil, 11.

23. Weil, 23.

24. Sergei Eisenstein, *Eisenstein on Disney*, ed. Jay Leyda, trans. Alan Upchurch (New York: Methuen, 1988), 21.

25. Roger Cardinal, "Thinking through Things: The Presence of Objects in the Early Films of Jan Švankmajer," in *Dark Alchemy: The Films of Jan Svankmajer*, ed. Peter Hames, 78–95 (Westport, CT: Greenwood Press, 1995), 89. Quoted in Paul Wells, *Understanding Animation* (London: Routledge, 1998), 26.

26. Paul Wells, *Animation and America* (New Brunswick, NJ: Rutgers University Press, 2002), 17.

27. Susan Sontag, *Regarding the Pain of Others* (New York: Farrar, Straus and Giroux, 2003), 18.

28. Sontag, 108.

29. Susan Sontag, "Freak Show," *New York Review of Books*, November 15, 1973.

30. Sontag.

31. Susan Sontag, *On Photography* (New York: Farrar, Straus & Giroux, 1973), 120.

32. Sontag, 4.

33. Quoted in Sontag, *Regarding*, 52.

34. Sontag, *On Photography*, 2.

35. Sontag, *Regarding*, 46.

36. Hillary L. Chute, *Disaster Drawn: Visual Witness, Comics, and Documentary Form* (Cambridge, MA: Harvard University Press, 2016), 14, 4.

37. Deleuze, *Cinema 2*, 58–59.

38. Sontag, *Regarding*, 46.

39. Sontag, 14.

40. Judith Butler, *Precarious Life: The Powers of Mourning and Violence* (New York: Verso, 2004), 34.

41. Emmanuel Levinas, *Entre Nous: Thinking-of-the-Other*, trans. Michael B. Smith and Barbara Harshav (London: Continuum, 1998), 85.

42. Sontag, "Freak Show."

43. Sontag.

44. Emmanuel Levinas, *Totality and Infinity: An Essay on Exteriority*, trans. Alphonso Lingis (Dordrecht: Kluwer Academic Publishers, 1991), 23. Emphasis added.

45. Dori Laub, "An Event without a Witness: Truth, Testimony and Survival," in Shoshana Felman and Dori Laub, *Testimony: Crises of Witnessing in Literature, Psychoanalysis, and History*, 75–92 (London: Routledge, 1992), 75.

46. Levinas, *Totality and Infinity*, 24.

47. Levinas, 25, 24.

48. Levinas, 23, 24, 297.

49. Quoted in Katherine Sarafian, "Flashing Digital Animations: Pixar's Digital Aesthetic," in *New Media: Theories of Practices of Digitextuality*, ed. Anna Everett and John T. Caldwell, 209–24 (London: Routledge, 2003), 215. In context, Gordon's point has to do with the ability to achieve an exacting verisimilitude in animated character performance, which he attributes to the total control that the animator maintains over the whole animated universe of a film.

50. Laub, 78.

51. "Bardin: Today a Great Many of People in Russia Are Seized with Depression— Our Nearest Neighbor Suddenly Has Become an Enemy," *Gordon*, October 17, 2014, http://english.gordonua.com/news/exclusiveenglish/bardin-46697.html.

52. "Bardin: Today"

CHAPTER ONE

1. "Walter Tournier, del joven militante al cineaste de animación," *La Izquierda Diario Uruguay*, December 8, 2016, https://www.laizquierdadiario.com.uy/Walter -Tournier-de-joven-militante-a-cineasta-de-animacion. Original translation.

2. "Primavera estudiantil: Primera muestra de cine politico," Información de interés, Universidad de la República Uruguay, September 13, 2017, http://www.universi dad.edu.uy/prensa/renderItem/itemId/41051. Original translation.

3. Shoshana Felman, "Education and Crisis, or the Vicissitudes of Teaching," in Shoshana Felman and Dori Laub, *Testimony: Crises of Witnessing in Literature, Psychoanalysis, and History*, 1–56 (London: Routledge, 1992), 3. Emphasis in original.

4. "Uruguay," *Freedom in the World 2013*, Freedom House (2013), https://freedom house.org/report/freedom-world/2013/uruguay.

5. William Kozlenko, "The Animated Cartoon and Walt Disney," *New Theatre* (August 1936): 16–18, 27.

6. Quoted in Katherine Sarafian, "Flashing Digital Animations: Pixar's Digital Aesthetic," in *New Media: Theories of Practices of Digitextuality*, ed. Anna Everett and John T. Caldwell, 209–24 (London: Routledge, 2003), 215.

7. James C. Scott, *Domination and the Arts of Resistance: Hidden Transcripts* (New Haven, CT: Yale University Press, 1990), 2.

8. Scott, 4.

9. Scott, 4–5.

10. Sébastien Roffat, *Propagandes animées: Le dessin animé politique entre 1933 et 1945* (Paris: Bazaar & Company, 2010), 152. Original translation.

11. Walter Benjamin, *The Origin of German Tragic Drama*, trans. John Osborne (London: Verso, 1998), 188, 186.

12. Benjamin, 164–65.

13. Wan Laiming and Wan Guchan, "Within the Popular Eastern Fairy Tale— *Journey to the West*, *Princess Iron Fan* Production Process," trans. Tze-Yue G. Hu, in Hu, *Frames of Anime: Culture and Image-Building*, 169–73 (Hong Kong: Hong Kong University Press, 2010), 170, 173.

14. Wan Laiming and Wan Guchan, 171.

15. Translation by Hongmei Sun in Sun, *Transforming Monkey: Adaptation and Representation of a Chinese Epic* (Seattle: University of Washington Press, 2018), 62.

16. William Moritz, "Resistance and Subversion in Animated Film of the Nazi Era: The Case of Hans Fischerkoesen," *Animation Journal* 1, no. 1 (Fall 1992): 4–33, 4.

17. Moritz, "Resistance and Subversion," 25.

18. Oliver Klatt, "The Life of Germany's Own Walt Disney," *Der Spiegel*, May 9, 2013, http://www.spiegel.de/international/germany/how-hans-fischerkoesen-trans formed-german-animation-a-898814.html.

19. Benjamin, *The Origin of German Tragic Drama*, 188, 186.

20. Moritz, "Resistance and Subversion," 23.

21. See Chris Robinson, *Unsung Heroes of Animation* (Bloomington: Indiana University Press, 2005), 13.

22. See Robinson, 13.

23. Hannah Arendt, "Lying in Politics: Reflections on the Pentagon Papers," in *Crises of the Republic: Lying in Politics, Civil Disobedience on Violence, Thoughts on Politics, and Revolution* (New York: Harcourt Brace & Company, 1972), 1–48, 42–43.

24. Quoted in John Canemaker, *Walt Disney's Nine Old Men and the Art of Animation* (White Plains, NY: Disney Editions, 2001), 85.

25. See Stefanie Van de Peer, "From Animated Cartoons to Suspended Animation: A History of Syrian Animation," in *Animation in the Middle East: Practice and Aesthetics from Baghdad to Casablanca*, ed. Stefanie van de Peer, 107–28 (London: I. B. Tauris, 2017), 115.

26. Benjamin, *The Origin of German Tragic Drama*, 164–65.

27. See, for instance, Noel Brown, *The Children's Film: Genre, Nation, and Narrative* (New York: Columbia University Press, 2017), 20.

28. Quoted in Cerise Howard, "The Passion of the Peasant Poet: Jiří Trnka, *A Midsummer Night's Dream* and *The Hand*," *Senses of Cinema* 66 (February 2013), http://sensesofcinema.com/2013/cteq/the-passion-of-the-peasant-poet-jiri-trnka-a -midsummer-nights-dream-and-the-hand/.

29. William Moritz, "Narrative Strategies for Resistance and Protest in Eastern European Animation," in *A Reader in Animation Studies*, ed. Jayne Pilling, 38–47 (Bloomington: Indiana University Press, 1998), 40.

30. Paul Wells, *Understanding Animation* (London: Routledge, 1998), 88.

31. Suzanne Buchan, *The Quay Brothers: Into a Metaphysical Playroom* (Minneapolis: University of Minnesota Press, 2011), 139.

32. See Karl F. Cohen, *Forbidden Animation: Censored Cartoons and Blacklisted Animators in America* (Jefferson, NC: McFarland, 2004), 94.

33. Jan Švankmajer, "Decalogue," trans. Tereza Stehlíková, *Vertigo* 3, no. 1 (Spring 2006), https://www.closeupfilmcentre.com/vertigo_magazine/volume-3-issue-1-spring -2006/decalogue/.

34. "Living Cinema," Pierre Hébert, http://pierrehebert.com/en/performance /living-cinema/.

35. Quoted in Shoshana Felman, "Education and Crisis," 3. Cf. Emmanuel Levinas, *Ethique et infini: Dialogues avec Philippe Nemo* (Paris: Fayard, 1982), 115.

CHAPTER TWO

1. See the Facebook page https://www.facebook.com/ExtremismKills/, where the video first appeared, or the YouTube channel https://www.youtube.com/channel /UCnUOgK6aTlB34Zjt5qdfqwg, where it was later reposted. The video has also been posted extensively elsewhere on the web.

2. See "Iranian Studio Making 'Conquest of Mecca' in Response to Saudi Animation," *Tehran Times*, January 6, 2018, http://www.tehrantimes.com/news/420076/Iranian-studio-making-Conquest-of-Mecca-in-response-to-Saudi. See also "War in Yemen," Global Conflict Tracker, Council on Foreign Relations, https://www.cfr.org/interactives/global-conflict-tracker#!/global-conflict-tracker.

3. Elaine Scarry, *The Body in Pain: The Making and Unmaking of the World* (Oxford: Oxford University Press, 1985), 62.

4. Scarry, 58.

5. Susan Sontag, *Regarding the Pain of Others* (New York: Farrar, Straus and Giroux, 2003), 11.

6. Scarry, 59.

7. Quoted in John Canemaker, *Felix: The Twisted Tale of the World's Most Famous Cat* (New York: Da Capo Press, 1991), 88.

8. Walter Benjamin, "The Storyteller: Reflections on the Works of Nikolai Leskov," in *Illuminations*, ed. Hannah Arendt, trans. Harry Zohn (New York: Schocken Books, 1968), 83–110, 84.

9. Canemaker, *Felix*, 48.

10. Canemaker, 70.

11. Quoted in Neal Gabler, *Walt Disney: The Triumph of the American Imagination* (New York: Random House, 2006), 42.

12. Bill Brown, "Thing Theory," *Critical Inquiry* 28, no. 1 (Autumn 2001): 1–22, 4.

13. Brown, 5.

14. Scarry, *The Body in Pain*, 66–67.

15. Norman McLaren, "Letter to Jean McLaren," September 26, 1949, GAA/31/C/1/1949, Norman McLaren Correspondence: Letters Written by McLaren to His Parents, Norman McLaren Archive, University of Stirling Archives and Special Collections, University of Stirling Library. Cf. "Norman McLaren's Chinese Odyssey," October 7, 2011, University of Stirling Archives, http://archives.wordpress.stir.ac.uk/2011/10/07/norman-mclarens-chinese-odyssey/.

16. Norman McLaren, "I Saw the Chinese Reds Take Over," *Maclean's Magazine*, October 15, 1950, 10, 74.

17. Emmanuel Levinas, *Entre Nous: Thinking-of-the-Other*, trans. Michael B. Smith and Barbara Harshav (London: Continuum, 1998), 85.

18. See Albert Ohayon, "*Neighbours*: The NFB's Second Oscar Winner," NFB Blog, February 27, 2011, https://blog.nfb.ca/blog/2011/02/27/neighbours-the-nfbs-second-oscar-winner/.

19. Michael J. Arlen, "Living-Room War," in *Living-Room War* (Syracuse, NY: Syracuse University Press, 1997), 6–9, 6.

20. Scarry, *The Body in Pain*, 75.

21. Scarry, 57.

22. Scarry, 71.

23. See Ronald Holloway, *Z is for Zagreb* (London: Tantivy Press, 1972), 9.

24. Giannalberto Bendazzi, *Animation: A World History*, vol. 3, *Contemporary Times* (Boca Raton, FL: CRC Press, 2016), 166.

25. "A Cartoon with a Message," *Motion Picture Herald*, December 9, 1939, 11.

26. See Timothy S. Susanin, *Walt before Mickey: Disney's Early Years, 1919–1928* (Jackson: University Press of Mississippi, 2011), 39.

27. Susan Sontag, *On Photography* (New York: Farrar, Straus & Giroux, 1973), 120.

28. While most of the live-action footage on which the rotoscoped portions of the short were based was filmed on the MGM lot, the animators' explicit goal was to evoke newsreel material. One article in an MGM promotional magazine likened *Peace on Earth* to "a current newsreel," only one that aims "to create fantasy out of grim reality." See Fred C. Quimby, "Animating Mother Nature," *Metro-Goldwyn-Mayer Short Story* (November–December 1939), 6–8, 8. (The details on live-action filming for *Peace on Earth* come from the account of animation historian Jim Korkin regarding Harman's recollections at the Cinecon 16 conference in 1980. See https://cartoon research.com/index.php/animation-anecdotes-138/.)

29. Sontag, *On Photography*, 4, 3; *Regarding*, 47.

30. On Harman's thoughts regarding his legacy and the importance of *Peace on Earth*, see in particular his 1973 interview with Michael Barrier. Cf. http://www.michaelbarrier.com/Interviews/Harman/interview_hugh_harman.htm.

CHAPTER THREE

1. See Paula Callus, "Animation as Socio-Political Commentary: An Analysis of the Animated Films of Congolese Director Jean Michel Kibushi," *Journal of African Media Studies* 2, no. 1 (2010): 55–71, 63.

2. Susan Sontag, *On Photography* (New York: Farrar, Straus & Giroux, 1973), 4.

3. Susan Sontag, *Regarding the Pain of Others* (New York: Farrar, Straus and Giroux, 2003), 46.

4. Ryszard Kapuściński, *Another Day of Life*, trans. William R. Brand and Katarzyna Mroczkowska-Brand (New York: Vintage, 2001), 96.

5. Walter Benjamin, "Theses on the Philosophy of History," in *Illuminations*, ed. Hannah Arendt, trans. Harry Zohn (New York: Schocken Books, 1969), 253–64, 255.

6. Julia Kristeva, "For Shoshana Felman: Truth and Art," in *The Claims of Literature: A Shoshana Felman Reader*, ed. Emily Sun, Eyal Peretz, and Ulrich Baer, 315–21 (New York: Fordham University Press, 2007), 316.

7. "Leaving the Village (2007)," Yantrakalā: The Machine Art, http://www.yan trakala.com/animation/ltv/.

8. Kristin Thompson, "The Concept of Cinematic Excess," *Cine-Tracts* 1 (Summer 1977): 54–64, 55–56.

9. Kamran Rastegar, "On Palestinian Cinema," in "Interview: Conversations Arbitrary and Definitive," special issue, *Bidoun* 8 (Fall 2006), https://bidoun.org/issues/8-interviews#rashid-masharawi-buthina-canaan-khoury-nahed-awwad-hazim-bitar-annemarie-jacir-and-ahmad-habash.

10. Scarry, *The Body in Pain*, 75.

11. Simone Weil, "The Iliad, or the Poem of Force," trans. Mary McCarthy, *Chicago Review* 18, no. 2 (1965): 5–30, 17.

12. Jonathan Murray, review of *Waltz with Bashir*, *Cinéaste* 34, no. 2 (Spring 2009): 65, 68.

13. Quoted in Murray, 68.

14. Garrett Stewart, "Screen Memory in *Waltz with Bashir*," *Film Quarterly* 63, no. 3 (Spring 2010): 58–62, 62.

15. See Clare Kitson, *Yuri Norstein and "Tale of Tales": An Animator's Journey* (Bloomington: Indiana University Press, 2005): 7, 10, 13.

16. Trans. Gaby and Vitaly Yerenkov. See Kitson, 12.

CHAPTER FOUR

1. See "Loss of *Lusitania* Shown on Films: Artist McCay Depicts Terrific Tragedy at the Press Club," *Washington Post*, May 3, 1917.

2. "'Sinking of the *Lusitania*' Will Be Released by Jewel," *Moving Picture Weekly* 6, no. 20 (June 29, 1918), 10.

3. Scott Bukatman, *The Poetics of Slumberland: Animated Spirits and the Animating Spirit* (Berkeley: University of California Press, 2012), 1.

4. D. B. Dowd, "Strands of a Single Cord: Comics & Animation," in *Strips, Toons, and Bluesies: Essays in Comics and Culture*, ed. D. B. Dowd and Todd Hignite, 8–34 (Princeton, NJ: Princeton Architectural Press, 2006), 19.

5. See, for instance, Annabelle Honess Roe, *Animated Documentary* (London: Palgrave Macmillan, 2013), 8.

6. Richard Crownshaw, "History and Memorialization," in *Writing the History of Memory*, ed. Stefan Berger and Bill Niven, 219–39 (London: Bloomsbury, 2014), 219.

7. Walter Benjamin, "Theses on the Philosophy of History," in *Illuminations*, ed. Hannah Arendt, trans. Harry Zohn, 253–64 (New York: Schocken Books, 1969), 255.

8. Andreas Huyssen, *Present Pasts: Urban Palimpsests and the Politics of Memory* (Stanford, CA: Stanford University Press, 2003), 101.

9. See Paula Callus, "The Rise of Kenyan Political Animation: Tactics of Subversion," in *Taking African Cartoons Seriously: Politics, Satire, and Culture*, ed. Peter Limb and Tejumola Olaniyan, 71–99 (East Lansing: Michigan State University Pres, 2018), 73–74; and Niamh Brannigan, "Blazing a Trail for the Development of East Africa's Digital Creative Media Industry," *African Brains: Innovation for Education*, March 8, 2013, https://africanbrains.net/2013/03/08/blazing-a-trail-for-the-development-of-east -africas-digital-creative-media-industry/.

10. Julia Kristeva, "For Shoshana Felman: Truth and Art," in *The Claims of Literature: A Shoshana Felman Reader*, ed. Emily Sun, Eyal Peretz, and Ulrich Baer, 315–21 (New York: Fordham University Press, 2007), 316.

11. For a further account of the incident in question, see Urvashi Butalia, *The Other Side of Silence: Voices from the Partition of India* (Durham, NC: Duke University Press, 2000).

12. See Brian Yecies and Ben Goldsmith, "Cinematic Hooks for Korean Studies: Using the 'Apache' Framework for Inspiring Students about Korea in and through Film," *International Review of Korean Studies* 7, no. 1 (2010): 47–72, 52.

13. Quoted in Paul Rankin, "Making Headlines," *Rave Magazine*, February 22, 2005, 3.

14. Shoshana Felman, "The Return of the Voice: Claude Lanzmann's *Shoah*," in Shoshana Felman and Dori Laub, *Testimony: Crises of Witnessing in Literature, Psychoanalysis, and History*, 204–80 (London: Routledge, 1992), 211.

15. Shoshana Felman, "Camus' *The Plague*, or A Monument to Witnessing," in Felman and Laub, *Testimony*, 93–119, 101.

16. Kristeva, "For Shoshana Felman," 316.

17. It is worth noting that the phrase "Polish concentration camps" has since been the subject of controversy and legislation in Borowczyk's native Poland for its potential confusion of German and Polish culpability.

18. Kristeva, "For Shoshana Felman," 316.

19. Quoted in review of "Picadon," *Bulletin of the Atomic Scientists* 39, no. 7 (August 1983): 52.

20. See, for instance, Catherine Munroe Hotes, review of "Picadon," January 29, 2010, Nishikata Film Review: A Journey through Visual Culture, https://www.nishikata-eiga.com/2010/01/pica-don-1978.html.

21. Quoted in "Takahata and Nosaka: Two Grave Voices in Animation," *Animerica: Anime & Manga Monthly* 2, no. 11 (November 1994): 6–11, 11.

22. "Takahata and Nosaka," 10.

23. "Takahata and Nosaka," 8.

24. "Takahata and Nosaka," 8.

25. "Takahata and Nosaka," 8.

FILMOGRAPHY

Films and series are listed chronologically. Dates represent the year of first release. In the case of animators working internationally, the country of origin is listed first followed by the country of production.

Matches Appeal (UK, 1899 [disputed])
Colonel Heeza Liar series (USA, 1913–17)
Gertie the Dinosaur (USA, 1914)
The Gasoline Engine (USA, 1916)
The Rudiments of Flying (USA, 1916)
What Next (UK, 1916)
Britain's Effort (UK, 1918)
The Sinking of the Lusitania (USA, 1918)
Out of the Inkwell series (USA, 1921–26)
Felix Turns the Tide (USA, 1922)
The Adventures of Prince Achmed [*Die Abenteuer des Prinzen Achmed*] (Germany, 1926)
Uproar in an Art Studio [*Dà nào huàshì*] (China, 1926)
Great Guns (USA, 1927)
Barnyard Battle (USA, 1929)
Bosko the Doughboy (USA, 1931)
Sankichi the Monkey: The Storm Troopers [*Osaru no Sankichi: Totsugeki-tai*] (Japan, 1934)
The Old Mill (USA, 1937)
Snow White and the Seven Dwarfs (USA, 1937)
Go to the Front! [*Shang qian xian*] (China, 1938)
Wang Lawu Became a Soldier [*Wang Laowu qu dang bing*] (China, 1938)
Peace on Earth (USA, 1939)
Of the Little Tree That Wished for Different Leaves [*Vom Bäumlein, das andere Blätter hat gewollt*] (Germany, 1940)
Pinocchio (USA, 1940)
The Troublemaker [*Der Störenfried*] (Germany, 1940)
Fascist Jackboots Shall Not Trample Our Motherland [*Ne toptat fashiskomu sapogu nashey rodiny*] (USSR, 1941)
Princess Iron Fan [*Tiě shàn gōngzhǔ*] (China, 1941)
Der Fuehrer's Face (USA, 1942)
Donald Gets Drafted (USA, 1942)

Daffy the Commando (USA, 1943)
Education for Death (USA, 1943)
Private Snafu series (USA, 1943–46)
Reynard the Fox [*Van den vos Reynaerde*] (Netherlands, 1943)
The Scarecrow [*L'épouvantail*] (France, 1943)
The Snowman [*Der Schneemann*] (Germany, 1943)
Tokio Jokio (USA, 1943)
Victory through Air Power (USA, 1943)
Commando Duck (USA, 1944)
Ferda the Ant [*Ferda Mravenec*] (Czechoslovakia, 1944)
Nimbus Liberated [*Nimbus libéré*] (France, 1944)
The Silly Goose [*Das dumme Gänslein*] (Germany, 1944)
Il Duce Narrates [*O Ntoútse afigeítai*] (Greece, 1945)
Momotarō, Sacred Sailors [*Momotarō: Umi no Shinpei*] (Japan, 1945)
Springman and the SS [*Pérák a SS*] (Czechoslovakia, 1945)
Cherry Blossoms [*Sakura*] (Japan, 1946)
The Little Soldier [*Le petit soldat*] (France, 1947)
The Revolt of the Toys [*Vzpoura Hracek*] (Czechoslovakia, 1947)
Bunker Hill Bunny (USA, 1950)
Neighbours (Canada, 1952)
Good Will to Men (USA, 1955)
We Shall Never Die (Israel, 1959)
Moonbird (USA, 1960)
The Hole (USA, 1962)
The Games of Angels [*Les Jeux des Anges*] (Poland/France, 1964)
The Hat (USA, 1964)
Assault and Peppered (USA, 1965)
The Hand [*Ruka*] (Czechoslovakia, 1965)
Pink Panzer (USA, 1965)
Escalation (USA, 1968)
Drought [*Susza*] (Poland, 1969)
Mickey Mouse in Vietnam (USA, 1969)
Missile Pencils (North Korea, n.d. [ca. 1970])
A Lesson Not Learned [*Urok ne vprok*] (USSR, 1971)
In the Jungle There Is Much to Do [*En la selva hay mucho por hacer*] (Uruguay, 1973)
Firing Range [*Poligon*] (USSR, 1977)
Pica-don (Japan, 1979)
Tale of Tales [*Skazka skazok*] (USSR, 1979)
Dimensions of Dialogue [*Možnosti dialogu*] (Czechoslovakia, 1982)
Barefoot Gen [*Hadashi no Gen*] (Japan, 1983)
Conflict [*Konflikt*] (USSR, 1983)
There Will Come Soft Rains [*Budet laskovyy dozhd*] (Uzbekistan/USSR, 1984)
Barefoot Gen 2 [*Hadashi no Gen 2*] (Japan, 1986)
Grave of the Fireflies [*Hotaru no Haka*] (Japan, 1988)
Raining Fire [*Hi no Ame ga Furu*] (Japan, 1988)
Flora (Czechoslovakia/USA, 1989)

Lip Synch series (UK, 1989)

Summer with Kuro [*Kuro ga Ita Natsu*] (Japan, 1990)

The Death of Stalinism in Bohemia [*Konec stalinismu v Čechách*] (Czechoslovakia, 1991)

Kayoko's Diary [*Ushiro no shoumen dare*] (Japan, 1991)

Kinshasa, Black September [*Kinshasa, Septembre Noir*] (Zaire/Belgium, 1992)

November 1992 Sarajevo [*Studeni 1992 Sarajevo*] (Croatia/Bosnia and Herzegovina/ Belgium, 1995)

Black Notebook [*Carnet noir*] (Burundi/Belgium, 1996)

The Cake [*Kolač*] (Croatia, 1997)

Silence (UK, 1998)

Between Science and Garbage (Canada, ca. 2001)

Birthday Boy (South Korea/Australia, 2004)

Endangered Species (Canada, ca. 2004)

Nagasaki 1945: The Angelus Bells [*Nagasaki 1945: Angelus no Kane*] (Japan, 2005)

Special Forces (Canada, ca. 2006)

Leaving the Village (Nepal, 2007)

Men in Black/Operation Homecoming: Writing the Wartime Experience (USA, 2007)

Persepolis (Iran/France, 2007)

The General's Boot [*Hidā Al-Jinrāl*] (Syria/Saudi Arabia, 2008)

Tolerantia (Bosnia and Herzegovina, 2008)

Waltz with Bashir [*Vals Im Bashir*] (Israel, 2008)

Fatenah (Palestinian territories, 2009)

The Barbarians [*Les Barbares*] (France, 2010)

Don't Forget (Australia, 2010)

Point of Mouth (Bosnia and Herzegovina/Sweden, 2010)

White Tape (Israel/Denmark, 2010)

Sentenced to Death (Australia, 2011)

1947: Haunting Dreams (India, 2012)

Nyosha (Israel, 2012)

Children of War (Kenya, 2013)

Fortress [*Krepost*] (Russia, 2013)

Frozen (USA, 2013)

Bear Story [*Historia de un oso*] (Chile, 2014)

Battle of the Persian Gulf [*Nabarde Khalije Fars*] (Iran, 2015)

Conquest of Jerusalem (Iran, 2015)

The Extremists' Game Destroys the Innocent (country unknown, 2015)

The Last Day of War [*Posledniy den' voyny*] (Russia, 2016)

Saudi Deterrent Force (Saudi Arabia, 2017)

BIBLIOGRAPHY

Arendt, Hannah. "Lying in Politics: Reflections on the Pentagon Papers." In *Crises of the Republic: Lying in Politics, Civil Disobedience on Violence, Thoughts on Politics, and Revolution*, 1–48. New York: Harcourt Brace & Company, 1972.

Arlen, Michael J. *Living-Room War*. Syracuse, NY: Syracuse University Press, 1997.

Bachelard, Gaston. *The Poetics of Reverie: Childhood, Language, and the Cosmos*. Translated by Daniel Russell. Boston: Beacon Press, 1971.

"Bardin: Today a Great Many of People in Russia Are Seized with Depression—Our Nearest Neighbor Suddenly Has Become an Enemy." *Gordon*, October 17, 2014.

Bendazzi, Giannalberto. *Animation: A World History*. Vol. 3, *Contemporary Times*. Boca Raton, FL: CRC Press, 2016.

Benjamin, Walter. *Gesammelte Schriften*. Vol. 1. Edited by Rolf Tiedemann and Hermann Schweppenhäuser. Frankfurt: Suhrkamp, 1972.

Benjamin, Walter. *Illuminations*. Edited by Hannah Arendt. Translated by Harry Zohn. New York: Schocken Books, 1969.

Benjamin, Walter. *The Origin of German Tragic Drama*. Translated by John Osborne. London: Verso, 1998.

Bottomore, Stephen. "Smith versus Melbourne-Cooper: An End to the Dispute." *Film History* 14, no. 1 (2002): 57–73.

Brannigan, Niamh. "Blazing a Trail for the Development of East Africa's Digital Creative Media Industry." *African Brains: Innovation for Education*, March 8, 2013.

Buchan, Suzanne. *The Quay Brothers: Into a Metaphysical Playroom*. Minneapolis: University of Minnesota Press, 2011.

Bukatman, Scott. *The Poetics of Slumberland: Animated Spirits and the Animating Spirit*. Berkeley: University of California Press, 2012.

Butalia, Urvashi. *The Other Side of Silence: Voices from the Partition of India*. Durham, NC: Duke University Press, 2000.

Butler, Judith. *Precarious Life: The Powers of Mourning and Violence*. New York: Verso, 2004. Reprint, Berkeley: University of California Press, 2012.

Brandon, Laura. *Art & War*. London: I. B. Tauris, 2012.

Brown, Bill. "Thing Theory." *Critical Inquiry* 28, no. 1 (Autumn 2001): 1–22.

Brown, Noel. *The Children's Film: Genre, Nation, and Narrative*. New York: Columbia University Press, 2017.

Callus, Paula. "Animation as Socio-Political Commentary: An Analysis of the Animated Films of Congolese Director Jean Michel Kibushi." *Journal of African Media Studies* 2, no. 1 (2010): 55–71.

Callus, Paula. "The Rise of Kenyan Political Animation: Tactics of Subversion." In *Taking African Cartoons Seriously: Politics, Satire, and Culture*, edited by Peter Limb and Tejumola Olaniyan, 71–99. East Lansing: Michigan State University Pres, 2018.

Canemaker, John. *Felix: The Twisted Tale of the World's Most Famous Cat.* New York: Da Capo Press, 1991.

Canemaker, John. *Walt Disney's Nine Old Men and the Art of Animation.* White Plains, NY: Disney Editions, 2001.

Cardinal, Roger. "Thinking through Things: The Presence of Objects in the Early Films of Jan Švankmajer." In *Dark Alchemy: The Films of Jan Svankmajer*, edited by Peter Hames. Westport, CT: Greenwood Press, 1995.

"A Cartoon with a Message." *Motion Picture Herald*, December 9, 1939.

Cavell, Stanley. "Words of Welcome." In *Cavell on Film*, edited by William Rothman, 205–20. Albany: State University of New York Press, 2005.

Chute, Hillary L. *Disaster Drawn: Visual Witness, Comics, and Documentary Form.* Cambridge, MA: Harvard University Press, 2016.

Cohen, Karl F. *Forbidden Animation: Censored Cartoons and Blacklisted Animators in America.* Jefferson, NC: McFarland, 2004.

Cook, Malcolm. *Early British Animation: From Page and Stage to Cinema Screen.* London: Palgrave Macmillan, 2018.

Crafton, Donald. "Arthur Melbourne-Cooper's Shadow of Doubt." Preface to Tjitte De Vries and Ati Mul, *"They Thought It Was a Marvel": Arthur Melbourne-Cooper (1874–1961), Pioneer of Puppet Animation.* Amsterdam: Amsterdam University Press, 2009.

Deleuze, Gilles. *Cinema 2: The Time-Image.* Translated by Hugh Tomlinson and Robert Galeta. Minneapolis: University of Minnesota Press, 1989.

De Vries, Tjitte, and Ati Mul. *"They Thought It Was a Marvel": Arthur Melbourne-Cooper (1874–1961), Pioneer of Puppet Animation.* Amsterdam: Amsterdam University Press, 2009.

Dowd, D. B. "Strands of a Single Cord: Comics & Animation." In *Strips, Toons, and Bluesies: Essays in Comics and Culture*, edited by D. B. Dowd and Todd Hignite, 8–34. Princeton, NJ: Princeton Architectural Press, 2006.

Eisenstein, Sergei. *Eisenstein on Disney.* Edited by Jay Leyda. Translated by Alan Upchurch. New York: Methuen, 1988.

Felman, Shoshana, and Dori Laub. *Testimony: Crises of Witnessing in Literature, Psychoanalysis, and History.* London: Routledge, 1992.

Fritsch, Matthias. *The Promise of Memory: History and Politics in Marx, Benjamin, and Derrida.* Albany: State University of New York Press, 2012.

Gabler, Neal. *Walt Disney: The Triumph of the American Imagination.* New York: Random House, 2006.

Gaudreault, André, and Tom Gunning. "Le Cinéma des premier temps: Un défi a histoire du film?" In *Histoires du cinema: Nouvelles approaches*, edited by J. Aumont, A. Gaudreault, and M. Marie. Paris: Publications de la Sorbonne, 1989.

Giessen, Rolf, and J. P. Storm. *Animation under the Swastika: A History of Trickfilm in Nazi Germany, 1933–1945.* Jefferson, NC: McFarland, 2012.

Gray, Frank. "Smith versus Melbourne-Cooper: History and Counter-History." *Film History* 11, no. 3 (1999): 246–61.

Gunning, Tom. "The Cinema of Attractions: Early Cinema, Its Spectator and the Avant Garde." In *Early Cinema: Space, Frame, Narrative*, edited by Thomas Elsaesser, 56–62. London: BFI, 1990.

High, Peter B. *The Imperial Screen: Japanese Film Culture in the Fifteen Years' War, 1931–1945*. Madison: University of Wisconsin Press, 2003.

Hotes, Catherine Munroe. Review of "Picadon." January 29, 2010. Nishikata Film Review: A Journey through Visual Culture.

Holloway, Ronald. *Z Is for Zagreb*. London: Tantivy Press, 1972.

Hori, Hikari. *Promiscuous Media: Film and Visual Culture in Imperial Japan, 1926–1945*. Ithaca, NY: Cornell University Press, 2018.

Howard, Cerise. "The Passion of the Peasant Poet: Jiří Trnka, *A Midsummer Night's Dream* and *The Hand*." *Senses of Cinema* 66 (February 2013).

Hu, Tze-Yue G. *Frames of Anime: Culture and Image-Building*. Hong Kong: Hong Kong University Press, 2010.

Huyssen, Andreas. *Present Pasts: Urban Palimpsests and the Politics of Memory*. Stanford, CA: Stanford University Press, 2003.

"Iranian Studio Making 'Conquest of Mecca' in Response to Saudi Animation." *Tehran Times*, January 6, 2018.

Kapuściński, Ryszard. *Another Day of Life*. Translated by William R. Brand and Katarzyna Mroczkowska-Brand. New York: Vintage, 2001.

Katz, Maya Balakirsky. *Drawing the Iron Curtain: Jews and the Golden Age of Soviet Animation*. New Brunswick, NJ: Rutgers University Press, 2016.

Kitson, Clare. *Yuri Norstein and "Tale of Tales": An Animator's Journey*. Bloomington: Indiana University Press, 2005.

Klatt, Oliver. "The Life of Germany's Own Walt Disney." *Der Spiegel*, May 9, 2013.

Kozlenko, William. "The Animated Cartoon and Walt Disney." *New Theatre* (August 1936): 16–18.

Kristeva, Julia. "For Shoshana Felman: Truth and Art." In *The Claims of Literature: A Shoshana Felman Reader*, edited by Emily Sun, Eyal Peretz, and Ulrich Baer. New York: Fordham University Press, 2007.

"Leaving the Village (2007)." Movies. Yantrakalā: The Machine Art. www.yantrakala.com.

Levinas, Emmanuel. *Entre Nous: Thinking-of-the-Other*. Translated by Michael B. Smith and Barbara Harshav. London: Continuum, 1998.

Levinas, Emmanuel. *Ethique et infini: Dialogues avec Philippe Nemo*. Paris: Fayard, 1982.

Levinas, Emmanuel. *Totality and Infinity: An Essay on Exteriority*. Translated by Alphonso Lingis. Dordrecht: Kluwer Academic Publishers, 1991.

"Living Cinema." Performance. Pierre Hébert. www.pierrehebert.com.

"Loss of *Lusitania* Shown on Films: Artist McCay Depicts Terrific Tragedy at the Press Club." *Washington Post*, May 3, 1917.

McLaren, Norman. "I Saw the Chinese Reds Take Over." *Maclean's Magazine*, October 15, 1950.

McLaren, Norman. "Letter to Jean McLaren." September 26, 1949. GAA/31/C/1/1949. Norman McLaren Correspondence: Letters Written by McLaren to His Parents. Norman McLaren Archive. University of Stirling Archives and Special Collections. University of Stirling Library.

Mollet, Tracey. *Cartoons in Hard Times: The Animated Shorts of Disney and Warner Brothers in Depression and War, 1932–1945*. London: Bloomsbury, 2017.

Moritz, William. "Narrative Strategies for Resistance and Protest in Eastern European Animation." In *A Reader in Animation Studies*, edited by Jayne Pilling, 38–47. Bloomington: Indiana University Press, 1998.

Moritz, William. "Resistance and Subversion in Animated Film of the Nazi Era: The Case of Hans Fischerkoesen." *Animation Journal* 1, no. 1 (Fall 1992): 4–33.

Murray, Jonathan. Review of *Waltz with Bashir*. *Cinéaste* 34, no. 2 (Spring 2009): 65.

"Norman McLaren's Chinese Odyssey." October 7, 2011. University of Stirling Archives. University of Stirling.

Ohayon, Albert. "*Neighbours*: The NFB's Second Oscar Winner." February 27, 2011. NFB Blog.

Pikkov, Ülo. "On the Topics and Style of Soviet Animated Films." *Baltic Screen Media Review* 4 (2016): 17–37.

"Primavera estudiantil: Primera muestra de cine politico." September 13, 2017. Información de interés. Universidad de la República Uruguay.

Quimby, Fred C. "Animating Mother Nature." *Metro-Goldwyn-Mayer Short Story*, November–December 1939.

Rankin, Paul. "Making Headlines." *Rave Magazine*, February 22, 2005.

Rastegar, Kamran. "On Palestinian Cinema." In "Interview: Conversations Arbitrary and Definitive." Special issue, *Bidoun* 8 (Fall 2006).

Rescher, Nicholas. *Imagining Irreality: A Study of Unreal Possibilities*. Chicago: Open Court Publishing, 2003.

Review of "Picadon." *Bulletin of the Atomic Scientists* 39, no. 7 (August 1983): 52.

Robinson, Chris. *Unsung Heroes of Animation*. Bloomington: Indiana University Press, 2005.

Roe, Annabelle Honess. *Animated Documentary*. London: Palgrave Macmillan, 2013.

Roffat, Sébastien. *Animation et propagande: Les dessins animés pendant la Seconde Guerre mondiale*. Paris: Editions L'Harmattan, 2005.

Roffat, Sébastien. *Propagandes animées: Le dessin animé politique entre 1933 et 1945*. Paris: Bazaar & Company, 2010.

Sarafian, Katherine. "Flashing Digital Animations: Pixar's Digital Aesthetic." In *New Media: Theories of Practices of Digitextuality*, edited by Anna Everett and John T. Caldwell, 209–24. London: Routledge, 2003.

Scarry, Elaine. *The Body in Pain: The Making and Unmaking of the World*. Oxford: Oxford University Press, 1985.

Scott, James C. *Domination and the Arts of Resistance: Hidden Transcripts*. New Haven, CT: Yale University Press, 1990.

Shales, Tom. "A Duck for All Seasons." *Washington Post*, June 24, 1984.

Shull, Michael S., and David E. Wilt, eds. *Doing Their Bit: Wartime American Animated Short Films, 1939–1945*. 2nd ed. Jefferson, NC: McFarland, 2004.

" 'Sinking of the *Lusitania*' Will Be Released by Jewel." *Moving Picture Weekly* 6, no. 20 (June 29, 1918): 10.

Sontag, Susan. "Freak Show." *New York Review of Books*, November 15, 1973.

Sontag, Susan. *On Photography*. New York: Farrar, Straus & Giroux, 1973.

Sontag, Susan. *Regarding the Pain of Others*. New York: Farrar, Straus and Giroux, 2003.

Stewart, Garrett. "Screen Memory in *Waltz with Bashir*." *Film Quarterly* 63, no. 3 (Spring 2010): 58–62.

Sun, Hongmei. *Transforming Monkey: Adaptation and Representation of a Chinese Epic*. Seattle: University of Washington Press, 2018.

Susanin, Timothy S. *Walt before Mickey: Disney's Early Years, 1919–1928*. Jackson: University Press of Mississippi, 2011.

Švankmajer, Jan. "Decalogue." Translated by Tereza Stehlíková. *Vertigo* 3, no. 1 (Spring 2006).

"Takahata and Nosaka: Two Grave Voices in Animation." *Animerica: Anime & Manga Monthly* 2, no. 11 (November 1994): 6–11.

Thompson, Kristin. "The Concept of Cinematic Excess." *Cine-Tracts* 1 (Summer 1977): 54–64.

Torre, Dan. *Animation: Process, Cognition, and Actuality*. London: Bloomsbury, 2017.

"Uruguay." *Freedom in the World 2013*. Freedom House, 2013.

Van de Peer, Stefanie. "From Animated Cartoons to Suspended Animation: A History of Syrian Animation." In *Animation in the Middle East: Practice and Aesthetics from Baghdad to Casablanca*, edited by Stefanie van de Peer, 107–28. London: I. B. Tauris, 2017.

"Walter Tournier, del joven militante al cineaste de animación." *La Izquierda Diario Uruguay*, December 8, 2016.

Wan, Laiming, and Wan Guchan. "Within the Popular Eastern Fairy Tale—*Journey to the West, Princess Iron Fan* Production Process." In *Frames of Anime: Culture and Image-Building*, by Tze-Yue G. Hu, 169–73. Hong Kong: Hong Kong University Press, 2010.

"War in Yemen." Global Conflict Tracker. Council on Foreign Relations.

Weil, Simone. "*The Iliad*, or the Poem of Force." Translated by Mary McCarthy. *Chicago Review* 18, no. 2 (1965): 5–30.

Wells, Paul. *Animation and America*. New Brunswick, NJ: Rutgers University Press, 2002.

Wells, Paul. *Understanding Animation*. London: Routledge, 1998.

Wieviorka, Annette. *The Era of the Witness*. Translated by Jared Stark. Ithaca, NY: Cornell University Press, 2006.

Woolf, Virginia. *Three Guineas*. In *"A Room of One's Own" and "Three Guineas,"* edited by Anna Snaith. Oxford: Oxford University Press, 1992.

Yecies, Brian, and Ben Goldsmith. "Cinematic Hooks for Korean Studies: Using the 'Apache' Framework for Inspiring Students about Korea in and through Film." *International Review of Korean Studies* 7, no. 1 (2010): 47–72.

INDEX